William Humphrey:

Destroyer of Myths

William Humphrey: Destroyer of Myths

Texas Writers Series

by Bert Almon

University of North Texas Press
Denton, Texas

First Edition 1998

5 4 3 2 1

Requests for permission to reproduce materials from this book
should be directed to:

Permissions
University of North Texas Press
PO Box 311336
Denton TX 76203-1336
940-565-2142

The paper used in this book meets the minimum requirements
of the American National Standard for Permanence of Paper
for Printed Library Materials, z39.48.1984. Binding materials
have been chosen for durability.

Library of Congress Cataloging-in-Publication Data

Almon, Bert, 1943–
William Humphrey : destroyer of myths / Bert Almon.
    p.   cm. — (Texas writers series ; no. 6)
Includes bibliographical references and index.
ISBN 1-57441-044-X (alk. paper)
1. Humphrey, William—Criticism and interpretation. 2.
Texas—In literature. I. Title. II. Series.
        PS3558.U464Z513   1998
        813'.54—dc21   97-39058
                                      CIP

for Olga,
and to the memory of my parents,
Lynn B. and Theola Almon

Table of Contents

Preface

William Humphrey set out from Texas in 1944 to achieve greatness. He was so intent on becoming a writer that he had no interest in publicity. As a result, little is known about Humphrey, who told his agent once that he didn't want a certain New York journalist even to know the color of his eyes. While I have focused on his writing, I have also attempted to illuminate his ambitions, which means understanding where he came from, what he wanted to achieve, how he learned about craft, and how he conducted his career. I rely heavily on his archives and letters to explore these matters and this study greatly increases the available facts about the man. As an overall approach I have used his own claim that his work tries to destroy certain myths, but I have tried not to be reductive. While he attacked myths and ideologies throughout his career, there is variety in his work— which includes superb sports writing and a memoir— and he often refitted his workshop. We can see a tragic element in his career: he found his sales and reputation declining book by book for all his attempts to renew his work, and he became an embittered man.

Many people have helped me with this project. I owe the most gratitude to the late William Humphrey, who answered my questions during his final illness and gave me permission to quote from his unpublished work. He wrote to individual libraries on my behalf, giving me permission to have his letters and journals copied.

I have silently corrected typographical errors when quoting unpublished materials. The notebooks were the workshop of a dedicated novelist: they are frank and lively records of his mind rather than polished compositions and there is no point in preserving his slips of the pen. Whenever possible I have cited dates of journal entries, but entries were dated only intermittently. He often kept several notebooks going on the same project, which makes dating particularly complicated.

In my efforts to understand William Humphrey I have benefitted a great deal from libraries and librarians. The Harry Ransom Humanities Research Center at the University of Texas holds most of William Humphrey's papers and I am grateful for the hospitality that a visiting scholar always receives there. Cathy Henderson, the head librarian, answered queries by mail and assured me that her staff would give me every assistance. My work in Austin was facilitated by Barbara Laborde-Smith, who made the complexities of this great repository clear; by Pat Fox, whose patience in managing the flow of documents was exemplary; and by John Kirkpatrick, whose skill in reading difficult handwriting was indispensable. All citations to manuscript materials by Humphrey are to the Harry Ransom Humanities Research Center, University of Texas, except for letters to the author of this study and letters in the following collections. The letters of William Humphrey and Katherine Anne Porter are held at the University of Maryland at the McKeldin Library. Beth Alvarez, the head of special collections, photocopied the correspondence herself in order to speed up my request. The papers of William Humphrey's friend and publisher Seymour Lawrence are held at the University of Mississippi in The Mississippi Room. Debbilee Landy helped me with those letters. Columbia University has the correspondence of William Humphrey with his agent, Annie Laurie Williams, and his letters to F. W. and Barbara Dupee through 1965. Later letters to the Dupees are in the collection of Barbara Dupee. I am grateful for access to these files.

I met Mr. Humphrey only once, briefly, in 1977. Two people who knew him shared their knowledge in phone interviews with me: Ken Harrison, who filmed one of his stories, and Barbara ("Andy") Dupee, who knew him from his days at Bard College. I appreciated their impressions of the man. When the Columbia Library informed Barbara Dupee that I wanted to examine their holdings of Humphrey's letters to her and her late husband, she immediately copied additional letters still in her possession and mailed them to me, an act of real kindness.

Several people shared their expertise as I wrote this book. My colleague, Ted Bishop, an authority on the Bloomsbury Group, provided background on Ian and Trekkie Parsons and Leonard Woolf, Humphrey's close friends in England. Dave Oliphant, with his deep knowledge of all things Texan, gave me information and encouragement. Sarah Greene, the exemplary editor of an exemplary small town newspaper, *The Gilmer Mirror*, sent me her excellent articles about the Cherokees in Texas. She will learn herein that her articles were an important source for a novelist she admires. Pat Twiford of the Clarksville Chamber of Commerce sent me abundant information on Clarksville and "Old Red," the clock celebrated in Humphrey's writings. Robert Morse visited Dorothy Humphrey's birthplace in Brooklyn on my behalf.

I profited a great deal from my correspondence with James Ward Lee, who proposed that I write this book. Lee was Humphrey's first substantial critic and a perceptive one. He read my first draft with extraordinary care. He accepted graciously his role in the opening chapter of this book. Fortunately he is proof against the slings and arrows of outraged authors, and Humphrey's claim that he was a bad critic has not destroyed his enthusiasm for the writing. James Ward Lee is the dean of Texas critics. It is true that he was born in Alabama rather than Texas, but—as the saying goes—that was an accident.

Charlotte Wright at the University of North Texas Press has given me encouragement and careful editorial work on the manuscript. She has patiently helped me with the use of the -en dash and -em dash and even canvassed her colleagues for information on wild boars. Fran Vick, the director of the Press, supplied some of that information.

The Faculty of Arts of the University of Alberta financed my research with a grant from the Endowment Fund for the Future, and a sabbatical leave from the University gave me the time to write it.

Chapter 4 incorporates some passages from an article of mine published by *Southern Quarterly*. I am grateful for permission to reprint. My interest in William Humphrey began when I was commissioned to write a review of *Farther Off from Heaven*. The magazine was *Southwest Review*, and the editor—one of the great ones—was the late Margaret Hartley. Her encouragement of my early poetry and criticism has not been forgotten.

My biggest debt is to my two research assistants. My wife, Olga Costopoulos-Almon, accompanied me to Austin and helped me carry out my work. She has been a constant source of insight as I wrote this book. I have always appreciated her clear handwriting, but I was especially grateful for it one crucial afternoon at the Harry Ransom Center when my laptop screen froze just as I came upon a crucial diary entry. Our daughter, Meli Costopoulos, spent many days at Columbia gathering and transcribing Humphrey's correspondence. This was a generous sacrifice of her own research time.

1

An Unhappy Guest at the Barbecue:

William Humphrey and "Texas Literature"

The death of William Humphrey on 20 August 1997, ended the career of a distinguished writer: an American writer, a southern writer, a Texas writer. Texas has produced many fine regional novelists, but so far the only writers of first rank—writers who transcend regional labels—are Katherine Anne Porter, William Goyen, Larry McMurtry, and William Humphrey. All have displayed ambivalence toward their native state while drawing much of their subject matter from it. In fact, Mark Busby gave his *Larry McMurtry and the West* the subtitle, *An Ambivalent Relationship*.

William Humphrey left Texas in 1944 at the age of nineteen, and lived for many years in Italy, France, England, and New York, but the creative core of his work can be traced to his first thirteen years, spent in Clarksville, county seat of Red River County in the northeastern part of the state, bordering on Oklahoma. His most memorable works (two novels, *Home from the Hill* and *The Ordways*; his stories of the Red River Valley, *A Time and a Place*; and an outstanding memoir, *Farther Off from Heaven)*, take place in or near a town very much like Clarksville, though it is sometimes unnamed or called Columbia, Blossom Prairie, or New Jerusalem. Many of his short stories are set elsewhere, and his harrowing psychological novel, *Hostages to Fortune*, takes place in the Hudson Valley of New York State and seems to represent a desire to transcend the regional. But his last novel, *No Resting Place*, dealing with the Cherokee Removals of the 1830s, has a framing story set in the Red River Valley in 1936, built around a pageant in honor of the Battle of San Jacinto. At the end of the pageant, the students and crowd sing the unofficial anthem of Texas, "The Eyes of Texas Are Upon You," which asserts that "you cannot get away." Humphrey, as we shall see, is deeply distrustful of "Texas Literature," but he did not manage to escape it.

At the time of Humphrey's birth, 18 June 1924, Clarksville was a town of about 2,000. For all its small size, it had a long history, antedating Stephen F. Austin's colony. The Sulphur River, which defines the southern border of the present county, was thought to be the boundary between the United States and Mexico. The actual border is the Red River, at the northern edge of the county, which now forms the border of Texas and Oklahoma. American settlers moved into the area thinking they were still in the United States. A good introduction to the Clarksville ambiance comes in a letter that Humphrey wrote to his agent, Annie Laurie Williams, to provide information for James T. Vaughn, the unit manager for the film of *Home from the Hill*, who was planning for the location scenes in Clarksville. The letter explains:

> I remember Clarksville with much affection. The square was not picturesque part by part, yet the total effect was picturesque. The courthouse (which was not in the square, but a block north, in a square of its own) was very nice—sort of Texas Gothic Revival, with a tower (all of yellow stone) about five stories high and a four-faced clock that boomed every quarter hour. It's rather a prosperous town, but the houses of even the citizens of

quality were without much distinction. It's Texas, after all, as you must remind Mr. Vaughn, and there are no FFV [First Families of Virginia] mansions with porticoes and Spanish moss (that's the stuff out of which they make the wigs for the darkies who serve the mint julips). Clarksville is one of the oldest Anglo-Saxon (as distinct from the Spanish) towns in Texas, and was the port of entry for nearly everybody from the US, including Davy Crockett and Sam Houston. And so it's not quite so raw as some of the western Texas towns. It is, as I am constantly telling everybody, a southern town, not a western town, and I never saw a cowboy in my life. Tell Mr. V that I think of myself as a southerner, of my characters as southerners, not westerners, and this is what he can expect to find in Clarksville. (9 August 1958)

Clarksville was settled by southerners and remained a part of the southern American cultural area for many years, with cotton as the supreme crop, though the opulence and pretensions of the "First Families of Virginia" were not a part of its social world. Humphrey recalled that when he returned in 1969 after thirty-two years away, his southern town had become western, with the decline of cotton-growing. By that time the kingship of cotton had been supplanted by cow-calf operations, cowboy boots were the new footwear, and the "Sulphur Bottom," the wilderness around the Sulphur River, so familiar in his fiction, was almost gone.

Readers of Humphrey's work quickly become familiar with the town square that he describes for the benefit of Mr. Vaughn, though he fails to mention the statue of the Confederate Soldier. The courthouse north of the square was built in 1884–85, a period when Texas towns competed to build impressive courthouses. The impressive clock tower, called "Old Red," is as important in his writing as the Sulphur Bottom. In Humphrey's childhood the chimes were a part of the fabric of his life. In 1961, the clock was converted to electricity and one night, "the night it got later than ever before," the clock malfunctioned and struck at least 120 gongs before it was permanently disconnected. In early 1985, when there was a rumor that the courthouse would be replaced with a modern structure, Humphrey responded by writing to the local paper and suggesting that he would be selling the grave that he and his Brooklyn-born wife had bought for themselves in the local cemetery. He had hoped, he said, to lie near the Hanging Tree and hear the clock strike till judgment day. One of the best descriptions of "Old Red" comes in "The Human Fly," in which a daredevil attempts to scale the courthouse of "New

Jerusalem," as Clarksville is called in that story.

Clarksville had one of the first colleges in the state, McKenzie College, founded in 1854, but the institution did not survive the nineteenth century. As Humphrey mentions in *Farther Off from Heaven*, there was a College Street in Clarksville but no college. The history of Clarksville's Carnegie Library conveys something of the cultural deprivation of the town where Humphrey spent his youth. In 1902 the great philanthropist, Andrew Carnegie, gave the town $10,000 to build a library, on the condition that the residents provide $1,000 a year to maintain it. In 1910 the library board had to default and the library was vandalized. Carnegie sued to recover his money, but the board members were all women, and at the time women had so few financial rights that they could not be held responsible. The story of the library is told in Eugene W. Bowers's and Evelyn Oppenheimer's book, *Red River Dust*, a local history that Humphrey seems familiar with. Bowers and Oppenheimer observe that one of the books in the library was Alphonse Daudet's *Sappho*. After the closure, there was no library in Clarksville for fifty-five years, and "Sappho never had to compete with Lady Chatterley nor any of her latter-day counterparts, at least not along the Red River" (75). As a result, young Humphrey developed his interest in literature after moving to Dallas.

Humphrey's parents, Clarence Humphrey and

Nell Varley, were children of poor farming families, which put them at the bottom of the social scale. Humphrey's father, as we shall see in discussing *Farther Off from Heaven*, became a successful mechanic as a way of escaping from the life of a sharecropper. He was a superb hunter, with a superb knowledge of the Sulphur Bottom. Humphrey's own love of the wilderness, which made him one of America's finest writers of sporting narratives, began in Clarksville, the town which imprinted its sights and sounds indelibly on his imagination.

The circumstances leading to Humphrey's departure from his home town insured that the imprint would last. Early on the morning on 5 July 1937, Humphrey was awakened by his mother and told that his father had been injured in a car crash the night before. Clarence Humphrey died three days later, and had the biggest funeral the town had ever seen. His son, however, refused to attend. When in 1977 he told an interviewer in El Paso about this misfortune, he remarked that time does not heal wounds (Ligon 3), and this one remained open. Fathers and sons are a preoccupation of his fiction, a central theme in every one of his novels.

The best sources for information on Humphrey's youth are two large red leather books he purchased on 21 July 1988, with entries running from that date until 6 May 1992. In these diaries he talks about his childhood, his university days, his feelings about Texas literature and many other highly personal topics, as well as his progress on the stories collected as *September Song*. He seems to have decided to reflect in considerable depth on his formative experiences, writing sketches and short essays. Humphrey was always a very private man, which makes the detailed self-revelations in the diaries particularly interesting. In writing his childhood memoir, *Farther Off from Heaven*, he was concerned to tell his parents' story as much as his own. He describes how his mother, left penniless after the cost of the funeral, left Clarksville the following day for Dallas, where her married sister Donna took in the mother and son. This was the height of the Depression and Donna, who had two children, was married to a night-shift waiter in a pancake house. Humphrey's mother had been a housewife and had no work experience, but she soon found a job filling mail orders for Sears & Roebuck for eleven dollars a week. Humphrey, who had been an exceptional student in Clarksville, did poorly at Adamson High School in Dallas, and his mother was called in to discuss his performance. She told the school that he was grieving for his father. Humphrey's 1991 comment on this scenario was that he was grieving for himself, for the loss of his happy childhood, a loss he blamed on his father's reckless driving.

Not long after his arrival in Dallas he had one of

those experiences that define a writer's life. He discussed it in a sketch, "My First Book," written in August 1988 in a *September Song* diary. He had been lonely, worried about being a mama's boy, missing his father. Furthermore his bicycle, a very expensive item during the Depression, had been stolen. Humphrey passed a bookstall on Elm Street and saw a copy of *Don Quixote* in the "Harvard Classics Five Foot Shelf" series on sale for a nickel. What impressed him as he stood there reading was the preface, which called the book a "supreme masterpiece." Here was a declaration that greatness could be achieved through writing:

> I stood there on the sidewalk for a long time deliberating whether to buy the book. It was not the money that deterred me, although I probably did not have a great deal more than that in my pocket. Looking back now on that decisive moment for me, a moment that would change my life, I think I may have had a vague sense that it was decisive, and that I was hesitant to take such a step. The large family from which I had sprung were uneducated, indeed illiterate tenant farmers. To buy a book would be to reverse my heritage. And I think now that I bought the book as an act of defiance against the interdiction of God that I remain ignorant. I had already rebelled

against this. He had let me down badly.
Though no church-goer, because of my pagan
father, I had certainly lived clean, worked
hard, and then had been rewarded by being
orphaned of my father, aged thirty-eight.

He took the step and paid his nickel, defying the divine decree.

Charles W. Eliot, the editor of what the flyleaf of
the Harvard Classics series calls "Dr. Eliot's's Five
Foot Shelf of Books," and the author of the preface
Humphrey read, was a scientist, an educational reformer and a President of Harvard. One passage he
wrote in the *Don Quixote* preface may well have influenced Humphrey's views of literature:

> Loose in structure and uneven in workmanship, it remains unsurpassed as a masterpiece of droll humor, as a picture of Spanish
> life, as a gallery of immortal portraits. It has
> in the highest degree the mark of all great
> art, the successful combination of the particular and the universal: it is true to the life of
> the country and age of its production, and
> true also to general human nature everywhere and always. (6)

Looseness of structure and unevenness of workmanship sounds like typical commentary on Humphrey's *The Ordways*, incidentally, but the relevance of the passage for Humphrey's work lies in the assumption that a novel can be a very particular portrayal of a time, a place, and a people, and still possess universality. Humphrey, as we shall see, was grateful to Katherine Anne Porter for showing him that he could write about the region and people of his origins, but his biggest intellectual stimulus during his youth was the friendship he formed with Jack Boss, an insurance salesman and part-time bookstore clerk. The dedication to *No Resting Place* expresses his gratitude: "To the memory of Mr. Jack Boss, who shaped my life." Boss, who died in the early 1940s, converted him to socialism and introduced him to literature, according to Humphrey's responses to my queries in a letter of 5 May 1997.

But Humphrey's first vocation had not been literature. At thirteen he won a scholarship to the Dallas Institute of Art after submitting charcoal drawings reproducing illustrations in an anatomy book. He devoted himself to painting so intensely that he later felt he had deprived himself of the joys of youth by doing so.

Humphrey's cousin, Wallace Floyd, hired the sixteen-year-old Humphrey to unload beer trucks at a dollar a day plus lunch, which must have been the summer before he entered Southern Methodist University. Entrance into the university was a kind of escape from his early explorations into painting as a possible career. (Ironically, he learned later from his navy physical that he was partially color blind: a career as a painter was itself a quixotic ambition.) He did not escape art entirely, however, for he married a painter, and a number of his stories have dealt with artists and the art world.

The teaching of modern literature was not common in the period when Humphrey started his education at Southern Methodist University. In 1991, in one of the *September Song* diaries, he recalls this incident:

> Professor Leesy to me at SMU in 1941—in answer to my question, "This course is called modern literature. Did it end with Swinburne & Hardy?"
> "Yes."
> Outside on the bench with classmates, I said, wouldn't you know it would be just our luck to come along when everything was all over. (18 November 1991)

Hardy would become one of his touchstones for the novel.

After a year at SMU he transferred to the University of Texas in Austin and enrolled in the premedical program. There he became a member of the Young Communist League, but also, the day after Pearl Harbor, decided to enlist in the navy. Decades later, in his *September Song* diaries, he questions his decision: he had almost drowned as a child—in *Farther Off from Heaven* he mentions that the town doctor even started filling out a death certificate for him—and he had nightmares about drowning for many years. The navy decided that he should continue with pre-med studies for the time being. Meanwhile, Humphrey quickly became disillusioned with communism, later explaining in his diary that his left-wing politics had been a product of his awareness that "the world was in flames" (18 November 1991).

After a year in Austin, Humphrey returned to SMU, where he decided to major in German, one of his best subjects. He once translated a fifty-page essay by Freud and became proficient enough in the language to come close to wrecking the business of his mother's small diner. He decided one day to tune in to a speech by Hitler, which outraged the patrons. He had learned to understand Hitler's politics from Jack Boss, he says in a November 1988 entry in his *September Song* diaries. A few years later in Chicago, Humphrey went for the first and only time in his life to a nightclub. There he met Thomas Mann and enjoyed a conversation in German with him.

Humphrey's interest in Freud was an enduring

one. He consulted Freud's essay on "Dostoyevsky and Parricide" when he was writing *Proud Flesh*, and he was fascinated with the mythological figure most important in Freud: Oedipus. A man whose childhood showed divided loyalties between his parents would naturally be interested in the Freudian family romance. The Oedipal situation is important in *Home from the Hill*, in which Theron feels a subliminal attraction to his mother; *Proud Flesh*, in which the Electra complex is crucial; and *Hostages to Fortune*, in which the central character suspects that his dead son suffered from an Oedipal fixation.

Humphrey was called up for a navy physical after he returned to SMU. The experience caused him great distress. He was a small man, and at the time of the physical he was only 4'11" and weighed ninety pounds. He recalls in his diary that his father had once bought one of the notorious Charles Atlas exercise devices, and that the ads for the product, "Are you a ninety-eight-pound weakling?" made him ruefully wish that he did weigh ninety-eight pounds. At the physical he found himself standing naked in line with huge Texas farm boys. A diary entry recalls bitterly an exchange at the physical: "Discharge, following my application to the CB's. Son, what have you done? Just gone to school, Sir. That's all. Just gone to school. My minuscule size" (December 1990).

He found himself discharged from military obligations for several reasons: his color blindness, a severe fall that had aggravated his childhood foot injury, and stomach ulcers. He was free to continue his education, but he did not last much longer at SMU. As he explained to Betty Ligon in 1977, he had developed an interest in writing and received some encouragement from an eminent French professor and writer on Texas subjects:

> I tried to write a short story and showed it to Lon Tinkle, then a French teacher at SMU. He gave me fifty cents to buy a meal because he thought I looked hungry and told me to take creative writing at night from George Bond. Twenty-five years later Tinkle (then *Dallas News* book editor) sponsored me for my honorary PhD, the only degree I ever got. (3)

Humphrey took a course from Bond, but did not find it very useful. His departure from SMU in 1944 was sudden, as he describes in his diaries:

> Dr. Schuller laying down his chalk. Humphrey? Humphrey! Where are you going? Are you sick? Bist du Krank? Wo gehts du?
> I had not known until I was asked.

"Chicago," I said, and opened and closed
the door behind me. (December 1990)

In Chicago, he later told Betty Ligon, he took "a
defense job for, get this, Chicago Screw Company" and
"began a crash course in reading everything from
Homer to the middle eighteenth century" (3). He had
written a five-act play with a cast of 350 about Benjamin Franklin, which he took to New York to show
to the producer Brock Pemberton. Clearly he would
have to serve an apprenticeship before writing something marketable, but he had fixed on a career. Freud
suggests that people become artists because they seek
fulfillment for their deprivations through fantasy. We
need not endorse all of Freud to see the sort of needs
that helped make Humphrey a writer: he was deprived, economically, socially and culturally, and he
felt his small size acutely. He was still brooding over
his height many years later. He wanted to make himself into a writer—a great writer, someone worthy of
the Harvard Classics—in compensation for what he
lacked, or felt he lacked. Along with fiction, he wrote
brilliant accounts of hunting and fishing that establish him as a successor to his father in those pursuits. One of the complaints about his work has been
his tendency to strain for greatness. While this seems
an unfair criticism of any writer, unless we believe
that writers should strain for mediocrity, the criti-

cism was made very astutely by one of the first reviewers of *Home from the Hill*, David L. Stevenson,
who wrote in *The Nation* that Humphrey wearies the
reader through "over-zealous attempts at greatness."
Humphrey, he said, "has not created a novel of deep
brooding insight, but one for seminars in technique"
(172).

The striving for greatness coexisted with an extreme reticence. Humphrey's life and contacts remain
practically unknown to the public, although his papers are now available for use, and the present study
will greatly increase knowledge of his life. In 1977,
during the writing of *Hostages to Fortune*, he copied
a lengthy passage from Paul Valery's essay on
Stendahl into the notebook for the novel. The passage seems to have fascinated him: the notebook has
an entry admonishing himself to find it, and when he
did, he incorporated it in two forms, a typescript
tucked into the notebook and a handwritten version.
Valery, writing about one of Humphrey's favorite novelists, explores a polarity also present in Humphrey,
a man very concerned with his literary fame on the
one hand, and obsessed with his privacy, out of which
literary works grow, on the other. Humphrey's papers
are filled with distressed passages about prizes he
has not won, and anthologies which have not included
him, and he repeatedly compares his progress with
writers like John Steinbeck (whom he especially

despised) and Saul Bellow. But he preferred life in the country, at an inconvenient distance from New York City, to the networking and schmoozing that helps keep a writer before the influential editors, reviewers, and critics.

The passage from Valery is so revealing that it needs to be quoted at length:

> We listen to the temptations of our talents at the expense of what perhaps lies nearest our hearts: of what is jealous, shy and incommunicable and desires to be so. This naive insular man and this lover of glory (which is no less naive) finally accept, as best they can, an identical destiny.
>
> How extricate ourselves from this clash of two capital instincts of the intelligence? One urges us to solicit, to force, to win minds. The other jealously recalls us to our irreducible strangeness and solitude. One spurs us on to appear, the other actuates us to be and to confirm ourselves in being. It is a conflict between that which is too human in man and that which has nothing human in it, and feels itself unique. Every strong, unspoiled person deems himself something other than a man, naively refusing and dreading to recognize in himself one of the indefinitely numerous

copies of a standard species or type.

In every profound personality some hidden virtue is incessantly engendering a hermit. In contact with, or at the memory of, other beings, they feel at times a particular distress, the sharp, abrupt sensation of which cuts into them and makes them shrink at once into an indefinable, intimate island. It is a reflex of inhumanity, of invincible antipathy, which may go as far as madness, as in the case of the emperor who wished that the whole human race had but one head that it might be severed at a single stroke. But in persons of a less brutal and more inward nature this energetic sentiment, this obsession of man by man, is capable of giving birth to ideas and to works. The victim of the ill of not being unique consumes himself in inventing that which separates him from the others. To become different is his mania. And perhaps it is not so much a question of placing himself above everything which works on him and torments him as it is of putting himself, so to speak, entirely aside, beyond all comparison. (116–18)

Valery goes on to say that "perhaps the great 'sin'—the metaphysical sin par excellence—to which the theologians have given the fine name of pride, has as root this irritability or need to be unique" (118). And such pride, he says, is an attempt to deny mortality, a refusal to be like those who die (in Humphrey's case, perhaps a refusal to be mortal like the father whose death had such a devastating effect). The passage by Valery concludes:

> And then, this horror of death produces from its depths a certain frantic will to be unlike, to be independence itself and different par excellence—that is, to be God. To refuse to be like, to refuse to have our like, to refuse to resemble those who are apparently and reasonably like us—all this is to refuse to be mortal and to wish blindly not to be of the same essence of those who pass and fade about us, one after the other. The syllogism which led Socrates to death more surely than the hemlock, the induction which forms its major premise and the deduction which concludes it, awaken a defense and an obscure revolt of which the worship of self is a readily deduced result. (118–19)

The thirteen-year-old boy discovered that his father, like Socrates, was mortal, and by extension, he himself was mortal. But great writers are not mortal: the

Harvard Five Foot Shelf of Classics offered immortality to Cervantes, certified by Charles W. Eliot and Harvard University. In a rather haughty letter written to his publisher, Alfred A. Knopf (26 October 1961) he said, with underlining for emphasis: "Publication in itself means nothing to me. *I don't want to create a seasonal stir. I want to be remembered after I'm dead.*" The letter, which says much about his working habits and plans, will be quoted in more detail later. In a talk Humphrey gave in the 1980s on the subject of "Why Do I Write Fiction?" he says: "But I wonder whether the main [reason] is not the fear of death, of going into the grave without having lived as fully as I might have, to cram into one life more lives than one, to experience in imagination adventures I have not, and never will, have" (186).

Humphrey's counter-impulse, his craving for privacy, while not rivaling Thomas Pynchon's, was very strong. He never traveled in a psychedelic bus like Ken Kesey or ran for mayor of New York like Norman Mailer. Nor did he do more modest self-promotion like appearing on talk shows or writing articles in popular magazines. Early in his career he wrote a letter to his agent, Anne Laurie Williams (31 August 1964) complaining about a columnist in the *New York Times*:

> Another letter from America this morning contained the nonsense about me written

by Mr. Lewis Nichols in his column for the
NY Times. This is the third such notice for
which I am indebted to Mr. Nichols, who in
addition to being intolerably nosy, has a genius
for getting anything wrong. I do not mean for
a moment to suggest that you or anyone in
your office had anything to do with this, in
what I am about to say: but—in future I mean
to make every effort to see that none of this
prying into my personal affairs gets into print.
It is nobody's business but mine how much
money I make, or where I live or how. If anyone asks you, you don't know where I am, or
where I'm going from there, or when I'll be
back, or what I'm writing, or what color eyes
I've got. I can't stop people like Mr. Nichols
from trying to pry, but I can at least make it
harder for them; in the future he's going to
have to make up his copy 100% instead of just
three-quarters of it, as he now does. And
should anyone show an interest in buying this
new book [*The Ordways*] for the movies, one
condition of sale is that they release no figure
whatever as to what they paid for it. I simply
won't tolerate this sort of snooping about, and
I call on you to help me put an end to it. I've
written my people at Knopf a letter in this
same vein today.

The *September Song* diaries of 1988 contain some interesting and angry reflections on one aspect of his fame, his status as a Texas writer. In 1985, James Ward Lee of the University of North Texas (or North Texas State University, as it was known then) invited Humphrey to come to Denton and take part in a Texas Sesquicentennial Celebration, a commemoration of the 150th anniversary of the independence of Texas. In the letter, which is preserved in Humphrey's archive at the Harry Ransom Center, Lee wrote "I know that you don't usually attend events like this." In the margin Humphrey wrote: "How does he know this about me?" There is a rough draft of Humphrey's refusal on the back of Lee's letter, along with a note that says, "Called to decline (didn't want this fellow to have anything in my hand)." The invitation to the event came from the critic who wrote the first full study of Humphrey, a writer who had praised the author on several occasions but had also been a stringent commentator, one who said in his pamphlet that "if *Home from the Hill* is not a great novel, it is a great Texas novel. . ." (*William Humphrey* 33) and that "to call *The Ordways* a novel is almost to abuse the term" (*William Humphrey* 37). These were not the terms used by Dr. Eliot to praise *Don Quixote*. They seem to stress the particular, not the universal. Lee recalled in an e-mail to me that Humphrey at first refused to take part in the conference, then changed his mind (26 May 1997). The novelist was not fond of Lee's criticism, as entries in several of his notebooks attest. A list of Humphrey's "bad critics," in responses to me postmarked 26 March 1997, began with Louis Rubin and Christopher Lehmann-Haupt (of *The New York Times*) and concluded with "James Ward Lee, of the University of North Texas Press." However, he says in his *September Song* diaries that he needed the fee and finally decided to come. He used William Owens, a distinguished Texas writer, as a go-between. The fee was eventually raised to $3,000.

The conference took place 24–27 September 1986, and included twenty-five Texas writers, among them Larry McMurtry, Elmer Kelton, Shelby Hearon, John Graves, Sandra Cisneros, Naomi Shihab Nye, and William Owens. The event disturbed Humphrey profoundly, and he was still brooding over it in his notebooks in 1988, as in this entry from one of his journals for *September Song:*

How tired I am of hearing about "Texas literature." You don't—at least I don't—hear about "Mississippi literature" or "Georgia literature" or "Massachusetts Literature," yet all these states have produced more worth reading than Texas has.

Literature is something that exceeds geographical—especially provincial boundaries.

These remarks were prompted by an essay by Dwight Chaney which poses the question whether I am a southern or a southwestern regionalist. As I said in the interview in *The Southern Review*, "any writer is a regionalist—and so is every critic."

The essay by L. Dwight Chaney, "William Humphrey, Regionalist: Southern or Southwestern?" appeared in the *Journal of the American Studies Association of Texas* in 1988.

In his diary entries about what he calls the "literary barbecue," he rages against his fellow participants, calling some of them "illiterates" or "cretins" or "Chamber of Commerce ranters." He wanted to publicly denounce the whole affair but did not want to have to return the fee. After Humphrey's talk, a young man asked him if he had deliberately omitted mention of Texas. The answer was yes: Humphrey told him that the "best way to dignify Texas and bring it into the world is to treat it as if it is already there, at least in some of its sons and daughters." Although there is no clear evidence in his notebooks or his drafts of *No Resting Place*, some of Humphrey's harsh tone in dealing with the Texas Centennial celebrations in that novel may have been influenced by his anger with the Sesquicentennial meeting.

Humphrey's reaction is not uncommon for a writer who fears being called regional. The year before the conference he had published his first novel set outside of Texas—*Hostages to Fortune*, with a protagonist who comes from Kansas, lives in New York, and seems devoid of ancestral pieties. It got some respectful reviews but did not sell very many copies. Humphrey writes magnificently about barbecues and dove hunting, but he is most interested in universal themes like family relationships, loss and reconciliation, wealth and poverty, crime and punishment. He must have been exasperated to get an invitation to appear as a leading Texas writer, on an occasion marked quite naturally by Texas pride, which he considered merely fatuous chauvinism. Judging from his papers, he admired William Owens and Marshall Terry among Texas authors, but his constant benchmarks were Austen, Stendahl, Proust, Dostoyevsky (whom he called the greatest novelist who ever lived), and Thomas Hardy.

While he aimed at dealing with universal themes and situations, Humphrey was still a vivid chronicler of the state of Texas, which, after all, had its own revolution, its own sacred battlefields, its own national government. A number of brilliant nonfiction writers had helped define Texas for Texans. The old triumvirate—which Larry McMurtry found it necessary to dethrone in a celebrated essay, "Southwestern Literature?"—was made up of Walter Prescott Webb, who wrote the history of the Texas Rangers as well as the classic *The Great Plains*; J. Frank Dobie, who was a magnificent and beloved folklorist; and Roy Bedichek, a brilliant amateur naturalist. This pantheon of elders should include Humphrey's friend William Owens, whose brilliant autobiography, *This Stubborn Soil*, chronicles a childhood in Pin Hook, Texas, a tiny village in Lamar Country not far from where Humphrey was born.

One of the best historians to deal with Texas, T. R. Fehrenbach, has suggested that the sense of peculiarity that Texans feel has its basis in the early period, 1835–61. Texas was a nation for a decade, it had an extensive Indian frontier, its ethnic mix was unique, and the struggle with the land was harsher than in most other parts of the United States. He says, quite shrewdly, that other states developed, while Texas *had* a history, one that its people learned in school:

> The Texan did not shed his history in the twentieth century; he clung to it. Texas history was taught in Texas schools before the study of the United States began. The Anglo held to his history; the Mexican to his; only the Negro faced an immense psychosis in Texas, because the black man's history was

not defined, and unbearable when it was. This Anglo history was shot through with the national myths all such histories have; it had its share of hypocrisy and arrogance. Parts of its mythology made both ethnic Mexicans and Negroes writhe. But in essence, it rang true. We chose this land; we took it; we made it bear fruit, the Texas child is taught. History, and the fact that he has never really left the land, made the twentieth-century Texan the most "European" of all American stock.

They had the longest frontier in America; they had battled in close combat with foreign races; they had subjugated peoples, and had been conquered themselves. They had learned that all people were not the same; parochial inside America, they were yet less parochial than those Americans who thought all the world was essentially the same. The great majority knew where their grandparents lay buried. They were as provincial as Frenchmen, as patriotic as Russian peasants. (712)

And, Fehrenbach points out, they held to the cult of courage of a warrior society.

Fehrenbach's ideas could be documented quite

fully from Humphrey's own writings. The struggle with the land is paramount in *A Time and a Place*. The Indian wars, wars of virtual extermination, are touched on in the story "The Last of the Caddoes," and explored fully in the concluding section of *No Resting Place*, which deals with the expulsion of the Cherokees and other tribes in 1839. The domination of the black race by the white is dealt with in several places, most notably in *Proud Flesh* and in "Mouth of Brass," one of Humphrey's best stories. The macho cult of the hunter is a major theme of *Home from the Hill*. As for knowing where your grandparents are buried, *The Ordways* has much to say about that. Humphrey questions these pieties, to be sure, and so frequently that, to reverse the song, his eyes are on Texas.

Along with the self-image of Texans, the fascination of the outside world with Texas made it impossible for Humphrey to untangle his literary status from his native state. Texas is recognizable all over the world, if only through the extreme image created by comic books and Westerns, through the television and the movies (we can think of *Dallas*), and through flamboyant politicians like Lyndon Johnson. Mississippi and Georgia do not have such recognition, for all their fine writers. Clothilde Luce, in 1996, wrote an amusing article for *Texas Monthly* called "Texas, Paris," about the French obsession with all things

Texan. Larry McMurtry, who is acutely aware of the
mythical image of Texas, attempted to deconstruct
this image in his novel, *Lonesome Dove*, but it and its
television offshoots appeal very much to those who
love the myth of the Western. McMurtry and
Humphrey face a similar problem: when they seek to
provide a critique of Texas myths in their work, the
appeal of the myths tends to overpower the critique,
even to crush it. McMurtry seems to have given in to
the mythology in his most recent novels, the collabo-
rations with Diana Ossana: *Pretty Boy Floyd* and *Zeke
& Ned*, novels which overlap some of Humphrey's
work in subject matter but take a traditional romantic view of the 1930s and the problems of the Cherokees. As Mark Busby remarks in his 1996 article
"Rewriting History," McMurtry used to be "antimythic,
deconstructing the various myths of the West. But
the two collaborative works with Ossana seem to
uphold rather than attack the myths of the West" (11).
Humphrey, on the other hand, never gave in.

T. R. Fehrenbach suggests in the preface to his
book *Lone Star* that Texas has a particularly strong
mythology, which he saw as his task to evaluate: "One
problem that faces every Texan historian contemplat-
ing a Texas readership is that all nations have their
national myths, and Texas became enough of a nation within a nation to formulate its own" (xi). He
notes that "many of Texas' legends, historically un-

proven and even historically insupportable, are fondly held and fiercely defended," and he says that his book "was not written to destroy myths but so far as possible to cut through them to the reality underneath" (xi–xii). William Humphrey, a novelist with a sharp satirical eye, wrote much of his work with the explicit goal of destroying myths.

While he was writing his third novel, *Proud Flesh*, he entered a long anguished meditation in a notebook on 6 November 1965, about his misunderstood intentions as a novelist. The comments were triggered by reading Kent Ladd Steckmesser's *The Western Hero in History and Legend*. Steckmesser examines the way in which four questionable figures, Kit Carson, Billy the Kid, Wild Bill Hickok, and George Armstrong Custer (the mountain man, the outlaw, the gunfighter, and the soldier) were turned into legendary heroes. Steckmesser's book impressed Humphrey, and he commented:

> Reading his piece has shown me again something about myself. Nearly every reviewer of *Home from the Hill* and of *The Ordways* spoke of me as a creator of myth. I am a destroyer of myths. My whole work has known the danger and falseness of myths. The myth of the hunter—the myth of the South, the myth of the West—the myth of the Outlaw/

vide Jesse Neighbours, the myth of Oil—and always the myth of Texas—I have attacked these in everything I have written. Yet I am called a creator of myths! Those who criticize my writing say that I live in the past. My writing has concerned itself with the past because I am concerned to show how deadening the past can be upon the present, how falsification, romanticization of the past—the urge to myth making, can be deadly. "Those who do not know the past are condemned to relive it," says Santayana and my writing has been in large part an effort to show it, so as to avoid reliving it. And this nobody has seen. I try so hard to write clearly—and I am completely misunderstood. One despairs of being taken at one's word.

And a few leaves in the diary later, he complained:

Either nobody sees what I am getting at, or else nobody cares. But I think it is an important thing to do, and I shall certainly go on doing it. I don't know of a more important thing to do than to show the truth, the dangers of romanticizing and sentimentalizing. The danger of making myths.

In a letter to him I mentioned this passage and said that I thought it applied to *Home from the Hill* and *The Ordways*. His comment (26 March 1997) was "You're right!"

While not too much should be made of his brief involvement with Marxism at the end of the 1930s, Humphrey would have heard a great deal about ideology in the original, narrow sense: a body of beliefs masking genuine power relationships in society—a form of false consciousness. As a reader of Freud from his early years, he developed a strong interest in the mythical patterns that reflect unconscious desires, but this is myth in a different sense, myth as a tool of discovery and analysis. Growing up in Texas, Humphrey came into contact with a number of ideological myths that upheld a racist social order: the glorious Lost Cause of the Civil War justified a great deal. In *The Ordways* he presents a critique of that myth and also looks at the mystique of the western hero. Another myth sees Texas as a land of oil wealth: there are endless jokes that see Texans as vulgar millionaires. The oil myth offered the illusion of a land of riches during the 30s: in *A Time and a Place* Humphrey deconstructed that fantasy, showing that the largesse of nature was bestowed in entirely arbitrary ways and could destroy lives as well as enrich them. He also took apart the Robin Hood myth of the outlaw (Bonnie and Clyde, and Pretty Boy

Floyd) that comforted the poor in the same period. And finally, *No Resting Place* dismantles some of the celebrations of Texas as a superior realm conceived in liberty by heroic patriots.

The misunderstanding most painful to William Humphrey must have been the critical response to his attempted destruction of the myth of the hunter. Over and over he has been accused of glorifying Wade Hunnicutt, the aristocratic hunter of wild game and women, the tragic hero of *Home from the Hill*. Critics like Gary Davenport and Mark Royden Winchell have insisted that Humphrey is unable to see Hunnicutt's flaws, that he is charmed by Hunnicutt and excuses him for his sins. A strange view, considering that the character alienates his wife, turns his adoring son against him, and brings about his own destruction at the hands of a man who believes that Hunnicutt is the seducer of his daughter.

But myths themselves are seductive by their nature, so perhaps the misunderstandings are not really strange. James Ward Lee compares Hunnicutt to legendary but historical figures like Davy Crockett and Big Foot Wallace, implying that Humphrey has given him a glamorous aura. We crave god-like figures to admire, and the omnipotence of Hunnicutt in the practices of venery may have charmed his creator a little, as well as many of his readers. While a story like "The Ballad of Jesse Neighbours" makes fun of the oil myth, readers are likely to be enticed by the glorious portrayal of the trip of a nouveau-riche family to Neiman-Marcus and may forget the absurdity of wealth that springs from a chance distribution of hydrocarbons. Where Texas is concerned, the world has an appetite for fantasy, as Larry McMurtry, would-be deconstructor of the cowboy mystique, could testify.

Humphrey's chief tool for destroying myth is irony, especially irony of situation. He rarely relies on direct commentary—he is a writer of fiction, after all—which compounds the chances that he will be misunderstood. He is a victim of irony himself, scorning Texas literature but finding himself an honored if unhappy guest at the literary barbecue, where he must have felt that myths were being perpetuated. His very choice of metaphors is revealing: the meeting was a "barbecue" and a dissenter would have been "lynched" like a miscreant in the cowboy movies.

Yet Humphrey and his wife purchased a grave under the Hanging Tree in Clarksville, not too far from Old Red, which can be seen as an act of ancestral piety. As a writer, he widened his geographical setting, but still, much of his writing draws its engrossing particularity from that sparsely inhabited county on the northeastern edge of Texas. In 1998, his novels in print are *Home from the Hill* and *The Ordways*, both recently reissued by Louisiana State

University Press in their "Voices of the South" series.
Red River County is not his only subject, but it seems
to be his enduring one. He received a respectful obituary in *The New York Times* the day after his death
from cancer. It was entitled, "William Humphrey, 73,
Writer of Novels about Rural Texas" (Gussow A17). If
he is remembered after his death, it will be as a Texas
writer.

2

Origins of a Style

Not long after he came to New York with his vast play about Benjamin Franklin, William Humphrey met his future wife, a married woman with a three-year-old child, Antonia. Born Dorothy Feinman in Brooklyn on 9 May 1916, she was eight years older than Humphrey. She had also been a member of the Young Communist League and belonged to the Red Dance Troupe, taking part in a performance called "The Scotsboro Boys Must Not Die" in the late 1930s. She was a painter, under the name "Dorothy Paul," the latter of which was her brother's given name. Dorothy Feinman and William Humphrey must have seemed extremely exotic to each other—a Jewish Brooklynite and a small town

Texan—though they were both artists and leftists.
In a letter (14 January 1969), Dorothy told Katherine
Anne Porter the story of their elopement: On his
twenty-first birthday they ran off with $75.00 that
Humphrey had saved from his job as a milkman, in-
tending to go to Mexico. But they wound up broke in
Dallas. According to Andy Dupee, the story among
their friends is that Humphrey met Dorothy while
he was working as a shepherd on her mother-in-law's
estate near Woodstock. I asked Humphrey in a letter
(26 March 1997) if he would tell me how he met his
wife. His reply was typically simple and direct: "I
won't." The exact circumstances of his employment
in this period—milkman or shepherd or both—remain
unclear.

They spent four years "on the lam," in order to
retain custody of the child, according to his interview
with Jose Yglesias (65). Humphrey found several jobs,
including one in 1946 at Manhattan's famous Gotham
Book Mart, operated by Frances Steloff, who was
known for cultivating and promoting modernist writers. Humphrey was her 3,000th clerk, he told
Katherine Anne Porter in a letter (5 November 1968),
and lasted a record three months because he knew
that his wife and child would starve if he did not. He
found the owner almost intolerable: a harpy with no
real interest in literature aside from poorly-printed
works on Theosophy in Yiddish, which she had to read

with her finger. Humphrey felt that she exploited writers by buying their editions of *Ulysses* "for a dollar and half" and then "asking a hundred" for them. Humphrey told Porter an amusing anecdote involving the English writer and editor, Cyril Connolly. Connolly was supposed to appear at the Gotham Book Mart at 7:00 o'clock one night for a party in his honor. Steloff had never met him. The writer came to the store at 4:00 to browse. Humphrey recognized him from his picture. "Have you ever seen Cyril Connolly?" he asked Porter. "He looks just like an ape. Ugliest man, as we used to say in East Texas, that God ever wattled a gut in." In a spirit of mischief, the young clerk let Steloff believe that Connolly, with his shabby briefcase, was a shoplifter, and when Connolly went into the rooms with signed editions of works like *Ulysses,* Humphrey was sent to fetch the cop on the corner. When he returned with the policeman, Connolly had introduced himself to Steloff, who tried to send Humphrey and the cop away by making frantic gestures. "I used to see Connolly on the streets of Lewes, the little town in Sussex where we spent three long summers, and I used to feel tempted to go up to him and tell him how he very nearly got picked up on suspicion of book theft at the old Gotham Mart." The three-month job ended when Humphrey became so exasperated with Steloff that he smashed three 100-watt light bulbs at her feet.

Humphrey eventually sought out W. H. Auden and Randall Jarrell to ask for literary advice. As Yglesias later reported:

Jarrell suggested that he [Humphrey] read Katherine Anne Porter, a writer from his part of the country, and with some of his last cash he bought a used copy of *Flowering Judas* and was carried away by it. "That good simple direct prose opened up a whole world to me," Humphrey remembers. (65)

He would eventually meet Porter, who was a permanent influence on his style because her approach to Texas was to perceive it as essentially part of the Deep South. Humphrey's East Texas was actually more southern in its mores than the area near Austin where Porter grew up.

The small family took refuge in rural New York. A letter survives in Humphrey's archive written on 26 August 1947 by D. L. Peterson, a radio broadcaster, addressed to "Dear Artist-Couple," offering them a small house in the country near Brewster. In return for chores like gathering eggs and milking goats, they would net twenty-five dollars a month. By early 1949, Humphrey had produced three publishable stories, which appeared in *Accent* ("In Sickness and in Health" and "Man with a Family") and *Sewanee Review* ("The

Hardys"). The creative promise shown by the stories got him a job interview at Bard College, in Hudson, New York. The invitation was written to "Mr. Humphrey" by Theodore Weiss, a poet and the editor of *Quarterly Review of Literature*, and it assured Humphrey that a good interview could make up for his lack of degree and experience. The interview must have gone well, for Weiss soon wrote to "Bill" to assure him that a job was likely, and Humphrey began teaching at Bard that fall.

Humphrey taught at Bard, a liberal arts college, for nine years. He made important friends on the faculty, including Weiss and his wife, Reneé, who co-edited the *Quarterly Review of Literature*. He was also very close to the seventeenth-century scholar Andrews ("Andy") Wanning, who became the model for Tony in *Hostages to Fortune*. The Henry James scholar and essayist F. W. Dupee was at Bard for some years before moving to Columbia University. He and Humphrey shared a radical background, both having been Communists. Dupee was the last editor of the Communist journal, *New Masses*, before he became disillusioned by the Moscow Purge Trials. After he and his wife Barbara ("Andy") moved to Carmel, California, Dupee was a frequent correspondent, and Humphrey's letters to them are particularly rich in biographical detail. Irma Brandeis, the one-woman Italian Department at Bard, and the muse of the great

Italian poet, Eugenio Montale, was another friend. And Humphrey's student, Nick Lyons, who shared his passion for fly-fishing, eventually founded an imprint, Nick Lyons Books. Humphrey helped scout fishing titles for Lyons, and published a little book of his own, *My Moby Dick*, through Lyons's association with Doubleday. Unfortunately, they had a bitter quarrel in 1988.

Humphrey's files contain a number of letters expressing various dissatisfactions with Bard, especially over job security and salary. But he came to its defense in 1964, six years after he had left, when *Esquire* announced that its college issue would contain an exposé of Bard. Protests from a number of sources led Byron Dobell, the managing editor, to query *Esquire* authors who had taught there. Like Ralph Ellison, Humphrey wrote an eloquent defense. Certainly the faculty included some brilliant people. The location, near the Catskills, offered beauty and opportunities for a sportsman who liked to hunt and fish. Indeed, after he decided to settle in the United States again in 1965, after years in Europe, he chose the Hudson area.

Humphrey placed a story, "Quail for Mr. Forester," in *The New Yorker* in 1950. In his 1989 interview with Jose Yglesias he recalled with bitterness his wrangling with the magazine over minor details, and the Humphrey correspondence contains letters from the fiction editor, William Maxwell, which do show a certain finickiness. Yglesias described Humphrey's version of the squabbles:

> There ensued much argument with his editor about the changes. At one point the editor said, "Mr. Ross [the chief editor] is in the hospital and he is very unhappy about the stubbornness you are showing—he would like to make you one of our stable." "I am not a horse," Humphrey replied: now he whinnies at his remembered effrontery. He was pleased to see in the final galley that a sentence was circled and a comment in the margin said: "This sticks out like sore thumb." He recalls that he had the satisfaction of writing: "That's what I told you when you put it in there!" (65)

Humphrey was proud of his independence: his correspondence with the editors of his books shows a stubborn certainty about his writing. It becomes clear in his letters to Katherine Anne Porter that he was a perfectionist, working on stories for years and taking them through many drafts. In the case of *The New Yorker*, this was his only appearance in the magazine, although he tried them again frequently. On 8 February 1968, his friend, the poet Theodore Weiss, commiserated with him in a letter about their problems getting work into the magazine. One of Weiss's few poems in *The New Yorker* was in fact a poem about William and Dorothy Humphrey.

Humphrey came to the attention of some influential writers and editors. Late in 1949, the literary agent Diarmuid Russell wrote him to say that one of his friends and clients, Eudora Welty, had noticed his writing and thought Russell might like to be his agent. Over the next few years Humphrey would get a number of letters from agents and from editors of major publishing houses, usually inquiring if he had a novel in progress. In May, 1950, he got his first overture from Knopf, where Elaine Shaplen said that his work had been praised to her by Pearl Kazin, the fiction editor of *Harper's Bazaar*.

The most important writer to notice his work in the magazines was Katherine Anne Porter, who, according to her biographer, Joan Givner, had seen his stories in *Accent* and thought they were influenced by her (Givner, *Katherine Anne Porter* 374). Naturally, when Humphrey wrote to her on 26 September 1950, asking her to read at Bard, she was interested in meeting him and agreed to come for a relatively modest fee. She told Humphrey that she had seen his stories and had already wondered what she could do to help him, and she said that at their last meeting Eudora Welty had given her news of Humphrey.

He told Porter that his first published story was based on one of hers and that he had long admired her work, keeping passages from it open on his desk. When *Home from the Hill* came out, he sent a copy to Porter with this inscription:

> To Katherine Anne Porter, whose stories fixed
> my standards, whose life gave me courage,
> and who taught me the great thing a writer
> can teach another: that the place and the life
> and the speech to which he was born is his
> place and his subject and his speech.

She had also given him practical help: his archive contains a rejection letter from *Harper's Bazaar* (May 1951) praising the style of a story, "Report Cards," and mentioning that it had been submitted to the magazine by Katherine Anne Porter. She recommended him to publishers like Harcourt Brace and Doubleday and tried to arrange a stay for him at the writers' retreat at Yaddo. She also recommended him for a Guggenheim Fellowship in 1954. When she first had him and his wife to dinner in her New York apartment on 14 October 1950, she prepared a huge Mexican dinner and invited another Texan, her protegé, William Goyen. The evening was not entirely successful: the beans were scorched and the seasoning was too hot: later she recalled that she had unknowingly fixed Mexican food for a man who had ulcers, and she admitted that the company (Goyen's) had not been congenial for Humphrey. Humphrey himself wrote that he was perturbed when he realized that Porter had gotten up the next morning to do the dishes (19 October 1950).

For many years they exchanged warm, intimate letters, like the undated one in the summer of 1955 in which he complained that he was having to kill off three people (presumably the Hunnicutt family) on a hot day, and went on to describe his wife's new pursuit of photography and his decision to give up trying to learn jazz clarinet. Still, their relationship was a complicated one and its difficulties have been described by Givner in her biography and in an article on the influence of Porter on Humphrey and William Goyen, "Katherine Anne Porter: The Old Order and the New."

To some critics, Givner's discussion of the relations of these two Williams—Goyen and Humphrey— seems biased against the young men who learned from the famous older writer. The chapter about them in the Porter biography is called "Disciples Must Be Very Hard for a Mere Human Being to Endure," a title that reveals her polemical slant. According to Givner, Porter deduced that because Humphrey was in a "publish or perish" situation at Bard College, and because he rewrote rejected stories before sending them out again, he was in a deep artistic crisis, compromising his art in order to sell it and secure his job. She wrote him a letter of admonition (6 January 1951). What Givner does not report is Humphrey's remarkably long and eloquent refutation of these charges in an undated letter shortly after. He stressed that he rewrote stories to make them better, not to tailor them to the market. He told her that he was not in a crisis: "If ever I should be (and my ego is so vast that it's unlikely that anything so external could ever so penetrate as to bring me to a crisis) I'll be honest enough to admit it, and the second person I shall tell will be you."

The editorial correspondence in Humphrey's archives bears out his claims to artistic integrity, not to mention the presence of a vast ego. He repeatedly resisted suggestions from editors, even some very good ones. It would be natural for an established author to assert himself against an editor—as he did with Jackie Farber at Delacorte when they were working on *Hostages to Fortune*. But he was just as intransigent (if not so pugnacious) with Herbert Weinstock at Knopf when they were working on the first novel. In fact, Humphrey resisted suggestions about that book from Alfred A. Knopf himself.

But Porter never quite gave up her belief that Humphrey would sell out for commercial success, and she made some disparaging remarks about him in interviews, like the one with Louis Rubin in 1960, but she then praised him to Hank Lopez in 1965 (Givner, *Conversations* 50, 133). In her interview with Lopez she acknowledged that Humphrey claimed her as an influence, but said she could not detect it, though it is clear in the early stories and in *Home from the Hill*, the book he so gratefully inscribed to her, that he "took" from her. In 1965, four years after she had spoken scornfully of him to Louis Rubin, she asked him to be her literary executor in the event that Glenway Wescott did not survive her. I asked him in a letter if he had any final comments on her, but he said no. When I suggested that the downs in their up-and-down friendship were not his fault, he concurred: "They weren't" (26 March 1997).

One claim growing out of Joan Givner's work on Porter was distressing to Humphrey: "Goyen wrote to Porter about a conversation in which Humphrey had told him that he hated all Southerners and never wanted to see the South again." In a notebook entry from 1988, Humphrey states that he only met Goyen twice, thirty-five years apart, and that the first meeting was at Porter's apartment in 1950, where the two young writers exchanged only a few words—because, Humphrey says, no one could say much when Porter began talking. Goyen's letter discussing Humphrey has been printed in Goyen's *Selected Letters* (163–64). It expresses concern about Humphrey's supposedly anti-southern state of mind in a condescending way and suggests that he was dominated by rancor. One factor in Goyen's response to Humphrey may have been a kind of literary sibling rivalry. Goyen had been Porter's disciple since 1947 and in a few months would become her lover. His febrile and symbol-laden fiction has a Texas setting but does not appear to have influenced Humphrey. Rivalry would probably have made him resistant to the influence of Goyen. Another writer Humphrey met through Porter at this time was Glenway Wescott. They had a long correspondence, and it is possible that Wescott's short novel, *The Pilgrim Hawk*, influenced the hawk scenes in *Hostages to Fortune*.

Porter's influence is clear enough once it is pointed out, but until Givner's biography documented it, only one commentator, Frank Kappler, seems to have spotted it. In his *Life* review of *The Ordways* he said that the book "has a perception approaching the Faulknerian but has the advantage of reading more like Katherine Anne Porter" (17). Porter was a stylist that a young writer could learn from without picking up identifiable mannerisms. Her style shows a classic poise and clarity, holding the stylistic midpoint between the minimalist extreme of the early Hemingway and the baroque extreme of William Faulkner, the writers who were most likely to influence a novice around 1949. The critical sport of spotting influences sometimes lets the big game get away. But Eudora Welty once said that Porter's style is "as invisible as the rhythm of a voice" (39), so perhaps the game was hard to spot. Porter's irony is perhaps the most readily identifiable mark of her writing, as Robert Penn Warren showed in his major essay, "Katherine Anne Porter: Irony with a Center," and irony does pervade her acolyte's writing.

In a letter to Porter (28 September 1950), Humphrey himself explains the influence her writing had on him:

> I spent a good while trying to learn to write, and did many foolish things without learning from any of them; I aped Henry James' late manner and set out to rewrite *Finnegans Wake*. Reading you was my great revelation; I knew then what I wanted to do. You were my one teacher. When I wrote I had copies of *Old Mortality* and *Noon Wine* and "The Cracked Looking Glass" open on my table at my favorite paragraphs. I stole my first printed story completely from "A Day's Work" (as you no doubt know). I wrote for you. You were the only person whose approval I wanted, and my wife and I asked each other constantly, "Do you think she has seen it? Do you think she will like it?"

Humphrey was perhaps still under the spell of Porter when he wrote a letter to a fan, Frederic Stout, in the summer of 1985. In the rough draft of the letter, he says:

> I resort to this kitchen simile: I would like it to be like Saran wrap: it should conform to the shape of the object and be transparent. It should be so memorable as to make the reader feel there is not and had never been any other way for it to be said. . . .

This rather classic ideal is far from the verbal extravagance of Humphrey's other early influence, William Faulkner, whose genius sometimes outpaces his talent (so much the worse for talent, we often feel).

In *Home from the Hill,* a passage near the end of the novel will illustrate Humphrey's skill at writing a long but absolutely lucid sentence. Theron is pursuing the killer of his father:

> Then he began to pass weevily little cotton patches and farmhouses each the same as the last, with a gray dirt yard smooth and hard as ironstone, a shade tree or a chinaberry tree with a car-casing swing, a high front porch under which a hog languished, brought in from the shadeless hog pen, a gray, never-

painted shotgun house with at least one windowlight stuffed with a towsack or tacked over with pasteboard, a wash bench at the back door with a water bucket and a gourd dipper hanging on the wall above the bucket, a backlot with a castiron washpot and an upended oil drum for scalding the hog in at hog-killing time, a weed-choked kitchen garden gone permanently to seed, with a drunken scarecrow, tatters of faded rag tied to the fence wire and rusty tin cans on top of the fence posts to scare off rabbits, and at each one three or four yapping, colorless curs that met him when he was still half a mile off to race alongside in the boiling white dust. (305)

In one sentence Humphrey has conveyed the texture of impoverished rural life in the South. Faulkner could be as inclusive but not always so controlled.

The lectures on the early English novel that he gave at MIT in 1965 began rather unusually with a stylistic comparison of Thomas Dekker and Ernest Hemingway, and the point of the comparison was to indicate that the gap between the written and spoken language has narrowed since Dekker's time. Humphrey generally avoids the mannered and ornate without falling into extremely colloquial diction. He uses dialect sparingly, for appropriate characters, like East Texas poor whites and black servants: here and there he throws in the earthy expressions that such southerners love. These are most common in *A Time and a Place*, his work about the impoverished victims of the Dust Bowl of the 1930s: a boy in "The Rainmaker" wears a slicker which had "been bought three or four sizes too big," so that he "rattled around inside it like a clapper inside a bell" (*Collected Stories* 300). The nouveau riche daughters of Dobbs in "A Job of the Plains" look absurd in their new clothes, "their topmost ribs showing like rubboards above the tops of their low-cut dresses" (249). In *Proud Flesh*, Lester Renshaw as a boy is described as so small he "couldn't hardly look into a standing rubber boot" (97). His brother Ballard is described as "the smallest of the lot but like the Oxo cube, with the whole bull in it" (223). The sneezes of a black servant, Jug, are "loud enough to be heard by everybody within three axle greasings" (136). Such expressions, which are both vivid and hyperbolic, work well to convey the grotesque or the comic in *A Time and a Place* and *Proud Flesh*. Humphrey naturally avoids them in a novel like *Hostages to Fortune*, which has no regional flavor—and no humor.

Stephen Cooper points out that "constant comparisons to Faulkner are also unfortunate because they set up an impossible standard and mask the originality of Humphrey's best work" (241). But the name of Faulkner has been invoked over and over again in discussions of Humphrey, and it would be foolish to deny that the influence was present at least through the writing of *Proud Flesh*. After that it seems undetectable, vanishing with the southern subject matter. Humphrey writes intricate sentences, but he rarely practices the kind of adjectival excess and syntactic entanglement that Faulkner is famous for. The most obvious influences lie in less stylistic realms: an interest in rural comedy, as in the story of Trixie the cow in *Proud Flesh*, a passage apparently modeled on the spotted horses episode in *The Hamlet* and narrated with the devices of slow motion narration that Faulkner is famous for. Similar tricks of motion and perception of motion are used for more serious purposes in *The Ordways*.

Humphrey's observations on Faulkner to Ashby Crowder in an interview are revealing:

> I was born about two hundred miles from William Faulkner, and William Faulkner was born the year my father was. But by the time I came on the scene, nothing had changed in that particular era; everything was just exactly the same. I consider myself a contemporary of William Faulkner because I grew up in the very same way. About the only dif-

ference was, well, there wasn't any; I can't
think of anything. And about two hundred
miles away. It would be very odd indeed if
some of my writing didn't sound like some of
his, wouldn't it? (827–28)

Humphrey is perhaps replying to Louis Rubin's complaint that "*Home from the Hill* tries to use William
Faulkner's social and human values, William
Faulkner's insights, in order to describe an experience that was not really Faulknerian at all" (*Curious
Death* 284). Any writer expressing as Humphrey does
the southern preoccupations with history (especially
the legacy of the Civil War), folklore, race, and family,
is likely to sound like Faulkner from time to time.
Humphrey shows a special concern with family: his
first novel was, in its early stages, called *The Hunnicut
Tragedy*; his second was finally titled *The Ordways*;
and his third, *Proud Flesh*, was first called *The
Renshaws*.

Elizabeth Janeway's extremely favorable review
of *The Ordways* formulates quite well the relationship of the early Humphrey to Faulkner. Speaking of
our literary debt to Faulkner and Humphrey's debt
to Faulkner as a model for writing about the South,
she says:

This isn't a debt that should irritate anybody,

either the reader or Faulkner. Humphrey has written two fine novels; this one, I think, better than the first. He's too good a writer to copy Faulkner, any more than he's copying Chekhov or Mark Twain, both of whom are recalled by various pages in *The Ordways*. What Humphrey does is to accept the vision that Faulkner and others have bequeathed to their heirs, and build on it. I suppose this means that he is not a primary writer. His books are less original than those of his masters, smaller and more constructed, and with a touch of conscious synthesis about them. Just the same, he stands up to the impossible comparison well. (1)

Harold Bloom's theory of the "anxiety of influence" has some relevance for Humphrey's relationship to Faulkner. Katherine Anne Porter was surprised when Humphrey wrote her a letter (undated) a few days after the Nobel Prize was announced in 1950 to say that he was upset over the award because Faulkner was his "pet hatred." She replied that she had been delighted by the award and was devoted to Faulkner's work. Amusingly, she thought the only other writer deserving the prize was Osbert Sitwell! As Humphrey's first novel was about to be released, his editor at Alfred A. Knopf, Herbert Weinstock, warned him that some reviewers would detect Faulkner in the work, and when the early reviews came in, Weinstock told Humphrey that the *Saturday Review* had given the book to a reviewer (Walter Havighurst) who saw it as derivative of Faulkner. Indeed, Havighurst said that "the title is from Robert Louis Stevenson, but the tale is from William Faulkner" (15). Before the reviews began to appear, Katherine Anne Porter told Humphrey in a letter that the boar hunt in his novel seemed pure Faulkner (12 January 1958) and Humphrey wrote back admitting that Faulkner was the source. In *The Ordways*, Humphrey to some extent purged himself of the Faulknerian ethos of family and history through parody, but the notebooks for this third novel, *Proud Flesh*, contain several warnings to himself not to fall into sounding like the older novelist, especially in the treatment of black characters.

Stephen Cooper, like a number of other critics, places Humphrey as a realist, saying that "he also has remained firmly in the realist camp, eschewing the self-conscious and self-reflexive experimentation of so many writers of the last three decades" (234). He has been praised by James Ward Lee, one of his best critics, for the vivid portrayal of life in East Texas, most recently in an article in the *Dictionary of Literary Biography*: "The best thing about *Home from the Hill*, about all of Humphrey's best work, is the sense of time and place" (150). Lee goes on to note that Humphrey's regionalism is at the same time universal: "though the book depicts the customs, folklore, and language of rural northeast Texas, at its core the novel is about people who could have lived anywhere at any time," which distinguishes work like his from mere local color. Humphrey certainly admired the great realists like Balzac, de Maupassant and Stendahl. In 1958, he sent Wright Morris, a novelist he respected (and another realist), a gift through Harry Ford—an edition of Stendahl. It was Stendahl who defined a novel as "a mirror that strolls down a highway." In "Why Do I Write Fiction?" Humphrey quoted Guy de Maupassant's description of the writer as a person who cannot stop observing himself and everything he has experienced: "He has seen all, noticed all, remembered all, in spite of himself . . ." (184).

Humphrey's literary taste was slanted toward the novelists who are strong on character and given to sharp observation. He loved nineteenth-century novels: he taught the works of Giovanni Verga and Alessandro Manzoni at Bard, and he often referred to Jane Austen. His admiration for Dostoyevsky, a writer constantly before his mind in his notebooks, shows that his kind of realism does not preclude an interest in some departures from the norm. In *Proud Flesh* the characters are, like Dostoyevsky's, so extreme in their emotional responses that the category of realism has to be stretched, though not necessarily broken. He was astonished himself, thinking the novel had become wild. Among twentieth-century novelists, Humphrey preferred Conrad.

His favorite novelist, though he ranked Dostoyevsky higher as an artist, was Thomas Hardy, a writer with a strong sense of place and a deep interest in the ironic twists of life. Humphrey's pervasive sense of the ironic and his rather melodramatic plot situations, for which he is often criticized, owe much to Hardy. Both writers have been criticized for their structure, their tendency to use melodramatic turns of plot. Elizabeth Tebeaux entitles her study of Humphrey's short stories, "Irony as Art: The Short Fiction of William Humphrey," and she asserts that he creates characters who live in a world without God and without meaning, a world which—although she does not directly make the comparison—suggests Hardy's characters also, struggling with chance and "the purblind Doomsters" of fate, as he calls the forces of circumstance in his poem, "Hap."

And yet, as Tebeaux says, Humphrey was concerned for his characters, and her comments could apply to Hardy as well:

While Humphrey deals harshly with the lives, fates, and feelings of many of his characters, and while he clearly believes in a uni-

> verse that yields no heroes, no meaning, no
> justice, no divine comfort, and no answers to
> the problems of experience, he clearly cares
> for his characters. Much of the perplexing
> charm of his stories comes from the collision
> between the poignant concern and his un-
> yielding belief that life ultimately has noth-
> ing for any of these people or for any of us.
> (331)

She suggests quite plausibly that the biographical
source of this "pervasive cynicism" lies in his early
life in Clarksville, in the losses he experienced (334).
His feeling of loss and betrayal after the death of his
father comes through very clearly in his late notebooks: he felt deserted by God and let down by his
father, and could see no point to his misfortunes.
Humphrey often quotes the Bible, but always the most
somber books of the Old Testament: Job, Ecclesiastes,
and the Apocryphal Ecclesiasticus.

His early stories were published as *The Last
Husband, and Other Stories* in 1953. Along with the
New York edition from William Morrow, they were
also issued by Chatto and Windus. This English publication came about after Humphrey was mentioned
to the firm by Joseph Summers, a Milton scholar who
taught at Bard, and it would eventually enrich the
lives of William and Dorothy Humphrey through their

friendship with the publisher, Ian Parsons, and his wife, Margaret ("Trekkie"), who would introduce them to many English writers. The early stories were also included in *The Collected Stories*, and citations hereafter will be to that volume.

The book is uneven, as might be expected in an early work. Two stories in particular seem weak: the title work, and "The Fauve." "The Last Husband" is William Humphrey writing in the mode of John Cheever and not doing it very well. The story focuses on a commercial artist who works in New York and commutes from a suburb. The artist, Charley, meets Edward Gavin, a fellow commuter who sometimes gets on or off at a stop three miles from the community in which they both live. In a rather complicated narrative, Charley begins to understand Gavin's bizarre behavior. Gavin claims that his wife, Alice Metsys, is extremely jealous and has him followed by detectives. So he keeps his secretary in the next town without telling his wife, or so he claims. Charley at last understands that the secretary is actually Gavin's mistress, and that the purpose of the affair is to make Alice jealous: she is actually indifferent to her husband. Marriage means so much to Gavin that he betrays his wife in order to make her feel the importance of the marital bond. Hence he is truly the "last husband," an "inverted sentimentalist" (162) in a rather corrupt world of cocktail parties and artists who have sold out for money. In a rather clever plot twist, Gavin eventually betrays his mistress for yet another woman, Katherine, who is pressured into offering the cozy 1950s domesticity that "the last husband craves": aproned and cheery, she becomes the kind of house-wife whose image could be seen everywhere in popu-lar magazines and early television comedies. Eventually the first mistress is eliminated from Gavin's life and he shuttles between Alice and Katherine: a commuter indeed! The story is clever but the writing is diffuse and there are too many mi-nor characters, like Alice's sister, Victoria, who has triumphed as a commercial artist by vulgarizing the great modern painters. Charley makes a dull Nick Carraway to Gavin's Tom Buchanan. Perhaps the story is merely outdated, as commuter stories about New York pseudo-sophisticates no longer seem very interesting.

In "The Fauve," Humphrey satirizes the members of an artists' community in a small town called Redmond. The protagonists are James and Rachel Ruggles, two painters. James has devoted himself to his art with no success at all. The other artists in the town have prospered and ceased to live in a Bohe-mian style but James and Rachel have no choice. James has the admiration of his wife, born Rachel Rivich in Brooklyn (Humphrey is perhaps making a playful allusion to his own wife's background). In an

attempt to raise the standards of the artistic community, the Redmond Gallery uses a bequest to set up a
prize at the annual exhibition. The prize goes not to
James but to his rather child-like wife, creating a very
awkward situation, especially at the party the couple
hold to celebrate Rachel's windfall. One of the central ironies of the story lies in the title. The Fauve
was an artistic movement which includes some very
fine painters, most notably Matisse. They got their
name in 1905 when the critic Louis Vaucelles reviewed
their Salon and dubbed them "wild beasts": *fauves*.
The artists of Redmond are not wild beasts. The ones
who have succeeded seem fat and complacent domestic animals.

The story fails because of the confusion in another of its ironies. James, who is so devoted to his
art, is not honored, and he suspects that the community would like to disown him. Perhaps the prize to
his wife was a hint. But the question is, what is the
quality of his art? Does the irony lie in the rejection
of a true artist by a group of commercial sellouts, or
is the story about a man who thinks he is a great
artist but has deluded himself? Two perceptive readers of the story believe that James is a bad artist:
William Humphrey's mentor, Katherine Anne Porter,
and James Ward Lee. Lee says that the reader sees
at once that James is not talented. Porter "took it to
be a story about a third-rate painter with a bad case

of megalomania, a natural-born cad and boor" (Givner 375), and was corrected by Humphrey, who said that James was a genius. She did eventually come around to his view of the story, saying in a letter (21 October 1950) that she had mistaken the story for one like her own: "That Tree," in which one character was a bad poet. And she thought that the comic tone had confused her as well. In fact, few readers would be likely to get past Ruggles's self-pity, vanity, and misogyny (not to mention anti-Semitism) to see him as anything except the butt of satire. The difficulty with a story like this, which uses the points of view of James, Rachel, and a objective narrator, is that Humphrey gives us no real basis for judging James's art. We cannot see the pictures, so the significance of Ruggles's failure is not clear. One thing is certain: the story is diffuse and drab in style, dominated by brief paragraphs.

As mentioned earlier, two of the early stories were imitations of Katherine Anne Porter. While Porter could detect the influence, no other reader would be likely to do so. "In Sickness and in Health," with its portrait of an aging and sickly husband, owes a little to Porter's "The Cracked Looking Glass," a much more subtle depiction of the marriage of an older man and a restless younger woman. Humphrey's story is more a sketch than a satisfying work. Much better is his "Man with a Family," inspired by Porter's "A Day's Work."

In Porter's story, Halloran, an Irish New Yorker, has lost his job and what little respect his wife has had for him. After a series of humiliations while seeking work, he returns home and in a rage throws a flatiron at the wall. As a retaliation for that action and his failures, he is beaten by his wife with a wet knotted towel. Humphrey's story also deals with a failed husband, but it is set on a Texas farm and presents a subtle picture of Dan, a farmer who seems cursed by his own neurotic will-to-failure, which makes him constantly accident-prone. Neither he nor his wife and in-laws can understand why his injuries escalate. There is an estrangement from his wife that he can hardly articulate: he feels mysteriously left out. His failures as a farmer make him feel more and more unworthy, and he steadily punishes himself through injuries that make him a greater failure. At the end of the story, he has gone out to mow hay for his father-in-law, though he is not supposed to work with his broken leg. His father-in-law has hung a cowbell on the mower so that he can ring it if he needs help (another humiliation), and when he hits a rock and is mortally injured, he thinks first that he won't ring the bell. In his dazed state, he imagines the bell dancing away over the field. The ending perhaps owes a little to Porter's "The Jilting of Granny Weatherall," in which the dying woman hallucinates her death as the blowing out of a light. Humphrey's story ends:

"Then Dan watched himself get up, get the bell, and begin swinging it with all his might, pointing at the body on the ground as though he wanted everybody to come see what he had gone and done with himself now." (51)

The stories set in Texas are the best in the collection. The most important thematically is "Quail for Mr. Forester," the work that led to Humphrey's conflict with *The New Yorker*. Set in "Columbia," a small town in East Texas, it deals with the passing of what Katherine Anne Porter called "The Old Order" in a sequence of stories. Mr. Forester is the last representative of the leading local family, which lost most of its possessions—but not the family home—after the Civil War. The narrator is a young boy who has heard a great deal about the Civil War. His parents decide to invite Mr. Forester, who has descended socially by opening a hardware store, to dinner for fresh game. The evening is essentially comic. John M. Grammer has described some of the incongruities of the story:

> But as the evening wears on, the old man becomes something of a disappointment. He errs first by revealing that General Hood was not only "a great soldier and a great gentleman," but also "a cagey cotton buyer"—a detail the family would rather not have heard. ...And he makes matters worse by trying to

tell a story from the Civil War: it wasn't Hood, the boy reminds him, but Stuart, who, despite a painful wound kept his vow never to touch alcohol; and it was at Spotsylvania, not Chancellorsville. In conversation it transpires that Mr. Forester does not really resent the modern world which has deprived him of his former eminence; he doesn't even mind keeping a store. He is merely puzzled when the mother suggests that his city taxes ought to be remitted in recognition of his historical significance—that he should be maintained as a kind of public monument. (6–7)

The detail about remitting taxes surely echoes Faulkner's "A Rose for Emily," in which the taxes on Miss Emily's fine house are exempted on the imaginary grounds that her family had special rights in recompense for service given the community by an ancestor. In Faulkner's story, Miss Emily is shielded by the myths of the glorious past, and the myth of the southern lady, though she herself has broken both myths by taking up with a Yankee. The hospitable family in Humphrey's story bullies the old man into a deep sigh of regret for a past that he doesn't really lament, and he walks off into the night supported by his stick at every step, whereas he had arrived touching it lightly to the ground every third step. As he

goes, the boy thinks, "I felt that there was no hope for
me in these mean times I had been born into" (27).
Humphrey is fulfilling his role as destroyer of myths
in this story. He does an even fuller job in *The
Ordways*. The ideology of a glorious old order was a
barrier to a realistic understanding of the southern
situation. It was kept alive by romantic stories like
the ones the boy in the story has come to love.

"The Hardys" seems universally acknowledged as
one of Humphrey's best stories. Even Mark Royden
Winchell, who generally does not like Humphrey's
early work, sees the manipulation of the point of view
as "the mark of an extremely talented craftsman"
(*William Humphrey* 28). The plot is minimal: Mr. and
Mrs. Hardy, married for fifty years, are introduced to
the reader on the morning that their farm will be sold.
Mr. Hardy had a first wife, Virgie. He can hardly remember her: when he tries to visualize her face, he
can only summon up the face of his present wife,
Clara. But Clara has lived in a painful state of jealousy all these years, imagining that he still loves
Virgie. In fact, he thinks of his first wife during the
story only because he is selling the house and comes
across things that evoke memories. The point of view
shifts brilliantly between the husband and wife, showing us their lack of communication and the ironies
that arise as a result. Mr. Hardy is reticent, a quality
that his wife attributes to his English origins. There

is a real life model for this marriage: in *Farther Off from Heaven*, Humphrey describes his maternal grandparents, the Varleys, an Englishman married to an American, and depicts exactly this state of irrational jealousy. And he creates a similar couple in *The Ordways*, the narrator's grandparents. Marriage is often full of misunderstandings and frustration in Humphrey's stories.

"Report Cards" is a story that Humphrey had great trouble marketing. In a letter he asked Katherine Anne Porter for her advice on it, mentioning that it had been turned down by almost every magazine in the country (10 October 1950). He had worked on it for a year and a half. It is a modest story, never accepted by a magazine, in which young Thomas Erskine pursues academic excellence in the third grade. His mother Harriet sees education as a way of raising him above the little world of their East Texas town. Humphrey's memoir, *Farther Off from Heaven*, makes it clear that he is using his own experience in the story. The social hierarchy is underscored: the Hazeltine children (poor white trash) fail in school and remain at the bottom of society; Katherine Spence, who is well-to-do, clearly envies Thomas's mother for having such a successful child. Education is one way out for the lower classes, and on the day of the story, Thomas and his mother learn that he will be skipped a year in school. An interesting bit of Texas folklore arises in the story: the boy was born on 18 June, and was teased that if he'd been born on 19 June, he would have been black. This is one of several references in Humphrey's work to "Juneteenth Day," celebrated by Texas blacks because news of Emancipation reached them belatedly on 19 June, 1865. Humphrey's own birthday was 18 June, a private joke implying that the story has an autobiographical source.

Another story with a young protagonist, "The Shell," is among Humphrey's best. It deals with one of his most frequent themes, the father-son relationship. The father, like Humphrey's own, was a superb hunter who died when the boy was on the brink of adolescence, before he could initiate his son into all the skills of hunting. Four years afterward, the boy still hoards a shell belonging to his father, thinking that he must not use it to hunt quail until he is good enough, because missing with his father's shell would be unthinkable. When he finally decides that the season to use the shell has arrived, he is terrified of missing and balks again and again. The story skillfully creates the atmosphere of quail hunting, and the relationship between the boy and his disappointed hunting dog, Mac, is superbly done. When the last day of the season arrives, he forces himself to use the shell, which by this time has become a dud. The experience liberates him: he knows he has kept the shell, a sym-

bol of his grief, for too long. When he next commands
the dog, it knows that "it was his master's voice speaking now, a hunter's voice" (79).

The story naturally calls Hemingway to mind,
particularly the story "Fathers and Sons." James Ward
Lee comments that "the theme of the youth's attain-
ing hunting prowess and manhood together has gotten to be almost a cliché, but the introduction of the
father's shell as a retarding influence gives the story
freshness and vitality" (*William Humphrey* 8). Perhaps the most interesting element in this good if
slightly derivative story is the way that it anticipates
Humphrey's first novel, *Home from the Hill*. The
father-son bond through hunting is important in both,
and like the boy in this story, Theron Hunnicutt wants
to excel but feels that it would be wrong to want to
exceed his father. The mother in the short story says
at one point, "It's the hunters the girls really go for,
isn't it? Us girls—us Southern girls like a hunting
man! I did. I'll bet all the little girls just—" (70). Like
Theron, the boy in the story is not much interested in
girls, not when he has hunting to master. In *Home
from the Hill*, we are told more than once that the
South is "a place where even the womenfolk felt that
no man was a man who was not a hunter" (74).

A final look at a southern mother comes in "A
Fresh Snow," a story in which a woman who has married and moved north thinks about her background

on a snowy day as she waits for her son to come home from school. With great economy, Humphrey shows us how alien she feels in a world where snow is normal and no one thinks about the Civil War. She recalls the custom of cleaning graves once a year, an event that Humphrey deals with in both *Home from the Hill* and *The Ordways*. She realizes that dead relatives are not significant for northerners the way that they are for southerners. When her son comes home in his snow gear, she realizes that his voice is nasal, not southern, and she refuses to let him go back out to play with his friends, forcing him instead to drink cocoa and sit on her lap like a smaller child, "his head against her breast, while she told him all about the South, where he was born" (201). The conclusion of this plotless little story is quite plaintive: the boy could no more be a southerner than he could revert to an earlier age.

The remaining story in the collection, "Sister," is an eccentric one, formless and close to pointless, a sketch of an eccentric young girl in a rather confused family. She has a huge collection of cats, nineteen in all. James Ward Lee's description of the work in his pamphlet as a character sketch rather than a story is fair enough (7–8), although *Harper's Bazaar* published it and Pearl Kazin was so impressed with Humphrey that she recommended him to Elaine Shaplen, an editor with the Alfred A. Knopf firm. In the talk reprinted in Ashby Bland Crowder's collection, *Writing in the Southern Tradition*, Humphrey summed it up very well, indicating that the story is about "an adolescent girl neglected by her parents in favor of her brother, who exacts her revenge by inflicting on them a house full of smelly and obnoxious cats" (186–87).

In *The Last Husband,* William Humphrey served his apprenticeship. The stories show occasional echoes of Porter, Faulkner, and Hemingway. The best of them—"Quail for Mr. Forester," "The Shell," "Report Card," "Man with a Family," and "In Sickness and Health" are excellent works. His best effort in the form, the unified and less derivative book on the 1930s in Texas and Oklahoma, *A Time and a Place*, is much better. Humphrey would return to writing short stories in the late 1980s with a large collection, *September Song*, but this final work is an uneven book.

On the basis of the stories, Humphrey began to get overtures from agents and from publishers like Alfred A. Knopf and Viking, asking if he had a novel. When he submitted his unfinished manuscript of *Home from the Hill* to Knopf in 1955, one of the editors, Henry A. Carlisle, told him he had never been so impressed by an unfinished work before. The novel took years to edit. Humphrey was thirty-three when it was published and had developed a strong sense of his abilities (to put it very mildly), which contrasts with the misgivings about his work that he manifested when he first began to correspond with Katherine Anne Porter.

3

The Myth of the Hunter:
Home from the Hill

William Humphrey had difficulty finding a title for his first novel. The initial agreement with Knopf in 1955 referred simply to "a novel about the Hunnicutt family in Texas," and it was referred to by the editors as *The Hunnicutt Tragedy* for a long while. Alfred A. Knopf, Jr., and the chief editor on the book, Herbert Weinstock, wanted to use the rather stilted title, *With All These Powers*, based on a quotation from Darwin: "with all these exalted powers Man still bears in his bodily frame the indel-

ible stamp of his lowly origin." That title would have
expressed the tragic force of the book, juxtaposing the
exalted spiritual urges of human beings with the
Darwinian struggle to survive: the demigod and the
blood-stained hunter. Henry Robbins, another Knopf
editor, suggested *Steps of the Hunter*, which would
have brought out the father-son dimension of the book.
At one point Knopf suggested that Humphrey read
the Bible to find a portentous title—it was a great
age for grand titles—but the author replied that he
had already read the Bible through twice for that
purpose.

Finally, Humphrey came up with the quotation
from Robert Louis Stevenson's poem "Requiem."

Under the wide and starry sky,
Dig the grave and let me lie.
Glad did I live and gladly die,
    And I laid me down with a will.

This be the verse you grave for me:
Here he lies where he longed to be;
Home is the sailor, home from the sea,
    And the hunter home from the hill.

The poem was a good choice. It manages to sound a
bit like a ballad as well as an epitaph, and the death
wish fits the character of Hannah Hunnicutt quite

well. The idea of digging a grave is appropriate in a relatively traditional society like Clarksville: the folk tradition delights in talk about graves, and there are several major scenes in the town cemetery. At the last moment the publicity department at Knopf wanted to expand the title to "The Hunter Home from the Hill," and Herbert Weinstock agreed, saying that the length of the title would be distinctive. Fortunately, this ungainly change (doubtless meant for readers who would not recognize the source) was not acceptable to the author.

Humphrey worried a good deal about the dust jacket copy, which he felt should refer to the aristocratic nature of the Hunnicutt family. He was trying to write a modern tragedy, but he was not interested in creating neurotic heroes. He was particularly concerned about one sentence in the proposed copy, and wrote to Weinstock:

> That same sentence goes on to say that Theron tried heartbreakingly to form himself in his father's image (aristocrat, man's man, and majestic hunter). The word "heartbreakingly" (though I know it's not meant that way) may seem to suggest that Theron was ill-suited by nature to become any of these three things. Seems to suggest that he was unsuccessful in all his attempts to be a

> man's man, etc. Brings to mind the image of
> another of those all-too-frequent browbeaten,
> ineffectual, un-heroic modern heroes forced
> to compete with an overpowering father, and
> foredoomed to failure. (13 May 1957)

While the novelist wanted to create a modern tragedy, he clearly wanted a character like Theron to have
a traditional dignity and forcefulness, which is perhaps one reason he seems stiff and stylized. It is difficult to have a modern tragedy without a modern
hero. Theron and his father are not meant to be Willie
Loman & Son. Hence they are slightly archaic figures. In a greater novel, *The Sound and the Fury* (to
flog him in the customary way with Faulkner's example), we are aware of a modern world impinging
on the doomed family, a world in which Jason
Compson can lose his money playing the Yankee commodities market.

Humphrey also wanted the copy to say something
about the secondary characters in the book, feeling
that "Mr. Halstead and Libby do occupy considerable
space in the book, are important to the plot; and one
of the things that pleased me was that the dramatis
personae was not small and tight, not confined to the
members of a family."

Perhaps the new novelist's most surprising comment about dust-jacket copy involved the question of

comparing the author to other writers. Humphrey said:

> I'd be much happier if no comparisons were made to any other writer. I confess to thinking I'm a much better novelist than R. P. Warren, so I don't much enjoy being compared to him. On the other hand I would be embarrassed to see myself compared in print to the writers with whom I privately compare myself.

Robert Penn Warren had won the Pulitzer Prize for fiction in 1946, and won it again for poetry in the same year when this comment was made. Humphrey was taking on a certain obligation to succeed by making this kind of hubristic remark. He managed to live up to the burden, however, producing a best-seller.

The initial success of the novel is easy to account for: it has a lucid style, a dramatic (even melodramatic) plot built on family conflict, a love story, and an interesting, slightly exotic setting. Readers of the 1950s would find the southern materials familiar from their reading of Faulkner—the fall of a prominent family, colorful folkways, picturesque black characters—and the emphasis on hunting would evoke Hemingway as well. Humphrey began his career at its commercial apogee: nothing he wrote later had

the same success. And unfortunately, critical opinion
seems to have turned against the book. Its rather convoluted plot has been scorned by a number of critics,
including James Ward Lee, Mark Royden Winchell,
and Craig Hudziak. Hudziak complains that the book
"contains more than a touch of melodrama, and the
last third of the novel is too much a series of coinci-
dences" (447). Winchell's comments on the novel are
scathing. In "Beyond Regionalism: The Growth of
William Humphrey," he says, "My television movie
guide describes the film version of *Home from the Hill*
as 'a turgid study of southern landowner and his relationship with wife, son, and illegitimate offspring.'
The novel offers us little more" (287). In his pamphlet
on Humphrey in the Western Writers Series, Winchell
even refers to the novel as "a potboiler aspiring to
high art. And it is an unusually nihilistic potboiler at
that" (16).

The book is neither nihilistic nor a potboiler. It is
too well written and insightful into both place and
character to be a potboiler, though it certainly kept
the pot boiling in the Humphrey household for years.
As for nihilism, it is no more nihilistic than other bleak
works like *The Sound and the Fury* and *Macbeth*, to
put Humphrey in the most exalted company. To lower
the company to more realistic terms, it suggests not
high tragedy but a tragic idyll. John Bayley uses this
term for the kind of novel to distinguish Hardy's *Tess*

of the D'Urbervilles from the naturalism of Flaubert (184), and it could be applied to Humphrey, who has written a rather melodramatic tale of love and murder in a backwater region, the sort of novel that Hardy wrote so well. In a greater novel, *The Sound and the Fury,* we are aware of a modern world impinging on the doomed family, a world in which Jason Compson can lose his money playing the Yankee commodities market. The clear influence of Faulkner has kept commentators from noticing that the ambiance of Humphrey's work is influenced by Hardy's Wessex. And although Humphrey satirizes Albert Halstead for assuming that his daughter's romance will follow the pattern of "old jokes and ballads," he acknowledges that for Halstead these forms were "so much a part of his native place that they were a part even of him" (238). Hardy and the ballads have assumptions about the "way of a man with a maid" that may have been overthrown in our time, but many of those assumptions were still intact in the southern world of the 1930s.

The novel begins with a framing narrative set in 1954, the "present." In a brilliant sequence of six chapters that constitute a prologue and carefully balance exposition and suspense, we are introduced to a setting and a collective narrator. "Frame" is a bit of a misnomer, as Humphrey does not return to this story at the end of the novel, though he was pressured to do so by his editors. Actually, the fictional world of Humphrey's first three novels is defined in this elaborate opening. The setting is a town square (very much like Clarksville) on an early September morning in 1954 (3). The aroma of the cottonseed mill wafts its "hot sweet nutty smell" downtown and the first bale of cotton of the year holds a place of honor on a platform wrapped in red bunting. Naturally there is a statue of a Confederate soldier. Into this little world enters a black hearse with Dallas plates, capturing the attention of men whittling on the northeast corner of the square. It passes under the shadow of the monument. The history of the Lost Cause is not important in this novel, although it will be in *The Ordways*. But a certain social order is implied by the monument: this is a traditional society which hasn't changed much since the Civil War.

The hearse scene reminded critic Walter Sullivan of the arrival of a hearse and limousine to pick up Peyton's body in William Styron's *Lie Down in Darkness*. That limousine is driven by the formal Mr. Llewellyn Casper; the hearse by his slow-witted assistant, Lyle Barclay. Styron's Casper and Barclay are not much like Humphrey's hearse attendants and they have a greater role in the novel. There are indeed some similarities in the openings of the two books, with the slow progress of the hearse serving almost as a introductory cinema shot, something to serve as background for the credits. Sullivan also notes that "there is something Styronesque about the family group: the neurotic mother, the father with his women, the child caught in the parental crossfire and running swiftly to his doom" (382). The elegiac tone of Humphrey's book probably does owe something to *Lie Down in Darkness*, but that is not anything that should cause discomfort. Humphrey was a great admirer of Styron's fiction and exchanged letters with him.

The hearse in *Home from the Hill* attracts attention, though it has entered the town almost by stealth. A sense of mystery is created as we follow the men in the square, who quit whittling to come and look when the hearse parks by the confectionery. We get an immediate sense of the social milieu through the terse utterances of the men gawking at the vehicle. As James Ward Lee has observed, the names and the speech of the characters capture the flavor of East Texas precisely: names like Peyton Stiles and Otis Wheeler, phrases like "I God! Hit's a Rolls-Royce!" The "I God" is, in fact, a phrase that Sullivan especially objects to, feeling that it has a labored small-town quality. The novel reveals that Clifford Odum "was taking advantage of that established right of townsmen to examine a visiting car and had raised the hood" (5). The men on the town square play an important role in the book: they exemplify the male community

that loves cars and guns. They are the associates of
the male protagonists, Wade Hunnicutt and his son,
Theron. They cannot be called peers because Wade
represents an aristocracy of money and hunting prowess, but they serve, as Lee says in his 1967 pamphlet
on Humphrey, as a kind of Greek chorus. Their comments are the banalities of folk culture: "It beats me
what could make a young fellow want to go into that
trade," says Marshall Bradley, to which Peyton Stiles
replies "It's steady." And Ed Dinwoodie observes: "Yes,
and it's a business that's always good." Indeed, "The
worse things are the better it is."

The opening helps define the world of the little
Texas town by bringing outsiders into it, city slickers
from Dallas who do not explain their mission. Eventually the town, with its superior knowledge of the
Hunnicutt family, will be able to condescend to the
outsiders. The opening chapters keep the reader (like
the community) in suspense about the mission of the
hearse. Its occupants, a burly man in crumpled clothes
and a dapper one, do not appear to be ordinary em-
ployees of an undertaker. They have come to bury
someone, but they are reluctant to explain their mission. We are reminded of southern racial attitudes
when they ask the waitress in the confectionery
"where we might find a couple of niggers that'd like
to make a dollar." The waitress replies, "Well, they's
generally some boys hangs out in the alley back of

the place here in the good weather, waiting for odd jobs. No-count town niggers, too lazy to pick cotton." Humphrey has set his novel in 1954, a few months after Brown vs. Board of Education, the desegregation decision that would change the racial order of the South forever. Perhaps this choice of date was intentional, the Supreme Court decision being as important to the South as the loss of the Civil War. The outsiders with the hearse are not professional undertakers, hence their desire to hire gravediggers. When they finally state who the deceased is, Hannah Hunnicutt, the listeners are astounded. The news travels quickly through the community. The two outsiders are assured that they will not need to have a grave dug, an odd statement. It is their turn to be puzzled, and eventually they will be astounded by what they see in the cemetery.

The person to be buried is the wife of Wade Hunnicutt, and Humphrey skillfully protracts suspense by giving us Wade's background in the second chapter. He was the biggest landowner in the area— fifteen years after his death in 1939, the first Saturday in October is still known as Hunnicutt Day because that was the day that his sharecropping tenants paid him. Humphrey works hard to present Captain Wade (as he was known) as a local aristocrat. His status is conferred by the respect given him by the community. In this chapter Humphrey shifts from omniscient narration to a communal narrator, a device clearly borrowed, as commentators have noticed, from Faulkner's "A Rose for Emily." In Faulkner's story, the community feels pity for Miss Emily, realizing that her family has declined since the Civil War, leaving her the impoverished last member. But Captain Wade excites no one's pity, even in his fall. He served in the AEF in World War I, giving him his military title, one retained by community consent, although "Captain" is also a common term in the South for a boss. His garb may seem less than aristocratic, as he wears khaki trousers and a faded blue denim workshirt, but his shoes are made in Fort Worth at fifty dollars a pair, a huge sum in his lifetime, and his hat cost a hundred dollars, "the sort of extravagant small gesture of which legends are made in Texas" (12). And we learn later that he has two custom-made shotguns, one costing a thousand dollars, the other two thousand. In his lifetime he was always the center of the ring of men on the town square. He is a kind of projection of Humphrey's own plebeian father, the most skilled hunter of Red River County, into a loftier figure.

Along with prowess in hunting, the traditional vocation of an aristocrat, he is a hunter of women. Venery in both senses of the word is his vocation, and Humphrey uses hunting metaphors to talk about womanizing: Wade will cross any man's fence to hunt

game, and "in his other sport he was equally unmind-
ful of property lines, bag limits, and no-trespassing
signs" (13–14). He uses the techniques of still-hunt-
ing to capture women: he waits for them to come to
him, and his black servant, Chauncey, says "he had
to fight the women off with a wet towsack" (14). His
favorites were married women. Hence when Humphrey ends Chapter 2 by speaking of the day fifteen
years before when he entered town as an unrecogniz-
able corpse in the bed of a pickup truck, we suspect
that sex was involved in his killing. This proves correct, in an ironic way, though he is not killed by an
angry husband.

By making Hunnicutt into a kind of aristocrat
by common consent, Humphrey has met the traditional requirement that the tragic hero should be
superior to the ordinary man, but not perfect. The
novel shows the long process through which a man
becomes estranged from his wife and loses his son's
admiration, a particularly terrible fate that Hunnicutt
feels as bitterly as Henchard in Hardy's *The Mayor
of Casterbridge* feels his estrangement from his
daughter. Hunnicutt's death by violence is almost
anti-climactic. His wife also meets a tragic fate, madness brought on by her own actions. The son is more
a victim of his parents' troubled marriage than a tragic
hero, but he too contributes to his fate by his extreme
pride and deluded idealism.

Humphrey's third chapter brings the story to the cemetery where the three extraordinary tombstones of these characters lie, and where—in a southern Gothic touch, or a Hardyesque one—Hannah's open grave has been waiting for her all these years. Bud Stovall, the deputy sheriff, appears, demanding proof that "Miz Hannah" is in the coffin, and then the sheriff himself appears (and so does most of the town and half of the county). He too demands proof that Miz Hannah is in the coffin, and is told that she is being buried as she instructed. When he asks to see the instructions he is told that they can't be seen, because they are in the coffin. The sheriff enters the hearse to look at the coffin. But this is not enough: the community must be involved. The sheriff decides that after fifteen years he can't be absolutely certain of Hannah's identity, so the collective "we" of the narration has a look also, in a morbid scene that definitely calls "A Rose for Emily" to mind. The body is dressed in a sequined evening gown, the significance of which is revealed later, but for the present the fact that the golden sequins have tarnished into green conveys the decline of the family. The corpse is no Sleeping Beauty. It shows defiance and outraged pride, but it has not been embalmed. Pinned to the dress is a note with burial instructions: the deceased wanted no embalming, no viewing, no ceremony: instructions quite similar to Henchard's at the end of Hardy's *The Mayor of*

Casterbridge. But the viewing has occurred, and the community will lay the body to rest in the grave. It is the turn of the well-dressed young stranger, who has been coy about his mission and his cargo, to be astonished as he looks at the tombstone and reads that Hannah, like her husband and son, departed this life on 28 May 1939. His surprise ("Why don't it say wife to him?—nodding toward the Captain's stone") enables the community to reverse the situation of the morning and express its own knowledge: "'That's just what we said,' we told him. 'That was when we sent for you people.'" The chapter ends with the reader understanding at last that the two men driving the hearse work for a mental institution.

Chapter 4 returns to 1930 to explain why Miz Hannah was committed. The crisis came on the first Graveyard Cleaning Day after what the collective narrator calls "the tragedy." Graveyard Cleaning Day (often known as Graveyard Workday or Graveyard Decoration Day) is a dying southern custom that fascinated Humphrey. He made excellent use of it in *The Ordways*. In *The Encyclopedia of Southern Culture*, D. Gregory Jeane describes the custom:

> Cults of piety express veneration of deceased family members. One of the most widespread of these is graveyard workday[,] . . . an annual event where all people with relatives in

a particular cemetery gather to clean the cemetery. Activities include scraping all grass from the cemetery (creating a stark visual contrast with surrounding woodland or field), mounding all graves, taking or sweeping all debris from the grounds, righting fallen tombstones (when present) and mending fences to keep animals out. Associated with this daylong event is "dinner on the grounds," light courting, business dealing, and general renewing of family bonds and relationships. Thus, graveyard workday serves multiple functions within the community, much the same way that southern funerals are family-strengthening affairs. (464)

A broken family cannot be strengthened by ritual. In this novel, two Graveyard Cleaning Days are described. In the one before the tragic event, Theron's alienation from his parents is shown by his refusal to work with them. He prefers to clean the Reprobate's Field, where social outcasts and the very poor are buried. In the second, the community sees the three gravestones that Miss Hannah has had erected, and the grave she has dug for herself. The opening of the novel takes us to the cemetery to provide a kind of denouement in advance for the story.

We are kept waiting for the graveyard scene, however: more suspense. The bulk of Chapter 4 is our introduction to the other half of the unhappy marriage. Captain Wade has chosen a respectable but not beautiful wife (a shrewd strategy for a man who must consider married women hopelessly unfaithful). They have one child, but when Hannah learns from an anonymous note that her husband is constantly unfaithful, she is outraged and turns away from him. She is particularly outraged when she complains to her father and learns that he had known about Wade's reputation. Being part of the male complicity in such behavior, he understands Wade's sexual proclivities: "her husband was no different from any other man" (25). Indeed, he continues to regard his daughter with "astonishment and amusement, asking her what on earth she had expected of a twenty-eight-year-old man. He had been a little disgusted to speak of the sort of fellow she had apparently wanted for a husband. He was disappointed that she had not known beforehand and did not appreciate what a ladies' man she was getting in Wade" (24). Hannah decides to be "long-suffering" as the traditional expression puts it. Her mother calls her a "saint," a role of passive martyrdom, but one psychologically dangerous, for a saint can nurse a sense of outrage. Hannah's outrage is a Faulknerian reaction: as Andre Bleikasten has pointed out, outrage and astonishment are responses by Faulkner's characters when they confront the

appalling facts of human behavior. Hannah's outrage
finds its outlet after Wade's death when she has the
three tombstones placed in the cemetery: a black one
for Wade, a white one for their son, and a red one for
her. Black for Wade's villainy, and white for Theron's
innocence (we shall see what that innocence involves).
In a valuable article on "The Graveyard Epiphany in
Modern Southern Fiction," John T. Hiers suggests that
Hannah's red stone suggests that "Hannah perhaps
realizes that she too must accept some responsibility
for the shedding of their blood" (398). The red also
associates her with martyrdom, and she has been a
living martyr throughout her marriage. The reader
is told that Theron's tombstone does not mark a
tomb, a mystery which will be cleared up later. The
inscriptions on the markers astonish and perplex the
slick young man from the asylum: all three declare
that a member of the family "DEPARTED THIS LIFE
May 28, 1939," even though Hannah has lived another fifteen years beyond her alleged date of death.
The collective narrator observes that if the two strang-
ers, now revealed to be a psychiatric intern and a
violent-ward attendant, can look at these tombstones
and say "Crazy!" His interjection implies that the community was right to say the same and arrange her
committal. The community is now in control of the
situation. It understands its own.

There is one more chapter on Hannah, the "crazy"

one, a summary of her accomplishments, her enormous self-education so that she can educate Theron, on whom all her love is lavished once she closes the bedroom door to her errant husband. She learned Boy Scout lore, the ways of crystal radio sets, entomology. Theron is the young prince-in-the-making: his father will teach him to hunt, and his mother will insure his general knowledge. But the situation is a dangerous one, with the boy growing up in a house where the parents have no love for one another. Wade gives little thought to his wife, but she nurtures a deep hatred for him, while resolving for the boy's sake never to disillusion him with his father.

The sixth chapter returns to the cemetery, where it is the outsiders' turn to be snubbed (the intern is called "Hot-Shot" by the "we" of the narration: the city slicker is now condescended to). The young intern is puzzled by the tombstones, but the community cold-shoulders his inquiries. Theron's inscription says "only son of Hannah Hunnicutt," as if his father had nothing to do with his begetting. The intern decides that Hannah must have hated her husband so much that she proclaimed to the world that he was a cuckold, a shamelessness that proved her crazy. The community doesn't correct this erroneous idea. This, after all, is their world, not the world of Dallas asylums and Rolls-Royce hearses. "He was so pleased with his explanation that we let him keep it" (35).

The "we" includes a number of young people who are known as "the Captain's Company," putative children of other fathers, who nevertheless show a strong resemblance to Wade. It is wry for "Hot-Shot" to call the Captain a cuckold.

The opening chapters are a leisurely introduction to the isolated and traditional community in which the Hunnicutt tragedy occurs. The oddity of the tombstones is extravagant but not an absurdity in the death-centered South. In Paris, Texas, one county west of Humphrey's Clarksville, the largest cemetery has two extraordinary gravestones. One is a huge statue of Jesus, dressed in traditional robes — but wearing cowboy boots. The other is over the grave of a boy who died after the doctor instructed his family to pack him in ice to bring down his fever. The inscription reads: "Frozen to Death."

An extraordinary number of details in the opening chapters resonates with the rest of the novel. The tragedy grows out of the situation that exists in the Hunnicutt family. The succeeding chapters fall into several movements: the education of Theron as a hunter; his proof of manhood by killing a boar (recapitulating a feat of his father's); the celebration of his deed by a barbecue and the snubbing of the hero by the father of his chosen date, Libby Halstead; the clandestine romance of Libby and Theron; Theron's discovery of his father's true character and his decision to leave home; the return of a pregnant Libby from the college where her father has sent her; Theron's misguided marriage to Opal, a tenant farmer's daughter; Libby's marriage to Fred Shumway; and the tragedy that ensues on the day that Libby's child is christened. The novel appears to take its time but is written with great economy, preparing tragic complications for Wade Hunnicutt in particular, but also for his wife and son. Along the way it immerses us in a richly detailed world. Humphrey's pacing is excellent. In the first half of the novel, the narration expands and contracts with ease. Humphrey deals with Theron's childhood and coming of age (marked by the killing of a boar) in Chapters 7–16. The barbecue and dance celebrating the successful hunt occupies chapters 17–24; these chapters are a kind of genre picture of East Texas life and the narration is leisurely. The romance with Libby occupies 24–33 and the novelist takes his time letting the relationship unfold in an entirely convincing way. The time of Libby's departure is a turning point in the plot: Theron impregnates her, his mother tells him about his father, and a series of disastrous events work themselves out with intricate twists and turns over a period of nine months. Humphrey's advance in craftsmanship over *The Last Husband* is striking.

We are told in Chapter 4 that Wade wanted a son to make into a hunter, and that even Hannah wanted a son because "it was a man's world" (25). The novel uses the growth of Theron into manhood as a means of explaining the hunter's code and the man's world that it defines. The code requires courage, a profound knowledge of the wilderness, and an ability to use firearms. In fact, we learn that a male in small town Texas knows cars and firearms very early. "You could speak of a Texas boy's youth and manhood as his .410, his 20 and 12 gauge shotgun years. Certainly you could have of Theron Hunnicutt, who lived for hunting and who, more than a boy and not quite a man, died at about the 16 gauge" (11). This is an extraordinary way to mark stages in a male's life. Of course, mere possession of firearms does not make a hunter. The ethos of hunting is inculcated in Theron in several ways: by the lore—tribal lore, really—that he picks up on the town square from his father's associates; from the example of the father whom he adores, and even from his mother, who knows little about hunting but lives "in a place where even the women-folks felt that no man was a man who was not a hunter" (74), and from the books that he reads.

After the hearse scene, the men on the town square provide one last example of the group narrator before the novel shifts to an omniscient point of view and begins to tell the story of the family's downfall. In Chapter 7, the group narrator no longer speaks for the community at large but merely for the men who gather on the square. We learn about Theron's innocence in this chapter: his tombstone was white, after all. Innocence, unfortunately, implies ignorance as well as purity. His fight with a sexually knowing boy, Dale Latham, is described. When Theron is seventeen, Latham meets him on the square and asks the priggish young man a classic male question: "Getting much lately?" (36). The encounter leads to violence when the traditional accusation of cowardice is made. Or rather violence follows when Dale adds "And so's your old man" to his initial "You're yellow." Dale loses his front teeth. The willingness of Theron to defend the honor of his father is ominous: the reader wonders what will happen when the boy learns that his father is a philanderer, that his prey is human as well as animal.

By the time of this incident, Theron had been involved with the male camaraderie on the square for a couple of years, causing a change in the speech and tone of the hunters: "It was as if he had brought Mrs. Hannah." Precisely. The boy's prudish idealism is the product of his mother's influence. The men find him humorless and proud, but they also respond to his admiration for them: he perceives them as nobler than they are and fails to see where they fall short of his ideals. His trust and his humorless nature leads to the debacle of the snipe hunt, the traditional prank played on the novice hunter. Theron stands patiently with his open bag waiting for snipe long after another boy would have perceived the joke and left. A mark of his pride is his reaction afterward when he is addressed on the square as "Lieutenant." "He liked that. But, 'Sergeant will do for now,' he said." The collective narrator says, "Not 'Private,' you'll notice." The collective narrator then almost vanishes from the novel (45), which proceeds to use omniscient narration to explore the minds of the three protagonists.

One of Theron's formative influences is his reading. We learn that he read Scott, Marryat, Cooper, and "Southern historians of The Lost Cause." These are typical boys' books, though the southern history is not universal. From Marryat and Cooper he would imbibe tales of adventure in the wilderness, and as for Scott, the code of chivalry is so pervasive in his works that Mark Twain liked to blame the South's disasters in the Civil War, the "Lost Cause," on Scott. Humphrey is aware of this idea of Twain's and mentions it *The Ordways*. While this reading seems natural enough for a boy, it certainly encourages Theron's illusions about the hunter's code.

But his real mentor is his father, not Sir Walter Scott. The novel describes, in what can only be called loving detail, the boy's growth as a hunter under his father's guidance. Frederick J. Hoffman has referred to Theron as "a poor man's Ike McCaslin" and suggests that he learns "the intricacies of the forest and, presumably, of God" (103). Actually, there are no indications that Theron imbibes any spiritual values from Wade. The novel has no equivalent of Sam Fathers, or even of General Compson. The father wants his son to be better than himself, but this seems to involve only worldly success.

The father's influence is enhanced by Chauncey, the black servant, who serves as historian of Wade's exploits. Chauncey, Theron's "Uncle Remus, the Captain's worshipful man-of-no-work and the most hyperbolic of old Negroes" (150), tells Theron innumerable stories with "Cap'm Wade" as the hero. Theron comes to think of his father as superior to Robin Hood and the wilderness of Sulphur Bottom becomes a Sherwood Forest in his imagination. The most important narrative is "How Cap'm Wade Hunnicutt Killed the Last Wild Boar in East Texas." Most of the game hunted in East Texas in the twentieth century is defenseless: deer, birds, squirrels. If the hunter is to manifest courage as well as woodsmanship and marksmanship, a worthy opponent is needed, and bears are virtually extinct in that part of the south. Wade has killed a worthy animal foe, a boar. Chauncey's entrancing narratives intensify the boy's admiration for his father by casting him as a hero. They also add an archaic air to the novel.

The portrait of Chauncey is superbly drawn, with authentic details of speech and gesture. It is also conventional and makes a contemporary reader uncomfortable, for, as James Ward Lee observes, it has something of the "stage nigger" about it. This is a world before the Civil Rights movement, but in writing about such a world William Faulkner constantly reminds us of the paradoxes and struggles that arise in a racist society. His Lucas Beauchamp constantly challenges—with a measure of prudence—his definition by others as a "nigger." Chauncey as a loyal retainer challenges the system in only one way: he refuses to "mister" white men if they are hunters. White men who are hunters he calls by their given names. He is indulged, but as a frisky dog is indulged: he is Old Chauncey, "a certificate of reliability, such as is given a dog or a cunning old fox or a long-run locomotive, people speaking of Old Queen or Old Red or Old Ninety-seven," and he takes pride in this title (53). And we learn early on that like the mistresses of Wade Hunnicutt, Chauncey would, at least metaphorically, be willing to wash the Captain's feet and drink the water. Humphrey's notebooks reveal that he was deeply opposed to segregation and the servitude of blacks in the South, but he has no vision of a different order, a problem that damages his last southern novel, *Proud Flesh*.

The mother also contributes to the boy's formation as a hunter, endorsing the view that a man is a man only if he hunts. When in his last year of high school Theron misses classes to hunt, she reacts not by reprimanding him but by summoning the hapless principal to her home to inform him that she has given Theron permission to hunt instead of going to school. In effect, she pulls rank on the principal. She is, after all, a Griffin, a member of an older stock than the Hunnicutts (24), and she knows how to play the grande dame. The school board acquiesces, just as the civic leaders in "A Rose for Emily" decide to excuse Miss Emily's taxes. The collective narrator makes one of its rare later appearances in discussing this acquiescence: "We spoiled him you see. Small wonder if he took to a fault what no one around him thought could be one, or that he grew narrow and proud and intolerant. . . ." (74).

The Captain himself is the great influence on his son. But he has no understanding of what it might mean for his son to turn out better than himself. We are told that "the Captain's business in life was, in the final analysis, getting the most out of men" (65): that "most" involves his status as a landlord and employer. He admires his wife for her part in raising the boy. He is a little awed by Theron's virtues. He gives his wife the credit for the virtues, but he rises in his own estimation for having contributed to his son's formation. Humphrey is setting him up for an enormous fall, of course: the Captain is a man of power, rather than of moral virtue. But for much of the novel, the boy grows into a fine hunter under his father's tutelage, and it is a noble trait in the father to be delighted in his son's capacity for surpassing the model.

Theron is presented as unbalanced both in his idealism and in his obsession with hunting. Both are excessive. A priggish young man is a figure of fun, and a game hog, as Theron becomes, perverts a skill into a vice. The positive side of his obsession is physical courage. Part of Theron's education as a hunter has come from his visits to Wade's study, a masculine space, "disorderly but clean, man-kept" (47), filled with trophies and Indian artifacts and redolent of smells of "leather and steel and gun oil and boot grease." The chief trophy is the mounted head of the wild boar killed by Wade.

Theron gets his chance to prove his manhood by killing another wild boar, a creature rather scarce in Texas. This one supposedly worked his way over from Louisiana. Wade tells the man who has seen the boar, "my boy here will take care of him for you" (81), causing laconic surprise on the town square, though the hunters listening dare not express skepticism about the boy's fitness to "take care" of the beast. In effect, the father has set a test of manhood for his son, who responds eagerly and with a craving for glory that leads him to slip away on the crucial morning without his backup man, Pritchard.

The description of the hunt is brilliant writing. It inevitably invites comparisons with Faulkner's hunting scenes in *Go Down, Moses*, and Humphrey, as we have seen in the previous chapter, admitted to Katherine Anne Porter that Faulkner was the source. This is probably his most Faulknerian passage, in theme and style. The prose takes on an adjectival eloquence: "Its speed was incredible, hurtling and huge and direct, like a guided torpedo" (90). The style employs the rapid motion/slow motion effects familiar in the Mississippi writer. The rather formalized scene has a *deja vu* effect, as Humphrey has given a similar account in Chauncey's black dialect. The mystical dimensions of the struggle with Old Ben are not present. This is not a wise King of the Woods, pursued for many years by hunters who respect his greatness. Rather it is an interloper, not one of the noblest, although it has mythical resonances. If Theron is a poor man's Ike McCaslin, the boar is a poor man's Calydonian boar, a ravaging intruder to be killed without sorrow.

Humphrey does provide an ethical, if not religious, dimension to the hunt. Theron has to deal with the desire to surpass his father, a feeling of rivalry and envy. After killing his own boar, he wonders if it might be bigger than his father's. But he conquers that feeling: "he saw too that he had slain what the brute embodied" (93). When this boar's head is mounted on the wall along with his father's trophy, he refuses to contemplate the possibility that it might be bigger. Once his head clears of excitement in the woods, he takes on a hunter's *sprezzatura*, a nonchalance familiar to readers of Hemingway as well as Faulkner: the hunter does not brag or swagger. He chooses to cut off the pig's tail as a trophy. It is his father who has the trophy mounted. Theron does not replicate his father's amorous nonchalance, and this will initiate the tragedy. The son, like any legendary hero, has slain his monster and is ready to find love. But he is also his mother's son.

The love plot is initiated by the barbecue and dance that Wade throws to celebrate his son's victory. The barbecue is a feasting scene described in epic catalogues of food and drink. Commentators have relished the detail of Chauncey using a mop to apply barbecue sauce to the boar. There are many details worth savoring: the food, the clandestine drinking, the story-telling about the liquor runner and the Sheriff (who are both present and drinking). The reader gets an excellent sense of this society and its mores, the same society which will later bury Hannah Hunnicutt. Theron overhears Chauncey talking about him and realizes that he has achieved the status of legend himself. The barbecue is the high point in the relationship of father and son. Their trophies look like a "stereograph," and when the son contemplates them he recalls his first squirrel hunt, when he fired too soon out of his desire to succeed before his father. He now has the wisdom to understand that his father was a boy once and must have made the same mistake. The rapport between father and son appears complete. It rests on very few words—this is a hunter's code, after all, and the ethos (as Hemingway demonstrates over and over) of such a code is understatement.

But the destruction of the father-son relationship has begun, unknown to the characters. Theron has invited Libby Halstead to the barbecue and dance, his first date, but he is humiliated by her father, who sees him as a potential womanizer like Wade. Turned away by Albert Halstead (who is not a hunter, significantly), Theron does not dance at his own festival. The complications of the romance will eventually destroy the family. Part of the plot is set in motion when a mellow Wade Hunnicutt tries to talk sentimentally to his long-estranged wife. She anticipates a visit to her separate bedroom, the first since Theron's birth, but it does not happen, heightening the bitterness which will lead her to reveal to her son just what sort of man his father is.

If any part of Humphrey's novel has been insufficiently appreciated, it must be the courtship of Theron and Libby. Their story is one that Humphrey's favorite novelist, Thomas Hardy, would appreciate.

In fact, the customs of Hardy's Wessex are not much different from Humphrey's East Texas. Both novelists create tragic idylls in a traditional world where relationships of men and women follow ancient patterns and courtship is carried on in a country setting. Humphrey also gives us a world of potential seducers and ruined women, of double standards, of dramatic confrontations at the church door. Elizabeth Janeway describes this novel as tragedy with melodramatic trimmings (1), which aligns it more with Hardy and the Border Ballads than with Sophocles. *Home from the Hill* not only presents a world before desegregation but also one before the sexual revolution.

In this world the male is a potential seducer: Albert Halstead, a timid townsman, is not pleased by his daughter's beauty, feeling dread that someone will ruin her before she can be safely married. Theron, son of the local Don Juan, is turned out of Albert's house because tradition says, "like father, like son." Halstead turns out to be right in a way, though Theron is not a guileful seducer and the sexual relationship ensues from passion, not from seduction. The passion is engendered, ironically, by the romantic interest created by Halstead's action. The result—pregnancy— is the same as in a seduction, but the motives and the experiences of the characters are different.

Much of the interest for the reader lies in the callow nature of the characters Theron and Libby.

Their hesitations and uncertainties are dramatized convincingly, and the irony of the situation—an affair created and fueled by a misguided parental prohibition—envelopes their every move. Their first meeting, the day after the dance, comes about when she signals him with the mirror of her compact, a romantic gesture. They take refuge in his house when rain begins to fall. They are not, of course, Dido and Aeneas taking refuge in a cave, but rather two teenagers not sure what they think about each other. Libby has a romantic image of him because he is a hero and a bit of a mystery. She adapts very well to his pride and reticence, adding these to the image. Humphrey conveys their growing mutual interest during the first meeting with some powerful sexual images, like the fallen earring that she screws back into her ear so tightly that it hurts. They are driven to the attic by the return of Theron's mother, and in the attic— where Theron does not take advantage of the solitude to make a pass at Libby—she has a museum of Theron's whole life. One of the most important items is a gold-sequined dress of his mother's, one which he loved, seeing her as a Joan of Arc or a mermaid, and which she wore, inappropriately and at his insistence, to a birthday party he attended. The heroic chastity and stubbornness of Joan of Arc has more meaning than Theron perceives, and a mermaid is isolated from ordinary human concerns. The dress is the one in which Hannah chooses to be buried in 1954. The Oedipal suggestions of the attic scene are clear: Theron and Libby are in hiding from Theron's mother, and they come across the dress associated with his immature feelings for her. So far there has been no sign of an Oedipal conflict in the novel, but antagonism toward his father will begin shortly.

The clandestine lunch that Theron brings to the attic for Libby includes an apple, a means for the black servant Melba to practice divination on: she has told Theron that she needs an apple that both he and his beloved have bitten. The following vivid and concise scene with Melba is one of the best in the novel. Melba heats two apple seeds in a frying pan, each representing one of the lovers. If one seed moves away from the other, she says, the corresponding person will be untrue. Theron asks, "Don't you know any pleasant magic?" "Doesn't anything ever turn out happy?" (148). The first trial fails: the seed representing Libby splits from the heat, "revealing the white within. It resembled a burnt kernel of popcorn" (149). Libby's eventual pregnancy is prophesied here. A second trial leaves the seeds representing the lovers united, though "he never afterwards could be quite sure that she had not jiggled it to make the two seeds roll lovingly together."

The following chapter, a fine genre picture of a coon hunt, turns away from the romance plot and introduces Verne Luttrell, who will contribute to the catastrophe. Verne is not a noble hunter, and he is puzzled when the Captain decides to let a particularly courageous raccoon go. After the hunt we see Verne briefly with his pregnant wife, Opal, whom he strikes after she taunts him with the suggestion that the baby is not his own. She takes refuge behind the Captain, which will later cause Theron to believe that his father is the progenitor, bringing about a set of disastrous complications.

The growing relationship between Theron and Libby takes place mostly outdoors, by necessity. This idyll in the presence of nature, readily calling Hardy to mind, is overshadowed by Albert Halstead's plan to send Libby away. The sexual politics are entirely traditional: at one point Libby feels that Theron has the harder part, "with the lonely endurance which the code of manhood forced on him" (169), and she believes that he should make their decisions: "he was the man" (156). The final meeting of the lovers ends as we would expect with a sexual encounter—which Humphrey does not describe any more than Hardy would have. Libby realizes that Theron has some reservations along with his feelings of love and gratitude: she hardly knows how torn with self-doubt he is, feeling that he is exactly the person that Albert Halstead feared.

The next chapter initiates the tragic complications of the novel. Everything is carefully prepared, perhaps too carefully. Hannah waits up, brooding over her injuries. She looks over the class picture in which the photographer clearly focused on Libby as the prettiest girl in the class and remembers her own class picture, in which the cynosure was Kitty Travis. It was during her pregnancy with Theron that Hannah received an anonymous note telling her, "You are living in a house of cards," that her husband was betraying her with Kitty (174). The characters, as in any tragedy, are all living in a house of cards: the cliché is appropriate and has scope for the plot. Hannah also broods over Wade's failure to come to her room the night of the barbecue. So she is naturally in a poor state to see what appears to be Theron sneaking into the house. But it is Wade, not his son. And when the son does sneak in, hours later, she meets him to query him about the lateness and what he has been doing. After she learns his story, she feels sympathy for her son and then outrage that the angry Halstead has in effect said, "Like father, like son." In wishing to deny this folk saying (of course, father and son have both sneaked in, which increases her instability), she blurts out the truth. She has been primed to do this by her rehearsal of grievances earlier in the morning, and by her resentment that her son has suffered for the sins of his father. Theron's reaction goes beyond an Oedipal loyalty to his mother and hatred of his father: he turns angrily on them both. The reader can be excused for feeling that his stiff hostility is excessive. He managed to reach adolescence while still worshiping both of his parents, and now he rejects them—with sorrow and torment, but with no compassion.

The house of cards referred to long ago in the anonymous note has fallen at last, with fatal consequences. Wade begins to pay for his manner of life the next day, when he offers to go hunting with his son and gets the sobbing answer, "I'm never going hunting again!" (195). Wade's reaction is interesting. He feels "a sudden, sharp cold chill of loneliness. He felt lonely, yet not alone. He felt for a moment the strange and intolerable sensation of being alone with himself" (195). One of Humphrey's difficulties in the novel is to present the tragic experience as it befalls a man who has very little inner life. He makes a good try in the scene just before Wade's death. The plot, which has developed slowly to this point, moves quickly and with surprising turns. Complaints about its manipulative quality are understandable, but it is no more contrived than some novels by Hardy or Dickens, perhaps less than some of them. Ultimately the entrapment of fate is, as Northrop Frye likes to point out, the author's entrapment of the characters in the plot. After a life of ease, Wade Hunnicutt is going to pay for his offenses, and every event will relentlessly work against him. In a way, his son is responsible for his death, having made Libby pregnant, an act for which Wade will be blamed.

The depth of Theron's estrangement from his parents is measured by the events on Graveyard Cleaning Day, our second glimpse of this southern event in the novel. He discovers the Reprobates' Field. Theron chooses to clean plots in that field rather than work beside his mother, and he obsessively continues to hoe long after everyone else has left. There is a bit of macabre southern humor in the chapter: we get a little digression about Hugh Ramsay, who buried his amputated leg with its own tombstone.

The following chapter is one of the best in the book. When Wade Hunnicutt learns from his wife that Halstead has turned away his son, he seeks him out on the town square. Ordinarily, Hunnicutt would be a match for any man, more than a match for the timid Halstead. But he has no reply when told, "I don't want any son of yours around my daughter. There. Is that plain enough for you?" He can only ask, "You had never heard anything against the boy himself? Is that right?" Halstead "missed the plea, missed the paternity in it" (206–207) and simply repeats his statement, "I don't want any son of yours around my daughter." The Captain is dumbfounded for once; the spectators are fascinated. It is a scene to savor. He goes to the barber shop for a shave from Dub and sits in a daze staring at the ceiling. The group narrator is used for a moment: "We all looked up, and all saw nothing more there than Dub saw" (207).

There is worse to come. Opal Luttrell appears with her new baby, seeking protection from her abusive husband, choosing as her protector Wade Hunnicutt, the husband's landlord. Theron assumes that Wade has fathered the baby, an incorrect but suitably ironic assumption. To escape the noise of the infant, Theron goes to the attic, where he looks at his childhood toys and the collections his mother helped him create. Hannah realizes how disaffected her son is when he brings down the precious objects of his youth for the baby to play with, and destroy. She suddenly finds that she is an old woman at thirty-nine.

Compounding the plot, Libby has discovered that she is on the verge of motherhood, and comes home from college. Humphrey evokes her pain and confusion very effectively and he makes the scene of her homecoming completely plausible. Father and mother understand immediately why their daughter stands before them, making her revelation an anticlimax. Halstead's reaction is subtle: he achieves "a sense of grotesque self-discovery and of a law, going beyond, including his own case, an understanding that the thing you have lived in fear of is the very thing for which you have lived" (226). It seems almost satisfying: "how silly and wasteful, and even mocking, it would have been if after all the effort he had spent avoiding this one, some other perfectly irrelevant and unprepared-for catastrophe had come knocking at his door." Halstead is an interesting character, capable of change and never entirely reducible to his role as outraged father.

Halstead assumes that his daughter has been seduced by a college student, a city slicker. He is aware of the tradition of jokes and songs about the situation, but he also recalls Theron's interest in his daughter and brings himself to visit the Hunnicutt house, hoping to find a husband for Libby. The Captain receives him in the trophy-filled den, putting Halstead, who has always had contempt for hunting, at a disadvantage. The worldly-wise Hunnicutt surmises why Halstead has changed his mind and says, in another of those traditional male phrases, "We're not buying any damaged goods" (234). This cynicism is in fact self-destructive: Theron will not marry Libby but someone far less to the Captain's liking. But Wade's self-possession puts sarcasm into the smallest gestures. "He got up and handed Mr. Halstead his hat. At once Mr. Halstead grew flustered and apologetic. Just before relinquishing the hat, the Captain deftly corrected the crease" (236).

Unlike Wade, Halstead has learned from his ordeal. During his interview with the Captain, he had come to realize how deeply he loved his daughter, in spite of what he took to be an abandoning of his moral principles to do so. Humphrey doesn't sentimentalize the character: we see him dropping his hat on his way and worrying that his daughter will kill herself like a woman in the old songs and ballads: "the nearest that life had ever brought him to false love and undone maidens was in the words of old jokes and old ballads so much a part of his native place that they were a part even of him" (238). He rather comically assumes that she has already killed herself and expresses relief that she is all right when he sees her again. And he counsels her against having an abortion. The change from mere guardian of her virtue to her loving father is complete but terrifying to him: "He was trying to be all to her. What had he discovered to feel that he had to be?" (241).

The infernal machine grinds on, having been given new impetus by Wade. The characters have reached a state in which every move veers back against them, not an uncommon situation in tragedy. Not knowing that Libby is pregnant by him, Theron treats her coldly (out of guilt) when she summons him by her old device, a flashing mirror. The first to see the glare flashing on the ceiling is the baby, and Opal tells Theron that "he likes that bright spot up there" (243). The interview with Libby is terminated when Opal and the baby appear: Libby drops her compact, shattering the mirror, and runs away. The mirror is an emblem of their love, and breaking it signals something worse than bad luck.

Libby follows the traditional path for women in her situation: she quickly talks an old admirer, Fred Shumway, into marrying her. Single-parenthood would have been immensely difficult in 1939. The portrait of Shumway, an aspiring "oh gosh" businessman, is brief and indelible. Theron and Opal go to the Courthouse to arrange Opal's annulment from Luttrell, and they encounter the wedding party. The symbolism seems too contrived when Theron finds a grain of rice on Opal's collar as the baby chews on the annulment decree. Theron will soon marry her in a bad gesture of atonement for his father's imagined sins. This rice grain rather ponderously balances the one at the end of the previous chapter, which has already narrated Libby's marriage and the start of the honeymoon. As the "damaged goods," awaits her bridegroom in a honeymoon cottage in Little Rock, a grain of rice falls from her hair.

Theron's marriage, naturally, is a travesty: he does not consummate it, baffling his new wife. In this way he is indeed a poor man's Ike McCaslin, with a marriage in name only and a refusal to partake of his family's wealth. The portrait of Opal, the white trash bride, has been called class snobbery by Mark Royden Winchell (*William Humphrey* 15), but she does in fact have vitality and a strong affection for her baby. She wears Evening in Paris perfume and has no table manners, but she seems more sympathetic than the stiff-necked Theron and the arrogant Wade. Literature has a long line of gutsy women who survive: Opal is perhaps a Sister Carrie if not a Becky Sharp.

The plot seems to accelerate steeply in the final pages. Theron begins to haunt the home of Libby and Shumway, and he waits outside the church when the baby is christened. The christening scene is one of Humphrey's vivid portrayals of life in East Texas. It becomes a virtual shivaree attended by ribald folk aware that the paternity of the baby is in doubt. Fred Shumway is too naive to understand their amusement during the ceremony and takes it for jocular community approval. But the *sotto voce* comments attributing the baby's paternity to Wade Hunnicutt ("I God, he's done it again") devastate Albert Halstead. His unspoken reaction is ominous: "He'd done it again, I God. Well, he'd done it for the last time" (290). We are in the ballad world that haunts Albert Halstead, a world of dramatic confrontations and murder at weddings. Theron manages to have a conversation with Libby at the church and learns that the baby is his. Rather melodramatically he and Libby decide to renew their love and Theron goes to tell his father. In a coincidence that perhaps goes too far, he sees Opal and her baby on the town square, waiting for a bus to take her to Dallas where she will doubtless flourish.

Wade has not fared well. We see him on the lawn pretending to read the newspaper, unable to go in and face his wife and—a good touch—unable to face her inability to face him. He has taken the measure of his rejection by his son. He achieves a certain dignity. He will not whine: "But the one strength he had now was in acceptance of the judgment upon him":

> It was not pride, however, that had kept him from going to Theron and begging forgiveness. From the very severity of his punishment there came to him a measurement of how much he had been admired. More stunning than the thought that he had been disowned was the terrifying knowledge of how he had been adored. He had been stopped from begging for a little love by the awesome knowledge of how much had been his, how much he had thrown away. He could make no move then; he could only wait for Theron to come to him. Meanwhile, he could take it all. He was almost ashamed of his endurance. Upon so big and bluff-looking a man remorse sat with a strange and almost comic incongruity. It was as if the soul inside him hammering its fists against his tough frame was baffled and ashamed of its weakness. (297–98)

His masculine code leaves him only stoicism as a means of coping with his loss. The courage is worthy of a tragic figure, but we are still aware of his limitations. The character's inner life is severely limited: he has hardly needed anything more than an instinctual life.

He makes a more fortunate death than his wife and son. Theron comes home and declares that his marriage to Opal is over. Wade is denied the pleasure of learning that he had a grandson: Theron fears that the news would be received with mixed feelings. When Wade suggests that he tell his mother, a slightly Oedipal memory comes over the son: "He remembered the comforting, faintly soapy smell of her breast when she had hugged him as a child" (299). Theron wishes to bring his parents together again by giving them a moment of shared joy but after he leaves, Wade has only the chance to call out Hannah's name before a shotgun blast kills him. One side of his body is destroyed, which undoubtedly represents his failure to be a whole human being. Hannah assumes that some husband has finally taken revenge. There is no mystery about who the killer might be—we've seen Albert Halstead in a frenzy of rage, and the weapon, appropriately enough, is one of Wade's own shotguns, Albert not being a hunter. But there is one shock: Hannah reacts by revealing her true emotions in front of her son, who has returned after seeing his own car driving by at 70 mph. She sees Theron for a moment as an apparition of his father, recalling her mistaking of Wade for Theron the night they both came in late, and after screaming murmurs twice, "Some husband." And then she screams, "I didn't do it! It wasn't me! It wasn't me!" The denial points to her own suppressed murderous rage. Just as Wade was blamed wrongly for Opal's baby, he has been blamed with fatal results for Libby's: "Like father, like son" has worked in reverse. In one of his notebooks for *Proud Flesh*, Humphrey offers his own interpretation of Hannah's outburst, suggesting that she will eventually go mad out of guilt for her long time hatred of Wade, a hatred which she has evaded by concentrating on her love for her son.

The chase scene that follows is admittedly overdone in its symbolism. Theron takes his father's car (and remaining shotgun) to pursue his own car, which is being driven by a killer who turns out to be his girlfriend's father and the grandfather of his son. Along the way, Theron is mistaken for his father. Like father, like son, indeed. The son wants to avenge his father, who has been killed for the son's own action. The situation does seem contrived, especially with the use of the cars, which is as complicated as the hit-and-run scene in *The Great Gatsby*. He pursues the killer into the woods of Sulphur Bottom, a suicidal refuge for poor Halstead, who has no woodlore at all.

Theron's pursuit of the killer into Sulphur Bottom is based on a feat of William Humphrey's own father, as we shall see in *Farther Off from Heaven*, wherein Clarence Humphrey chased an escaped killer into the woods and waited until the man became lost and sufficiently hysterical to give up. Theron tracks Halstead in a similar way, and soon recognizes that he is dealing with an inexperienced man. He thinks of simply leaving him there to die in misery, hopelessly lost. But a tragic figure often seeks fatal knowledge, and Theron decides to turn back in pursuit. The complete catastrophe might have been avoided: the killing of Libby's father. When he comes upon the fallen Halstead, who has his back to him, he fails to recognize his quarry, and furthermore thinks he is dead. When Halstead suddenly reaches for the gun beside him, Theron fires before realizing who he is killing. Humphrey rather improbably grants Halstead—the man who had learned to love his daughter—a happy death; he has a smile on his dead face, which had not been touched by the shotgun blast. A forensic scientist might be able to judge the verisimilitude when Humphrey says, "There had been just time, as he felt the pain in his aching heart eased forever, for Mr. Halstead to smile" (310).

Humphrey goes too far with the smile. The conclusion of the novel is as mannered as the opening. On the other hand, he handles the aftermath for

Theron exactly right, by simply shifting, after a typographical mark, to the posse that finds Halstead's body. "Deputy Sheriff Bud Stovall was new to his job then, and eager to pursue." The Sheriff, a more experienced man, realizes that Theron is a better woodsman than any of them and that he will not be back. The reader can deduce Theron's hopelessness in the situation: it would have been a mistake for Humphrey to have taken us inside his mind. Finally the Deputy concurs in his boss's judgment: "Yeah . . . the body could not be recovered." With that statement the novel ends, and we know the rest: Hannah will place the tombstones in the cemetery, reserving an open grave for herself beside the stone commemorating a son whose body will never be recovered. We can infer that the reaction of Libby will be crushing, but Humphrey avoids damaging the impact of his ending by providing a denouement for her. He resisted suggestions from his editor, Herbert Weinstock, and his publisher, Alfred A. Knopf, to revert to the opening story of Hannah's funeral. We have already learned that Sam Shumway, our Fortinbras of a sort, will someday be head of the Chamber of Commerce. Our Hamlet has revenged his father in the worst possible way and has no choice but to disappear into the woods.

As Stephen Cooper says, the contemporary reviewers of Humphrey's early novels thought they were stronger than the later commentators have (241). In

1967, James Ward Lee's pamphlet on Humphrey suggested that the book was not a great novel but a great Texas novel, and he thought that "the chief flaw in the book is in the development of character" (26). His assessment of the characterization (30) is good: "In general, the main characters are adequate but not much more than that; the minor characters are very well done. . . . In great fiction we might find adequate minor characters and excellent main ones." Of course, Wade is a mythical figure, the heroic hunter, and limited by that role. We see him, Lee points out, through others. "Wade Hunnicutt is necessarily a remote character, for to delineate him fully would destroy the myth. He is the unknown and unknowable figure whose presence broods over the whole novel" (28). Lee links him with figures like Bigfoot Wallace and Jim Bowie, real people who have turned into legends. Hannah and Theron are rated "satisfactory"; Hannah never shows flashes of humanity; Theron is too predictable. These judgments seem accurate. What we need is a little of the unpredictability that Lee sees in Albert Halstead: "His fear for Libby, his own timidity but willingness to fight Wade over Libby, his final murder of Wade, give him a touch of the unexpected that Forster says round characters must have" (30). Humphrey's skill as a novelist actually works against him: we understand the central characters all too easily, as we hardly ever would in Faulkner or

Porter, his other great influences.

What Lee finds to praise is the style and the evocation of place. As he says, "the folkways of the people—their dress, speech, attitudes, manners and beliefs—play a prominent part in the book" (32). He supplements this judgment in a survey of Humphrey's writing in 1980, saying that "at its core the novel is about people who could have lived anywhere at any time." He says quite plausibly: "The ability to recreate a region exactly and yet not so limit the characters to it so that they lose believability is the heart of great regional writing and is what separates it from local color" (150).

Later criticism has been more concerned with theme than with setting and characterization. Clearly the novel focuses on the hunter's code, the macho code, that Wade Hunnicutt, the great hunter, lives by. Gary Davenport calls it "a single-minded and exclusive code: strictly masculine, of course—but also primitivistic and self-consciously simplistic" (495). He measures Humphrey's growth as a novelist by his gradual distancing of himself from it, as if the novel endorsed it. In *Home from the Hill*, he believes, Humphrey is fascinated and uncritical: "Captain Wade Hunnicutt . . . is an object of adoration to his son, but also, I think to Humphrey; the Captain's only real vice is a kind of lordly philandering, and it is treated with indulgence, almost as if it were the *droit du seigneur* of a gentleman hunter" (496). But it is precisely the Captain's philandering, his long record of faithlessness, that causes his downfall. Davenport ignores the ironies that surround his fall. It is appropriate to his hubris that he is blamed for characteristic actions — actions natural to his character — that he did not happen to perform. The start of his fall comes when his wife, who has played the role assigned to her by the code, to be the long-suffering saint, can endure no more. And it is the complete inadequacy of his code in a moral sense that leads Theron to reject him. The philandering half of Wade is symbolically blown away by a blast from his own shotgun.

Wade has deformed Hannah's character: playing the long-suffering wife is a masochistic and corrupting role. Her revenge, pathetic as it is, has been to befriend her husband's lovers, an act that baffles them: this is the victim's neurotic revenge, and not one that relieves her suffering. "Some husband," is her involuntary judgment on Wade, and the reader can agree. After his death, and Theron's disappearance, she plays the martyr to the point of madness. Katherine Anne Porter understood the novel better than most of its academic critics have. As Joan Givner points out in her article, "Katherine Anne Porter: The Old Order and the New," Porter saw Hannah as "an abject bitch," Wade as "a murderous hedonist," and Theron as a "blinded neurotic" (65). Unfortunately she did not publish these views but expressed them in a letter to Humphrey.

Mark Royden Winchell concurs with Davenport in believing that Humphrey adores Wade Hunnicutt. Certainly Humphrey relishes the life of the hunter: that is clear from much of his writing. And we can all admire skill and nonchalance. It is not clear that Humphrey admires Wade's amorous pursuits, however. In a notebook cited earlier, he expresses his annoyance at critics who fail to see that he wants to destroy myth. And the code is not, as Winchell claims, "destroyed by external forces without seriously considering contradictions within the code itself" (*William Humphrey* 14). It is the one-sidedness of a code that equates hunting game with hunting women that Theron reacts against. Like his father he aims to marry only once, but he fails to understand what a convenient marriage his father has enjoyed. Under the influence of writers like Cooper, he thinks his father is as pure as Natty Bumppo. Winchell says that Wade's "inability to keep his pants zipped is a mere gimmick necessary to bring the plot to its contrived resolution" (*William Humphrey* 15). The critic is using the language of the men who gather on the square to belittle the genuine theme of the novel. His claim that the book is a nihilistic potboiler is a double injustice: the nihilism is in the Captain's egocentric macho character, and the novel works out the consequences with painstaking craft. Winchell, who believes that Humphrey's writing improved after he turned away from southern materials, consistently denigrates the early novels. The title of his article in *The Sewanee Review* sums up his approach to his subject: "Beyond Regionalism: The Growth of William Humphrey."

With all its weaknesses, Humphrey's book is a finely-crafted work which seeks to destroy the Myth of the Hunter. It has come back into print and seems likely to endure as a southern standard. Humphrey is aware of the limitations of a world in which even women expect a man to hunt. Hannah herself is a victim of this basic assumption. The sexual politics of the novel would be intelligible in Hardy's Wessex, where the way of a man with a maid had persisted since time immemorial. The racial politics would change drastically after 1954, and the isolation of Northeast Texas would hardly outlast television (Humphrey makes one reference to "moving pictures," but his world seems locked into itself). The book has an elegiac tone: it is possible to reveal the inner contradictions of a world which one knows intimately while still commemorating its beauties of time and place, even such small beauties as Chauncey's mop and an unusually valiant raccoon.

The novel was a best-seller and a nominee for the National Book Award. The Book-of-the-Month-

Club purchased it as an alternate along with Rumer
Godden's *Greengage Summer*. MGM bought the rights
and set out to make the film. The French translation
appeared from the top publisher, Gallimard, in 1960,
and the book would appear in German and Spanish.
Humphrey's life was transformed. He could give up
teaching and spend years in Europe. It appeared that
he was about to live the literary version of the American dream.

4

Humphrey's Quixote:
Parody in *The Ordways*

On 24 July 1958, William and Dorothy Humphrey sailed for Southampton on the *Liberté*. During the sailing, the unit manager for the production of *Home from the Hill*, James T. Vaughn, tried unsuccessfully to reach Humphrey by radio in order to ask him questions about Clarksville, its weather, its crops, its likely places for filming. The president of the Chamber of Commerce had invited MGM to film outdoor shots there and the studio needed background to make plans. Mr. Vaughn sent his questions to Humphrey's agent, Annie Laurie Williams, and she relayed them to Humphrey, who

replied from a farmhouse in Dorset in a letter quoted
in the introduction to this study:

> As to the weather and the crops, tell Mr.
> Vaughn to read the book. It was cotton and
> corn and sorghum when I was a boy. Red soil
> and sometimes black soil. Hot from March
> till November. Sulphur Bottom is (was in my
> time, and I can't believe they can have changed
> such a big thing) a real place, and is called
> that. I believe I heard that it is entirely the
> property of one man, a big insurance broker,
> who lives in the town of Anon, some fifteen
> miles from Clarksville. If it's at all like it
> was when I was a boy, however, they'll need
> army tanks to get in there with a camera
> crew. And they will have to bring their own
> wild boar—so far as I know there never was
> one in Texas: poetic license on my part alto-
> gether, or as I have one rednecked character
> say, to protect myself, "Musta strayed over
> from Loozyanner." (9 August 1958)

Humphrey suggested his uncle, Bernard Varley,
a barber and a skilled hunter, as a source of information, and Bernard served as a consultant. He also
played the town barber in the movie. The role of Wade
Hunnicutt was supposed to be played by Clark Gable,

but Gable refused, claiming that he could not take the role of a man with a grown son. He would consider playing the father of a twelve or thirteen year old, but no one older. He was fifty-seven at the time. The role went instead to Robert Mitchum, and Humphrey's response to this news from Williams was droll:

> Someone sent me a clipping that said Robert Mitchum is being considered for the role in our movie. What role, it doesn't say—but that's hardly necessary with those sleepy, dope-filled eyes, he's just what I had in mind for Deuteronomy the hound-dog. If they don't get started pretty soon it's going to be a period piece. (15 March 1959)

Mitchum always regarded acting as a lucrative job, not as a mystique, but this role was perhaps his finest. Unfortunately, the script wasn't up to his talents. Eleanor Parker was cast as Hannah, and George Hamilton played Theron. Other parts were played by Everett Sloane and George Peppard.

Humphrey was back in the United States when the film opened in January, 1960, at Radio City Music Hall. MGM offered a special showing for him and his friends, but he found it inconvenient to go: he was living in Glendale, Massachusetts, with no access to

New York City by train, and he told his agent that he had a car but "it never runs" (13 January 1960). Most authors would not think of missing such an event. Williams suspected that he wanted to see the film when there would not be people around asking him what he thought of it. She thought that MGM had made a good movie, though it was not really William Humphrey's story. When he appeared at the University of Texas at El Paso on 3 May 1977, he said that he had never seen the film, and he made the same comment in 1989 to James Ward Lee.

It was probably just as well that Humphrey did not see the film. As Annie Laurie Williams perceived, it was not very faithful to the novel. Two very experienced screen writers, a husband and wife team, Harriet Franck and Irving Ravetch, wrote the script. They were considered southern specialists and had written the scripts of *The Long Hot Summer* (based on stories by Faulkner) and *The Sound and the Fury*, which ensured that Humphrey's novel was further Faulknerized in a Hollywood fashion. They would later write scripts for Faulkner's *The Reivers* and for *Hud*, based on Larry McMurtry's *Horseman, Pass By*.

William and Dorothy Humphrey planned to spend two months in England and Scotland and a month in Ireland, then to go to the Continent. On Humphrey's arrival in London, he immediately went to meet Ian Parsons, his English publisher, who asked him how long he'd been in London. Humphrey said, "thirty minutes." In a tribute to Parsons, Humphrey said that he regretted having taken so long to get to the Chatto and Windus office: he might have known Parsons for another fifteen minutes. The two became close friends, and Parsons introduced the Humphreys into the English literary world. Humphrey became very close to Parsons and his wife Margaret, known to everyone by her nickname, Trekkie. Trekkie became one of the Humphreys' most active correspondents, writing often from the pub "Juggs," which she and her husband owned near Lewes, Sussex. The Humphreys spent three summers (1961–63) in that area, staying in Oak Cottage in Telscombe, a village not far from Leonard Woolf's house at Rodmell. Woolf became so close to the Humphreys that he gave them a terra cotta figurine which Virginia Woolf had brought back from a visit to Greece. Humphrey also became friends with Stephen Spender and Peggy Ashcroft. He had hoped to meet Elizabeth Bowen, whose review of *Home from the Hill*, "Texas Beyond the Oil Wells," referred to the book as "a tragic masterpiece," by "a writer of genius" (506). She admired the structure, the design that opened with Miss Hannah's funeral and revealed the full mystery of Theron's fate only on the last page. The meeting seems not to have taken place.

After two and a half months in England, Hum-

phrey and his wife moved on to Paris. On their first
visit they found the city uncongenial, deploring the
drizzling weather and the Parisians, whom Dorothy
Humphrey referred to as "sour wretches." They decided to go to Biot, near Antibes, twenty-five kilome-
ters from Italy.

Humphrey didn't take to France at all on his first
acquaintance with it. His wife reported to Fred and
Andy Dupee in November 1958 that he had thrown
his language book into the waste basket with impre-
cations on the French and their lousy language. In
Biot he got by with a strange mixture of gestures and
words drawn from billboards, road signs, and book
titles, along with English words that he hoped would
be cognates. But eventually he came to love France.
Biot soon charmed him, and he loved exploring the
mountains in its hinterland. He observed in one of
his notebooks for *September Song* (21 July 1988) that
France felt like his second country, although he never
thought that his command of the language was very
good. But he was a favorite with the most prestigious
French publishing house, Gallimard, and even *The
Last Husband*, which he had come to think of as an
apprentice work, was well-received when a translation was published in 1987. As Dorothy Humphrey
wrote to Katherine Anne Porter from Paris (6 April
1969) the French had a great interest in the southern novel, to the point of cultishness. Sartre, who

wrote a classic essay dealing with time in *The Sound and the Fury* and a "southern" play, *The Respectful Prostitute*, may have something to do with the French interest in fiction south of the Mason-Dixon Line. Cultural references can be obscure: Jean Lambert, Humphrey's French translator, had to ask him about terms like the very phrase, "Mason-Dixon Line," along with "Bible Belt." Such queries make it clear how exotic the South must seem to French readers.

Humphrey and his wife visited Spain in the winter of 1959. They had intended to spend a month in that country and bought a rail pass in Barcelona. Humphrey, with his love of Don Quixote, must have relished touring in a train called "the Rozinante Limited." With his love of Cervantes, he might have been enchanted with the country. But in a typically irascible style, he described Spain to the Dupees this way:

> We went to Madrid and Toledo, to Seville, Granada, Alicante, Valencia, and back to Barcelona where the oranges ripen and the people rot. Oh, noble Spanish people, bewitching Spanish senoritas, with their noses too long and their eyes crowding one another. Oh, bullfights! Oh bullshit! (9 June 1959)

But irritability was not Humphrey's only note. In the same letter he told the Dupees about a visit to

Wareham in England, where he and his wife had gotten to know some of the people. This anecdote shows the comic gift that he would employ in parts of *The Ordways*:

> Went back to Wareham, where we were last fall, to see our pig-farmer, Mr. Mears and his wife. The "locals" of our pub The Pure Drop had just returned from a day in London, via private rail coach (first time in his 55-yr-old life Tom Mears has ever been to London) and all were full of the sights they'd seen. "We was standing outside one pub there," said Bob, "and Jack went in and come back out and told us they was a woman in there wearing a dress you could see her tits through. So we went in and looked. And Joe looked so hard the woman came over and said, 'do my breasts interest you?' 'Wot, me?' said Joe, 'no, ma'am.' 'They don't?' she says, 'why not then?' 'Oh,' says Joe, 'girls in our town goes about with one of them hanging out.' 'Why only one, then?' says the woman. 'Oh,' says Joe, 'because they both be alike.'"

The Italian atmosphere of Biot must have been an inducement to live in Italy. In the next two years Humphrey would live in Siena, Perugia and Rome.

He was in Lenno, on Lake Como, when the National
Book Awards were handed out in the spring of 1959.
Home from the Hill did not win. There may be a touch
of sour grapes in the letter he wrote to his agent imagining the ceremony:

> So you've been to the National Book Awards
> Shindig. Who got it? My own guess is Mal-
> amud. What an affair that must be! Have you
> ever seen such a TV production called Queen
> for a Day. I saw it once. They bring 6 or 8
> broken-down charwomen out and each one
> tells her tale of wretchedness. When all are
> done one is chosen by applause meter to get
> all the loot. All the rest drift offstage—pre-
> sumably to return to their drunken husbands
> and crippled children and wretched lives.
> That's how I visualize the authors waiting
> for THE ANNOUNCEMENT at the National
> Book Award Dinner. Glad I wasn't there. (5
> March 1959)

He was right about Bernard Malamud, whose short
story collection *The Magic Barrel* won the award for
fiction.

Humphrey wrote a great deal while in Italy, but
had difficulty bringing any of it into publishable form
because he was working on three major projects

simultaneously: two more "family novels" and a collection of stories. His long letter on 26 October 1961 to his publisher, Alfred A. Knopf, is worth quoting at length for what it reveals about his plans and his working methods. Knopf had been wondering when his author would complete another book. Humphrey replied from Rome, where he had leased an apartment for a year:

> As near as I can guess I'm no more than two-thirds done with this book. It is a picaresque. Which means that it is improvisational. It is perhaps precisely the sort of book which I, with my Flaubertian fretting over each word and over the carefully cadenced rhythm of sentence and paragraph, and with my dependence on plot (see *Home from the Hill*) ought never to attempt. Which is precisely why I am determined to do it. But, as it goes against whatever natural gifts I may have, it does not come easy. (No writing comes easy for me: I'm one of those that Hoffmansthal had in mind when he defined the writer as one for whom writing is harder than it is for other people). Now, a picaresque needs adventures and many characters, and these must be imagined—in a way it is like writing a great collection of short stories, so

that you start afresh, with little help from what has gone before, with each new episode. And yet it must all the same not seem episodic. To imagine adventures and characters requires time. . . . Moreover, this book is supposed to be comic—not altogether so, but basically. And there is nothing on earth harder than being humorous, nothing worse when you fail. I don't mean witty and I don't mean smart and diverting—I mean adding something to comic literature.

And that's what I want to do. I am very ambitious. I don't want to write a pretty good book. I want to write a great book. I don't care how long it takes. Unless and until this one seems to me the best that I can ever hope to do with the material, I won't publish it. Publication in itself means nothing to me. *I don't want to create a seasonal stir. I want to be remembered after I'm dead.* (25 October 1961)

He goes on in the letter to comment on his working habits, and the comment gives a sense of his lapidary approach to style:

My work here, except for interruptions for illness, has gone very well, better indeed than

ever before in my life. How many pages of
the novel I now have I don't know—it must
be around 525, maybe only 500—of which
twenty percent (my usual average—will be
discarded. I don't write a "first" draft. Before
I proceed, each page is polished and finished.
It may come to be thrown away entirely, but
it is a finished page. As I say, I believe that
what I now have represents no more than
about two-thirds of the final book. When you
send a man on a search for his son all over
the state of Texas, and on not one but two
separate trips, and then bring the book up
thirty years later and to a third generation,
you are not writing a novella.

The Flaubert reference is not surprising.
Humphrey admired the great stylist. His lectures on
fiction at MIT given when he taught there in 1965–
66, show more concern with style than with any other
aspect of the novel form, and Flaubert has been the
great emblem of the fastidious craftsman. But
Humphrey wanted to avoid repeating himself. In a
notebook from 1987, he quotes James Joyce: "Every
writer has just one book to write—and he writes it
again and again." He then says, "Like all generaliza-
tions about literature, that's partly true. It's not true
of me." He aimed at doing something different book

by book, and has suffered critical disdain for it. He tried to go beyond the meticulous plotting (or over-plotting) of *Home from the Hill* in his second novel, turning to the picaresque as a model, and although the book was a best-seller, the critics have called it formless and chaotic.

His other two projects were a short novel (which became *Proud Flesh*, a very long novel) and the story collection which became *A Time and a Place*. Of the book now known as *The Ordways* the letter to Knopf says:

> Sometimes it seems to me that the big novel (which has now got a title, incidentally: The Quest of Samuel Ordway) will occupy me for years. I hope not, and all my efforts go toward seeing that it does not, but if it does, it does. It (or I, if you choose) will not be hurried, conscious though I am of time's winged chariot at my back.

He continued with a defense of his working habits, which, in later years, he thought might have offended Knopf:

> I rather suspect, Alfred, that you think me, not exactly lazy, but susceptible to distractions, shall we say? If you do, you are wrong.

I suspect also that you think I've become something of a professional tourist these past few years. Again, if so, you're wrong. I am in Europe not to seek but to avoid distractions. I work from 9 to 5, six, more usually seven, days a week. I know not one human being in all of Italy, or aside from Ian and Trekkie Parsons in all of Europe, and have called on none of the people to whom friends have given me letters of introduction. My dissipations are confined to ice cream one night a week after dinner on the Piazza Navona. I do not live la dolce vita. I am not and apparently never will be prolific; but while I am not the best writer you ever knew, I am one of the most industrious, one of the least social, and possibly the one least in need of being reminded that time is passing. It is precisely because I have such a strong sense of mortality that I cannot be hurried in my work. This is the only chance I will get to leave a name behind me. To write *Home from the Hill* took me four and a half years; I now think that with a little more time I might have made a pretty good book out of it. As for the one I am now on, I think it is already a better book than that one; and to the list of superlatives that I've already used about myself let me add, I

am one of the most self-critical and least self-
infatuated writers you ever struck across.

The tone of these remarks (and others later in the
letter) to a man who was probably America's leading
publisher is surprising, and later Humphrey suspected that the letter was one of the causes of a sour
relationship with Alfred A. Knopf and therefore with
the firm.

Humphrey sent Knopf the fragments of his two
novels, and Knopf did not like what he saw, feeling
that *The Ordways* had too long an opening and that
Sam Ordway's adventures became improbable. Knopf
also felt that "The Renshaws," which would become
Proud Flesh after years of struggle, overdid the bru-
tality of the family and became improbable at times.
This upset the novelist, although Knopf's letter was
more tactful than Humphrey's long letter from Rome,
and Knopf next pointed out that he had never thought
it wise to read works-in-progress and discouraged
writers from sending them. Such exchanges, along
with Humphrey's failure to attend several events in
honor of Knopf, would not endear him to his publisher.
There was also a sharp disagreement over the dust
jacket of *The Ordways*. He was quite right about the
dust jacket, a kind of blue and maroon-brown combination, ghastly to behold. He also disputed the division of the proceeds from the sale of the book to

Columbia Pictures. Humphrey eventually felt neglected enough to be lured away to Delacorte by his
friend Seymour Lawrence.

An impediment to the completion of the book was
Dorothy's serious illness in Rome around Christmas,
1961. It appears to have been jaundice, wrongly di-
agnosed as influenza. She was hospitalized for a
month and then spent another month in bed at home.
Humphrey himself had a severe attack of kidney
stones in Rome. His comments to Annie Laurie Williams on his progress are relevant and witty:

> As to my work, well this has given it a
> setback, as you can imagine. Of course I shall
> let you show it to Clark and Brown when it's
> finished, but oh dear me, by then books as
> well as movies may have gone the way of
> vaudeville. I have about 450 more or less fin-
> ished pages of it, and I'm still just clearing
> my throat, this book is like Texas: once you
> start across it, you think you'll never get out.
> On the last page, if I ever reach it, instead of
> "The End" I shall write, "You are now enter-
> ing New Mexico." (24 January 1962)

Another impediment was his desire to write the stories that became *A Time and a Place*.

One of the stories from that collection, "The Ballad of Jesse Neighbours," appeared in the September 1963 issue of *Esquire*. It was a finalist—to the author's surprise—for an Edgar Award from the American Mystery Writers' Association. Certainly it ranks among his best stories, though it is hardly a mystery. He said to his agent, "I stand a chance of winning a statuette of Edgar Allan Poe, who along with Ella Wheeler Wilcox and Lord Bulwer Lytton has always been a favorite writer" (1 April 1964). He hoped that Hollywood might be interested in the story, and he mentioned to Williams that "The Ballad of Jesse Neighbours" would "be a perfect vehicle for Elvis Presley (22 November 1963). This might sound absurd, but the role of a simple country boy with a guitar would not have been beyond Presley's capabilities, although the ending—Elvis in the electric chair—would not have pleased his fans.

He had received a grant from the National Institute of Arts and Letters in 1962. Another mark of his prominence was a letter (22 December 1964) from Howard Gotlieb, Chief of Reference at Special Collections at Boston University inquiring about his papers. Mr. Gotlieb, who is still head of Special Collections and still a fan of William Humphrey, said, "A William Humphrey Collection would certainly be a distinguished nucleus around which this University could build a great literary center." Humphrey regarded such inquiries (one would come

later from Stephen F. Austin State University in
Nagacdoches, Texas) as premature attempts to write
his obituary and always declined until 1993, when
he sold his papers to the University of Texas at Austin.

A more practical mark of his fame was the offer
of the post of Glasgow Professor for 1963–64 at Washington and Lee University in Lexington, Virginia,
which indicated his stature as a distinguished writer.
He and his wife liked the countryside, though he had
a problem with the people, so many of whom were
"hopelessly sunk in piety and superpatriotism," he
said in a letter to Annie Laurie Williams (3 April
1964). The position only required that he deliver four
lectures over the academic year. One of the lectures
was on the historical novel, and he told Williams that
it would "be largely an attack" on *Gone with the Wind*,
which he was "rereading with great pain." It is a pity
that this lecture was not preserved in his archives:
Mitchell is usually classified as one of the prime pro-
ponents of the mythical and romantic image of the
Civil War South, something Humphrey would
deconstruct in *The Ordways*. But she also, as Darden
Asbury Pyron points out in *The Encyclopedia of Southern Culture*, "debunks and demythologizes" the South
and the War, and her characterization relies on modern psychology, particularly a Freudian view of the
Oedipal conflicts between generations (959).

After the year at Washington and Lee University, he and his wife planned to spend another year in Lexington, but the house they had been promised suddenly became unavailable, so after their third summer in a cottage in Sussex at Telscombe and two weeks in Scotland with Ian and Trekkie Parsons, they decided to head south. They had planned to spend a week in Paris, but they lost their passport and spent days at the Parsons's house in Sussex searching their luggage for it. Finally Humphrey went to London to order a new one, but by the time he came back to Sussex, the passport had arrived from Lincolnshire, where it had been lost in a pub. They went directly to Italy, and lived in the town of Alassio, on the Mediterranean, from October, 1964 to the middle of March, 1965, at a house called Villa Felice. That sojourn has been commemorated in a poem by their friend Theodore Weiss, published in *The New Yorker* in 1967 and reprinted in his collection, *The Last Day and the First*. The poem, "The Life of . . ." has the dedication "for Bill and Dorothy" (39). The opening section purports to be the direct speech of William Humphrey:

> "So there we were stuck
> in Alassio all that rotten winter
> in a rented house, no one around
> but puffed-up Germans, and nothing
> to read beyond a pair I can't abide,
> Boswell and Johnson, the latter worse

than his crony.
And nothing to do
but struggle on through that wretched
Life of . . . . How I loathed it!"

The second section of the poem, in the voice of Weiss,
suggests that life itself is a single book that we are
all stuck with in our "own Alassio." The third section
is spoken by Dorothy Humphrey, who reminds her
husband that eventually they came to love the town
in all its rich detail. When the poem appeared in
Weiss's collection, it had a charming pendant, a poem
called "The Life of . . . (Cont.)," dedicated to Irma
Brandeis, Humphrey's friend from Bard, letting the
original poem speak in its own defense against
Brandeis's criticism that it lacked resolution (41–42).
Humphrey's isolation from the fashionable literary
world should not make anyone think that he lacked
literary friendship.

Just before he left Italy in 1963, the manuscript
of *The Ordways* almost vanished by misadventure,
something much more serious than a misplaced passport. A prefatory note says that the manuscript was
"left aboard the Rome-Milan express on March 15,
1963" and recovered through the efforts of an employee, "Capostazione Michele Fortino of the Stazione
Terminal in Rome." The manuscript avoided the fate
of Hemingway's early stories, lost by his wife Pauline

(along with the carbons) on a trip from Paris to Italy, and T. E. Lawrence's *Seven Pillars of Wisdom*, the first manuscript of which was left on the London Underground. Humphrey's book was published on 1 February 1965.

Humphrey saw himself as a destroyer of myths. The picaresque is an irreverent form: after all, it was invented by his beloved Cervantes to make fun of another kind of myth, the exaggerated ideas about chivalry in the heroic romances. Humphrey's novel addresses two kinds of mythology, the southern myth of the Lost Cause, and the western myth of the cowboy. In a lecture at the University of Texas at El Paso in May, 1977, Humphrey mentioned that one inspiration of his novel was an article in *Time* magazine on the cowboy. The article was a review of what has become a standard work on the subject, *The American Cowboy: The Myth & the Reality*, by Joe B. Frantz and Julian Ernest Choate, Jr., published in 1955. Humphrey's attention must have been caught by the attitude of the reviewer to the question of mythology. As their subtitle implies, Frantz and Choate work very hard to distinguish the reality of ranching life from the world-wide image of the American cowboy perpetuated first by dime novels, then by pulp westerns and the movies. The *Time* reviewer, in the arch and dismissive tone for which the magazine was famous in its prime, belittles the authors for their careful discriminations of myth and reality: "The point not grasped by Messers. Frantz and Choate is that the myth is the only reality worth bothering about" ("Cornua Longa," 116). Humphrey would naturally have sided with Frantz and Choate. He would also have been interested in their discussion of the cowboy myth as something that began, like the practice of American ranching, in Texas. In his lecture in El Paso in 1977, he mentioned that the cowboy needed a Cervantes, not a Homer.

Their book may well have been the source for Humphrey's presentation of the myth through the mind of *The Ordways*' narrator, Tom. Tom imagines his lost Uncle Ned, who disappeared into the West with his kidnapper, as the consummate cowboy, a combination of "Kit Carson, Buffalo Bill, Pat Garrett, and Billy the Kid" (329). In the words of Craig Edward Clifford in his book on Texas and its literature, *In the Deep Heart's Core*: "At the end Ned returns out of the blue, not a gun-toting cowboy as the narrator has fantasized, but a car-driving goat rancher" (65). Clifford discusses *The Ordways* in his chapter on "Texas, Southern and Western," noting that *The Ordways* "says something about the puzzling unity of Texas, a state where South and West form part of the whole."

As Humphrey has said, "The South is tragedy, the West is comedy." Because Clarksville was a place where the South and the West meet, the novelist could take advantage of that collision to deal with both myths in a novel with a mixed, tragicomic tone. Indeed, Texas has a third important culture, the Spanish-speaking one heavily concentrated near the Mexican border, and Humphrey makes some use of that interface.

The South, the region that the novelist knows best, dominates his opening scenes. While the novel was at first called "The Quest of Sam Ordway," its later title—almost up to the point of publication—was "Look Away, Look Away," a line from the chorus of "Dixie," the unofficial anthem of the Rebel South. Only the publication of another book with that title forced a reversion to the rather bland family designation. Humphrey was not pleased, incidentally, with the title chosen for the French translation by the House of Gallimard: *Les Pionniers du Texas*, which sounds like the name of a history book.

The opening section is among Humphrey's finest achievements in style, leisurely but exact in tone and detail. He begins with a fine image for the location of Clarksville:

Clarksville is in Texas—but only barely. Take a map and place the index finger of your right hand on Clarksville, your middle finger will rest in Oklahoma, your ring finger

in Arkansas, and your little finger in Louisiana. It lies fifteen miles south of the Red
River, on the road from the ferry which transported the first colonists to Texas. Standing
on the edge of the blackland prairie, it was
the first clearing they came to out of the cane-
brakes and the towering pines which choke
the broad river bottom. Southerners, those
first settlers were, and in the towns of northeast Texas, such as Clarksville, the South
comes to a stop. Mountain men, woodsmen,
swampers, hill farmers, they came out into
the light, stood blinking at the flat and fea-
tureless immensity spread before them,
where there were no logs to build cabins or
churches, no rails for fences, none of the game
whose ways they knew, and cowered back into
the familiar shade of the forest, from there
to farm the margins of the prairie like a timid
bather testing the water with his toe. The
Texas of cattle herds and cowboys, of flat little
sun-swept towns with low sheet-iron buildings strung out along a single main street,
the Texas of the West, lies farther on, in time
as well as space. (3–4)

The town of Clarksville is not a Western town strung
along a single street. It has a town plaza and a statue

of a Confederate soldier, a monument whose meaning Humphrey explores—whose myth he destroys—
in the novel. To this town came the Ordways during
the Civil War: the family of the narrator's great-grandfather, who "drew back appalled from those vast and
lonely "prairies. . . "(4). Before the novel ends, the
Ordways will be linked symbolically with the vast
prairies.

After a long description of Clarksville, the novelist describes Graveyard Decoration Day, the annual
post-harvest event dealt with in *Home from the Hill*.
The emphasis in *The Ordways* is on the association
of the day with family traditions. It is an occasion
that brings in relatives who've moved elsewhere, and
it encourages the retelling (and therefore the perpetu-
ation) of family stories. Southerners have long memories. In "The Decline of Outrage," an essay from 1961
that Humphrey must surely have read (it is in a volume along with Walter Sullivan's harsh criticism of
Home from the Hill), James Dickey discusses the
southern cult of family memory. Dickey's suggestion
that the southerner holds to old ways because his
grandfather's ghost would be outraged or upset by
change (88) seems to be echoed by Humphrey's narrator:

> Undoubtedly the Southerner clings to cer-
> tain outmoded social attitudes and resists

> changes, which for his own part he knows he
> could learn to live with, because they are unac-
> ceptable to Great-grandfather, whose voice,
> should he think one moderate thought, he hears
> accusing him of capitulation, of betrayal, of un-
> worthiness of the name he bears in trust. (39)

Humphrey himself, coming from a dispossessed class, had a fairly short family history, but he showed a strong interest in it in *Farther Off from Heaven*, and his papers contain several letters from genealogists and other informants who tried to help him trace his family further.

The family stories of the Ordway clan are some-times tragic, sometimes romantic, sometimes comic. The narrator, Thomas, hears them year after year as his family works in the family graveyard in Mabry, a village in the Clarksville area where Humphrey's fam-ily lived for a short and happy time in the 1930s. The day the narrator, Tom, chooses to describe is in 1933. Presiding over the event are his grandparents, Samuel and Hester. The event is not too painful be-cause no Ordway has died for thirty-five years; there-fore it can be more nostalgic than mournful. But there are two sad facts worth noting. There is one person missing, a half-brother of the narrator who is said to be "out west." It is a strong rule in novels that a lost child will be found, of course, though Humphrey audaciously breaks that rule in his next novel, *Proud Flesh*. The mother, Agatha, died in childbirth, another familiar motif. The other fact is that Samuel Ordway's second wife, Hester, lives in jealousy of the first wife, fearing that her husband still loves her predecessor. She is particularly worried that he will die first and be united with his first wife in heaven. The situation is familiar from Humphrey's early story about the Hardys, though Samuel Ordway is not an Englishman like both Mr. Hardy and Humphrey's maternal grandfather, Mr. Varley, the source for this situation.

The jealousy has consequences. Young Thomas notes that he alone is treated coldly by his grandfather, unlike the other grandchildren. Thomas's mother explains that the grandfather knows that his wife watches him to see if he shows favoritism to grandchildren descended from the first wife, and his defense is to act distantly with them all. Thomas and his family always arrive first, while this resolution is still in effect, but it soon weakens and other grandchildren get different treatment. Humphrey is introducing his explorations of the complications of family love in this story. Samuel Ordway has gone through a terrible ordeal in the case of his missing son, Ned. Humphrey takes his time telling us that story, which forms the long middle section of the book.

In the meantime, he elegantly tells us the whole

story of the Ordway family, and modulates rather easily from whimsy to grim tragedy. The Ordways have a remarkably large contingent buried in the Mabry cemetery. All of their American ancestors are present, transported in kegs to Texas by the narrator's great-grandfather and namesake, Thomas, in 1863. We learn their stories; then we learn the story of the blinding of Thomas Ordway at Shiloh and the subsequent migration to Texas. Humphrey uses the story to destroy—the word "deconstruct" was not available to him—the myths of the Glorious South and its Lost Cause, the war commemorated by the statue of the Confederate Soldier on the town square in Clarksville. The story of Thomas Ordway shows the human horror concealed by the Memorial Day rhetoric common enough at one time in the South. Humphrey's own maternal great-grandfather was blinded and crippled at Shiloh, but the novelist had no idea how he came to Texas. He must have enjoyed working up an extravagant narrative of the journey. Humphrey's work seems to be permeated by mythical and biblical analogues, usually parodied or reversed in some way. Sam Ordway is an Odysseus searching for Telemachus. Thomas Ordway flees the burning South like Aeneas leaving Troy, a mythic echo noted by John Grammer, who says of the family: "Carrying the bones of the ancestors out of the devastated South, they enact an archetypal conservative paradigm: Aeneas carrying

Anchises on his shoulders out of burning Troy. The Ordways too hope not so much to found a new order as to resurrect an old one" (11).

Parody is a central method of the novel. Along with parodies of stories like the Prodigal Son and the quest of Telemachus, Humphrey parodies several works by Faulkner, as if to confront and purge himself of the anxiety of influence. We should recall Humphrey's ambivalence about the great southern novelist. He could tell Katherine Anne Porter that Faulkner was a pet hatred and deplore his winning the Nobel Prize. He could also admit to Porter that Theron's boar hunt was an imitation of Faulkner. He would caution himself in *Proud Flesh* to avoid Faulknerian characters and situations.

In praising the description of the Ordway journey to Texas, Louis Rubin noted that it is "at times worthy of Faulkner himself (and sometimes suggesting *Absalom, Absalom!* and *As I Lay Dying*)" (264). The parallels with *As I Lay Dying* are the crucial ones. We are never sure whether to laugh at Faulkner's hapless Bundren family or to look at them with horror and amazement. The story of Thomas Ordway, blinded at Shiloh and doomed therefore to be a hero in a war he hardly understood, is at times as grotesque as the scandal of the Bundren family. It is after his wife and two children are reduced to eating mule meat (a disgusting and yet ludicrous fate) that

Ordway decides to leave Tennessee forever on a journey that many would be taking at the end of the Civil
War. Humphrey's protagonist is not shiftless like Anse
Bundren, and for all its echoes of the Bundren journey to Jefferson with Addie's rotting body, the Ordway
trip is clearly motivated. Texas will be a new start.
Some of the grotesque humor of the journey comes
from the mistakes of observers who think that
Ordway, who must eventually ride on the wagon and
let his pregnant wife lead the oxen, is a shiftless character like Anse and too lazy to lead the team himself.
Thomas is not aware that his wife, Ella, is pregnant:
she will not let him touch her because he might in-
sist on stopping the journey. Faulkner's Dewey Dell
is pregnant but unmarried and hopes to find a way to
abort herself. Ella wishes to go to Texas to start a
new life, not to seek an abortion. The reactions of
people along the way, who find themselves helping
the Ordways, calls to mind the individuals who help
the Bundrens on their difficult journey. The scandal
of the Ordway journey is not the rotting body of a
dead woman, but the rotting wounds of Thomas
Ordway, who is buried alive in his blindness and his
shredded legs. Addie Bundren reminds onlookers
of the scandal of death, as André Bleikasten (126–
33) would put it in his useful work, *Faulkner's As I
Lay Dying*. Ordway forces people to confront the
scandal of a mad war. His blindness and the

unhealable wounds suggest the defeated South, brooding on its injuries.

In contrast with *As I Lay Dying*, the rotting body in *The Ordways* rides on the wagon rather than being carried; it is alive. The dead within the wagon are the Ordway ancestors. Humphrey's blind veteran carries southern attachment to kin and past to an extreme that out-Faulkners Faulkner. Ordway digs up the entire graveyard and seals his ancestors in barrels and kegs, and he brings the gravestones along. The hauling of the monuments is perhaps a minor echo of Faulkner's *Absalom, Absalom!* in which Colonel Sutpen orders marble tombstones for himself and his wife during the Civil War and has them hauled around in a wagon from battle to battle. His body servant refers to them as "Colonel" and "Mrs. Colonel."

In the opening section of Humphrey's novel, structured around the traditional Graveyard Working Day, the young narrator, a great-grandson of Thomas Ordway, says that he and his family referred to their reburied ancestors by the containers they were brought in: "Blackstrap" Dismas Ordway and "Old Sourmash," his wife; "Old Tenpenny" Aubrey Ordway and his wife, "Granny Blackpowder," and so on, an even more ludicrous touch than the naming of Sutpen's grave markers.

The strongest parallel with Faulkner's novel is the river-crossing scene. The Red River separates

Oklahoma from East Texas. Lacking a Moses to part this Red Sea, the Ordways must ford it, just as the Bundrens had to cross a dangerous river on the way to Jefferson. The Bundrens faced a stream about a hundred yards across, dangerously swollen from torrential rains and carrying occasional logs. Faulkner's prose conveys something portentous and dangerous about the stream:

> Before us the thick dark current runs. It talks up to us in a murmur become ceaseless and myriad, the yellow surface dimpled monstrously into fading swirls traveling along the surface for an instant, silent, impermanent and profoundly significant, as though just below the surface something huge and alive waked for a moment of lazy alertness out of and into light slumber again. (127)

The Ordways face a river about three quarters of a mile across, and apparently quite tranquil:

> On into the brooding stillness, and then their first glimpse of the river. Impossibly red, silent, sluggish, it was as unlike water as anything could be. It looked simply like a crossroad to the one they were on. Thick, motionless, semi-solid, it might have been a

> fresh-poured concrete highway; you felt that
> just by waiting overnight you would find that
> it had set, and you could walk across to Texas.
> (73–74)

There are touches of the Mississipian's style here, like
the brooding stillness and the interest in tricks of
perception. Both writers favor long languorous sentences and rich details. But Humphrey's style is always under control, no matter how elaborate the
syntax. Faulkner's river-crossing scenes, told in suc-
cession from the wildly poetic point of view of Darl,
the disturbed and immature mind of Vardaman, and
the headlong paratactic viewpoint of Tull, are mas-
terpieces of defamiliarization and crafty confusion.
In Humphrey's book, we are never left in doubt about
just what is happening to the Ordways as they try to
ford their river.

Their oxen are reluctant to enter the water, so
Thomas Ordway uses burning brush to force them
into the stream. We might recall that Addie Bundren
was carried through fire and flood. Like the Bundren
mules, the oxen struggle desperately in the water. The
dead weight of the past—the ancestral stones that
the Ordways are bringing to Texas—steadies the
wagon. Humphrey doesn't provide the elaborate slow-
motion and stop-motion effects of Faulkner's river
passage, though there are effective contrasts between

the "drowsy stillness" and "dreamy silence" of the setting and the struggles of the wagon in the slow but
implacable current. The wagon finally sinks but, held
steady by the tombstones, it rests on the riverbed and
is pulled from the water by the oxen. Ironically the
living child, the son Dexter, has been swept away into
the river. The casks and kegs containing the ancestors have been swept away also, but—with one
exception, a nail-keg, containing a great-grandfather—catch on a trotline and bob in a neat line, ready
to be retrieved more easily than Cash Bundren's
sunken tools. The missing keg will be found, but the
living son is lost, to be replaced by Sam, the first child
born in Texas, who will himself lose a son, though not
to death.

It is the imminent birth of that child which leads
Thomas Ordway to settle in the Clarksville, Texas,
area, near the hamlet of Mabry. After burying Dexter
in Mabry, the Ordways momentarily resume their
trek, heading for the plains. The wife had hoped to
settle on the prairie, in horse and cattle country, having developed a hatred for mules after the family's
experience eating one. But the plains represent a place
without history (at least to southerners of 1863), and
Thomas feels lost there: horrible as his fate has been,
it still has a place in the story of the South. And his
reaction to hearing Spanish spoken is one of terror:
"he shrank back as if a second bomb had burst, blind-

ing his ears" (86). He is too rooted in the South, its history and culture to accept an alien environment and he fears that his children will be foreigners. Almost forty years later, his Texas-born son will transcend this narrow sense of human possibility. But for himself, Thomas Ordway seeks out the cotton country around Clarksville to settle in and re-bury his ancestors. He lives out his life making useful objects of woven cane, creating pity and terror in the people around him, and gathering a reputation as a sage: a kind of Oedipus and Philoctetes at once, with his blindness and his stench. His presence on Memorial Day is a hideous refutation of the speakers who glorify the Lost Cause, for he is an "accusation and embarrassment," and the other veterans suspect him of "subversive reservations as to the truth and beauty of what they had done, even of doubts as to the justice of the cause for which they had fought" (31). But in fact he has succumbed to the myth of the glorious cause himself: ". . . when a man has given everything to a cause he cannot disavow it, but must cling to the last to that which has betrayed him." He embodies the doubts of his fellow veterans without sharing them. His last appearance at Memorial Day comes in 1888, when a glamorous statue of a Confederate Soldier is unveiled. He dies shortly after, a sign that the myth has triumphed over horrifying realities.

The monument itself is a subject of Humphrey's

satire. The first proposal was for a mounted figure, but that is deflated superbly by a former infantryman on the Board of Aldermen, the only man to vote against the monument when it was first proposed.

> "Horse?" said one alderman, the original abstainer, and the only former infantryman on the Board. A man not born to rule, but who had become a power to reckon with in the town and county just during the past few years, and who retained a certain amount of the enlisted man's rancor against his former mounted officers. "Rearing to charge? I reckon you mean, charging to the rear." (32)

For all the obsession with the glories of the war, the deciding factor for the Board turns out to be money: when an Italian sculptor comes to town, his price is $5,000 for a mounted statue, $1,000 for a standing one. Locals who travel elsewhere in the South discover that their statue is remarkably like a host of others, and their descendants traveling to Europe are reminded of home by the statues of Garibaldi in little Italian towns. Humphrey has deflated the reverence for the past in the statue episode.

The area where the Ordways settle is near the frontier of cotton and cattle country, which brings two radically different ways of life—and two mythologies—into proximity. The young narrator of the novel, Thomas Ordway's great grandson, another Tom, grows up with stories of great battles of the Civil War. After a while, he realizes that the war has long been over and that the South lost. He consoles himself for Appomattox with the myth of the West: "In my fashion I was repeating not only the history of my family, but of the country. For the West provided America with an escape from the memory of the Civil War" (89). The rest of *The Ordways* explores the myth of the frontier through the quest of Sam Ordway for his stolen son.

By shifting myths, Humphrey sacrifices the ideal of the well-made novel, and the critics have been harsh to him. But he is unrepentant, as his remarks to Ashby Bland Crowder make clear:

> The more I thought about the Civil War, and the more I thought about its aftermath—I don't want to schematize this and make it sound that I think it was quite as simple as this, but if you'll permit me to make a very thumping big generalization—I thought: the Civil War is one of the really truly great American tragedies. And the exploration of the West is a comedy; it's a farce. Indeed it's how Americans forgot the Civil War, by getting away from the South and going West. So

> I made the adventures of my grandfather in
> search of his son, which after all is the stuff
> of many a John Wayne film, into a farcical,
> episodic picaresque, so that the book is quite
> broken-backed. The first part of it is tragic,
> and the second part of it is comic. For this
> reason, many people don't like it. But I don't
> care what many people don't like. (25–26)

The exploration of myths is a legitimate aim of a novel
and can surely take precedence over a tight plot. The
picaresque adventures of Sam Ordway's quest are a
natural form for exploring the frontier experience:
what genre is more picaresque than the Western?
Fortunately, Humphrey has the comic talents to tell
us some hilarious stories along the way. He writes in
the tradition of frontier humor, exploiting the oddities of Texas, its mores, politics, and laws, and catching the Texas vernacular brilliantly.

Sam Ordway is the rather ordinary son of the
tragic Thomas. His horizons are limited to his plowed
fields. When his first wife dies giving birth to a third
child and first son, Ned, he relies on his neighbors,
the Vinsons, to help him with the new baby. After two
years, he remarries, and the Vinsons, who have become extremely fond of little Ned although they have
three children of their own, disappear with him on 7
May 1898, abandoning their farm and heading West.

For some time, Ordway assumes that they have left suddenly because of some crime Will Vinson has committed: the kidnapping of Ned would be merely a result of their haste. Finally, he understands that the theft of the child is the crime, and the motive is love, and his emotional education begins.

That education takes the form of a parody of the John Wayne Western, the sort of story in which a brave and skillful hero searches for a missing child, wife or treasure, letting nothing stand in his way. But Sam is no hero. He is apologetic, timid, slow to anger—almost impossible to anger. He packs a pistol when he sets out, a reminder of the heroic past: it had been given to his mother Ella by a sympathetic Rebel soldier when she left Shiloh with what she thought was the body of her husband. But the gun has never been fired, and its antiquity makes it unlikely that it can be, though it does go off with comic results in the trial scene. He is no horseman: as a farmer, he distrusts horses and would rather walk than ride. His vehicle for the long journey is his wagon, pulled mock-heroically by Dolly, his mare, and a mule, perhaps an even less glamorous mode of transport than Don Quixote's Rosinante. He is, as John Grammer notes, his own Sancho Panza, the naive countryman (13).

The western code of vengeance is a variant on the southern obsession with maintaining honor through violence. But there is no proper fire of ven-

geance in Sam's heart: "As he later said, it wasn't easy
to hate a man who had wronged you by loving your
child enough to steal him. A man who loved him more
than you yourself ever had" (151). As a hard-pressed
farmer, Sam had little knowledge of his son. Nor had
he knowledge of most people: he is unable to describe
Will Vinson or the missing son. A stranger who saw
Will briefly provides a better description of him than
Sam could manage. One function of the picaresque
scenes is to educate Sam: about his son, about his
second wife—someone else he has hardly looked at
carefully—about human nature.

Sam's quest leads him to Paris, the seat of the
county west of Clarksville. He later admits to his
grandson, the narrator, that "in those days Paris was
the end of the world, as far as I was concerned" (153).
He has to learn the business of searching for a lost
child very slowly. He decides to offer a reward and
wait for informants to come to him. The day appointed
is the day of an election rally, and Humphrey presents a marvelously funny parody of a southern political speech by Senator Clifford Venable, whose name
is clearly a play on "venerable" and "venal." He seems
a figure out of Mark Twain. Besides providing humor, the speech makes it clear how the twenty-four
years since the end of the Civil War turned the national tragedy into a glamorous myth to be manipulated to win elections. Venable creates a sophistical

argument that the South really won the Civil War, and his audience accepts it. Sam takes advantage of the political platform to address the audience and make a typically self-deprecating and gentle speech asking for assistance in finding his son. As a result a group of boys bring a lost child to him and ask for the reward. Sam's comic adventures with the wretchedly-behaved child as he searches for the father teach him something about the stress of paternity. When he finds the father, who begins to wallop the child for getting lost, he intervenes and is bitten by the child, which teaches him something about the loyalty of children to parents. When he returns to his room, he finds three callers: a Pinkerton detective, who sees a lost child as lucrative business; a political kingmaker, who sees Sam's rhetoric as a means to office and happy peculation; and a Baptist minister, who has news of Ned's whereabouts. The callers extend Sam's education in the ways of the world. The Pinkerton man's horrifying stories of kidnappings and murders make him aware of human depravity, and the political hack gives him a quick lesson in the corruption of political life. The minister turns out to be a con-man who cheats Sam out of most of his money: Sam's education is helped along in a manner typical of the picaresque narrative.

The adventures multiply. A brilliantly Dickensian visit to an orphanage creates pathos and has an enormous impact on the grieving father. The need to support himself and travel too leads to a picaresque solution: he joins a dilapidated circus, which shows him more of the world and teaches him more lessons. For a dirt farmer, joining the circus is an astonishing plunge into a world completely foreign to him. The circus scenes are superb: the African elephant, Topsy, is a fine comic invention. When she dies, the stench of her carcass causes such an uproar among the people of Zodiac, Texas, that the only solution is to move the entire town. Harriet Beecher Stowe's Topsy is a character in the novel that Lincoln once said caused the Civil War. Topsy's famous line, of course, is "I just growed," a comic explanation for the size of an elephant. Such events do in fact evoke García Márquez in their strangeness. Humphrey was formed in a realist tradition, but in this novel he begins to move toward a less realistic mode. In the closing portions of *Proud Flesh* he will move even further. Texas is known in folklore and humor for its oddities and enormities, and Humphrey exploits that ambiance.

In a valuable discussion of the novel, "Myth & Folklore in *The Ordways*," Patrick B. Mullen has surveyed some of the folkloric elements it uses, like the tall tale, the folk stereotype, and the Western folk hero. Sam's adventures become more improbable as he goes farther west, which is prophesied by one of the first tall tales he hears, an example chosen by Mullen, the claim by traveling salesmen in Paris that out west ". . . when you set off to visit your neighbor you ride a pregnant mare so as to have a way to get back again." The stereotypes are easily spotted: the crooked politician, the dirt farmer, the confidence man. And the figure of the western hero—deflated by its embodiment in Sam—is everywhere apparent.

And the deflation is most effective in the trial scene. Near Fort Worth, the place where the West of cowboys really begins, Sam is arrested when he is overheard rehearsing out loud his fearsome vengeance on Will Vinson should he find the man. It is assumed that he has actually killed someone. When no body is found, he is charged with intent to kill. That is to say, he is held to the highest moral standard: the intent is treated as comparable to the deed. His unsuitablity as an avenging gunman is made clear by the prosecutor, who quotes such clichés as: "And did you or did you not say while in that thicket, as the witness has testified he heard you say, 'Will Vinson, prepare now to meet your maker? Unquote'" (281). Ordway realizes his own foolishness:

> But my grandfather could hardly bear to recall the rest of his own words which the prosecutor had quoted at him. He had to sit there and listen to himself boast and rant and rave and threaten and pretend to beat and stomp

and murder Will Vinson, then had to confess
to a crowded courtroom full of men that he
had been alone in that thicket, and that he
was (had to say this three times before the
prosecutor was satisfied that everyone had
heard it) "just practicing." (281)

The code of revenge is deflated by the long series
of verbs—boasting and ranting and raving. The trial
itself is farcical: the legal system of Texas has long
been a subject of humor. Judge Roy Bean's infamous
trials West of the Pecos come to mind. The trial has
slapstick elements. The prosecutor accidentally fires
Sam's gun, and "from the rear of the courtroom came,
in a disgusted voice, 'Hellfire, Ed. You missed him a
country mile.'" The doddering defense attorney wins
acquittal rather easily:

Mr. Parker's defense was brevity itself. A famous jurist of the state, he began, had said
that in a Texas murder trial the first thing
to be established was whether or not the deceased ought to have departed. He believed,
he concluded that the same principle should
apply in cases of intent to kill. The jury, out
ninety seconds, returned a verdict of not
guilty, plus a pool of thirty-six dollars to be
presented to the acquitted with which to buy

himself a more reliable firearm. (285–86)

After Fort Worth, Sam Ordway plunges deep into the western frontier. As Frantz and Choate demonstrate in their book on the cowboy, American thinking about the West was long dominated by the image of the Great American Desert. Humphrey mentions in *Farther Off from Heaven* that his school in Clarksville had a map so old that Colorado and Utah were still blank and marked "Great American Desert." Frantz and Choate observe that "the Texas segment" of the Desert "lay in a trapezoidal area below San Antonio and stretching to the Rio Grande" (18). The Great American Desert was largely a myth, an exaggerated conception of the Great Plains as "a boundless, trackless, worthless area fit only for savage Indians and wild beasts, a land of cactus and prairie dogs, of shifting sands and tall eccentric whirlwinds of dust." Sam Ordway will enter this region and see both the loneliness and the beauty of it.

Humphrey evokes the vertiginous physical sensations of looking at and moving through the Great Plains very skillfully, and a prairie dog town is described in a brilliantly defamiliarized passage (287) in which the animals and their burrows are experienced by Sam before he can finally put a name to them. But the focus is on the psychological effects of the vastness of the land on its inhabitants, a realm of experience entirely new to an East Texas farmer.

Loneliness is emphasized: a half-mad denizen of Fort
Griffin, a ghost town, babbles on when he meets
Ordway, telling how he "et the coyotes" and even ate
much of the town—the temporary shelters made of
buffalo hides. A woman encountered in a shanty in
the middle of the plains tells Ordway about her friend,
Mrs. Blainey, from Clarksville, then confesses that
the friend is entirely imaginary, a device for keeping
sane. Such encounters are not random: they serve to
teach a man whose human sympathies have been cir-
cumscribed some lessons about human needs and the
effects of solitude. The encounter with the woman,
who is first seen struggling to hang out wash during
a western windstorm, is particularly important. Ordway observes in a letter home that the isolation of
the West makes "a hard life on women." His sympathy toward the wife he has left alone in Mabry begins
to grow as he travels.

After the encounter with the woman, Ordway
finds himself in a West very recognizable from books
and films, a masculine world of violence inhabited by
secretive people who conceal their pasts, even their
real names. Secrecy is carried to a point of absurdity.
He finds it easiest to ask about Will Vinson if he pretends to be his brother, Sam Vinson. Eventually he
learns that Will is going by the name of Ordway, probably to avoid complications if Little Ned uses the
name. The symbolism is excellent: each man has

become the other. Humphrey suggests that southern clannishness can be transcended. As the questing father searches for his son, he begins to identify more and more with the man he should hate. The western code of vengeance has no real hold on Sam Ordway's fundamentally easy nature. What Ordway, a decent enough man, has lacked so far is broad human sympathy, and he has been gaining it on his travels. As he tracks the Vinsons, he becomes aware of the privations and the joys they must have experienced while moving through a splendid but harsh country. His empathy reaches the point that he actually pays a debt left behind by his supposed brother. In a moving passage he remembers vividly the death of his first wife and puts in order his feelings about her and about his remarriage. The intensity of his feeling toward the second wife changes him, makes him a different man, and shortly afterward he finally has an intense recollection of the nondescript son he has lost: "And there his child all but stood before him, and my grandfather knew at last why the Vinsons had been unable to give him up" (315).

He is now prepared for his final trek, to the far south of Texas, across the Edwards Plateau toward the Rio Grande Valley. He has a clue: the Vinsons have mailed a letter from Utopia. Having no education, he doesn't realize that "Utopia" means nowhere. But the experience is worth the journey, although he doesn't

find his quarry. The journey makes him aware of
human diversity: he meets Swedish Texans—recent
immigrants—and ancient pictographs that represent
a far earlier race. And when he encounters Spanish,
he does not emulate his own father and turn back to
Clarksville. He is neither literally blind nor figura-
tively deaf. Indeed, he spends some time in south
Texas. But he is aware that his wife, pregnant when
he left her, will soon deliver a baby, and after a while
he is "looking now for a place to stop looking" (322).
He finds it:

> Somewhere west of the Nueces River east of
> Del Rio, north of Uvalde, south of Sonora,
> where the Balcones Escarpment rises sheer
> as a rampart above the hot plains of the Rio
> Grande Valley, he found it, recognized it: the
> spot where he could say, "If I had to lose him,
> if I just had to lose him, I'm glad at least to
> think that Will made it to here." (323)

It is a good place to grow up in, he concludes. The
Great American Desert is not, in fact, a desolate place
of exile. And of course he has grown up himself.
Ordway has learned to love his wife, his lost son, and,
in a sense, his enemy through his picaresque adventures.

The two major portions of this "broken-backed"

novel are not unrelated. The first shows a hopelessly
nostalgic mythos of the Lost Cause in its bloody be-
ginnings. The myth has a grandeur, if the waste and
misery are ignored, but it becomes a sterile ideology,
manipulated by demagogues. The Sam Ordway section of the novel shows the limitations of another ideology, the equally bloody myth of the frontier. Genuine
human loyalties transcend both of these myths. The
quest for an external object has turned into a quest
for wholeness and imaginative sympathy. Thomas
Ordway once regretted that he had not shown cowardice at Shiloh and saved his eyesight by running
away. But the hardness of his fate left him no choice
but to accept it, to value his courage and live out a
maimed life. Samuel Ordway is able to outgrow his
southern parochialism and the frontier code of vengeance. He is not maimed, but rather has achieved a
measure of wholeness.

The novel is tragedy first, then comedy. The epilogue, set in the 1930s, is extravagant romance. As in
The Winter's Tale and *Pericles*, the lost child is found.
Louis Rubin finds the epilogue sentimental (264–65),
and indeed it is: romance, with its stress on restora-
tion and renewal is likely to be sentimental. But the
ending has its ironies. The lost child appears, having
been told by the dying Will Vinson (a.k.a. Will Ordway)
about his true identity. There is a tearful reunion.
Resumption of family relations is eased by Ned's easy-

going nature, in which he resembles both of his
fathers. The shock comes when his occupation is revealed: he raises angora-goats, which puts him lower
in the frontier code of values than a sheepman, though
perhaps above the Prodigal Son, who herded swine.
Once again Humphrey is mocking the shallowness of
stereotyped codes. He invites the entire clan to visit
him in south Texas—immediately. The Prodigal Son
is going to kill the fatted calf—or kid—for his family.
The journey is an epic one, a cavalcade of cars through
Texas, and Will's journey of almost forty years before
is recapitulated, enabling him to display his cosmo-
politan knowledge of the world outside of Mabry and
Clarksville. The symmetry is interesting: we can recall that Thomas Ordway set out West from Mabry
with a wagon-load of dead ancestors and turned back
when he heard Spanish spoken: he couldn't endure
leaving the South. In effect, Humphrey is parodying
his own narrative. At the end of the novel, all the
living Ordways set out across the plains and don't
turn back: they relish their time in Spanish-speaking south Texas. They have an enormous fiesta, an
epic series of feasts and games. Life has been affirmed;
life-denying codes have been mocked and transcended. This denouement imitates life: Humphrey
told Ashby Crowder that the conclusion was inspired
by an incident of his childhood in 1928: his
grandfather's lost son (stolen by the neighbors as in

the novel) appeared and invited the whole family to Del Rio on the Mexican border (25).

The fate of the novel has been a curious one. It was a best-seller and received a number of highly favorable reviews. Elizabeth Janeway's front page review in *The New York Times Book Review* was especially positive. The movie rights were sold to Columbia Pictures, but the film was never made. The misgivings about the form of the novel, first expressed by Alfred A. Knopf, were shared by Humphrey's good friend from Bard, Irma Brandeis, who wrote him that she found something "integral" lacking in the work. It was a bad sign when Humphrey's editor on this book, Harding Lemay, wrote him on 25 June 1963, recognizing that it was a picaresque novel but wasn't quite sure what that meant or what good examples of the genre might be. Lemay also anticipated that the rambling form would not please all the reviewers.

Many later commentators have deplored the episodic nature of the novel, which seems ironic, considering that Humphrey has been criticized for overplotting his first novel. In his pamphlet, James Ward Lee complains that *The Ordways* is a novel in name only: "To call *The Ordways* a novel is almost to abuse the term. It is, at least, two novels, a short one about Thomas and Ella, and a longer one about Sam. To call the book a fictionalized family chronicle is more accurate" (37). Louis Rubin finds "the archetypal journey" of Thomas and Ella Ordway to Texas moving, and praises the description of Samuel Ordway's second marriage as well as the depiction of his reaction to the kidnapping of his son, but Sam's picaresque hunt for his child is considered almost meaningless: "the novel simply seems to disintegrate. The search, at first very moving, soon becomes funny; and then humor gets really slapstick" (264). The assumption is that Sam's comic adventures bear no relation to the tragic past of his father, Thomas. In effect, the novel has been judged and pronounced a failure by an eminent critic whose work combines historical awareness of southern literature with high New Critical standards of unity. Mark Royden Winchell's survey of Humphrey's work in *Sewanee Review* makes a similar dismissal of *The Ordways* on structural grounds: "He has not one coherent novel but the makings of three (a family trilogy perhaps)" (287). Humphrey's literary offense is to combine a "southern historical epic with baroque Faulknerian overtones" with "a western picaresque" account, a mixture that makes him "the raconteur who tells entertaining but ultimately pointless stories" (288).

Gary Davenport's sympathetic retrospective of Humphrey's career shows a different attitude toward the picaresque adventures of Sam Ordway. Davenport praises Humphrey's "penchant for comedy and for a sort of grotesque hyper-reality that often puts the reader in mind of Dickens or Kafka or perhaps García Márquez" (498). Unlike most of Humphrey's other critics, Davenport sees the triumph of the novel not in the opening section but in the story of Sam's quest, precisely the portions objected to by Lee, Rubin, and Winchell. A more relaxed conception of fiction is at work, surely: the presence of García Márquez in Davenport's list of analogues is significant. To anticipate the trial scene, Humphrey's offenses against modernist conceptions of the novel might earn him a discharge in a postmodern courtroom and commendation from the jurors.

A shift in literary sensibility can reveal the virtues of works which have been dismissed for offenses against the dominant conventions of the time in which they were written. The point is not to give *The Ordways* full postmodern credentials, but to suggest that current assumptions about the nature of fiction (even the term "novel" seems out of style) are more generous to such a work than were the New Critical assumptions of the 1950s and 1960s. Humphrey's picaresque plot, his comic "hyper-reality," his interest in comparing and deflating mythologies, southern and western: these can be seen as strengths rather than as a failure to create a well-made novel. Parody runs throughout this work, and not merely parody of the western revenge story. Even the "archetypal" and tragic journey of Thomas and Ella Ordway has its elements of the grotesque. The function of parody in both of Humphrey's generational tales is similar: to point out the inhumanity of a restrictive mythos. Sam Ordway is the character who finally manages to transcend mythology, and his adventures give him a fullness of humanity that his father, who was maimed literally and emotionally by the Civil War, could never attain.

5

Remember the Red River Valley:

A Time and a Place

Humphrey received an award from the Texas Institute of Letters for *The Ordways*, but unlike his first novel, it was not on the short-list for the National Book Award, nor did it receive any other national recognition. But it did receive good reviews and reasonable sales, appearing for a while on best-seller lists. He was upset that Knopf did not seem to promote the book very well. The company may have felt that he was not working to promote it either: he was again in Italy and Annie

Laurie Williams noted that he was probably glad to be out of the country on publication day so that he would not have to duck interviews. Humphrey was also upset by the invocation of a Mississippi novelist in the comments, saying in a letter (8 February 1965) to his agent: "Once again the reviewers seem to have trouble spelling my name—it usually comes out F-a-u-l-k-n-e-r—but then how can you expect people to know how to spell who don't know how to read?"

Hollywood was slow to take interest. Williams reported that Olin Clark at MGM had consulted its producers; however, Clark's view was that the book was charming but lacked dramatic drive. Williams thought Humphrey would be worried about artistic merit of any film made, but in the same letter in which he complained about reviewers, he said:

> You're mistaken in thinking I'm as interested in getting a good picture as I am in getting a good price. Money, Money, that's what interests me. What I do not want is to be dependent, as I was the last time, on the success or failure of something beyond my control, namely the picture. Thus it seems to me that yours is the right suggestion, i.e. a big (I love that word!) cash price. (8 February 1965)

Humphrey hoped to support his art as a novelist

through a movie sale; the art of the movie was irrelevant. He did not like movies anyway.

Columbia Pictures finally bought the rights, but the Hollywood sale would come to nothing. Humphrey's archive contains an apologetic letter (4 February 1966) from a script-writer at Columbia named Dan, whose scenario the novelist had read. The outline had referred to East Texas as West Texas, perhaps a pardonable geographical error from the distance of Hollywood, and Humphrey apparently thought Ella Ordway was presented as "a bitch in heat." Humphrey had reacted angrily to these shortcomings of the script. He was also angry with the Alfred A. Knopf firm over its share of the film rights to the book, believing that he had given them a percentage of his net without having to—and they had then demanded a percentage of the gross instead. On 11 May 1965, he instructed his agent to "be insistent and if necessary unpleasant" with them about matching the money given them by Columbia to promote the book. In a letter dated 13 June 1965, he thanked her for "standing up to them on this matter."

Humphrey was offered the post of writer-in-residence at MIT for the 1965–66 academic year. He and his wife were ready to settle down in the United States. In one of his letters to Williams from Alassio (8 February 1965), he talked about how tired he and Dorothy were of "roaming, tired of looking at other people's whatnots on whatnot shelves, etc." After a trip to Sicily they sailed to the United States in August 1965 and stayed in a friend's guest house at Poughkeepsie, New York, while house-hunting. They found a house near Hudson, in the area where they had lived when he taught at Bard. The house, called High Meadow and built in 1795, came with 165 acres. It had a fine view and an apple orchard. Apples would become rather important to Humphrey: his book of stories, *September Song*, was at first to be called *Comfort Me with Apples*, and the protagonist of the longest story is an apple-grower. The location was excellent for a trout fisherman: from it the Berkshires and Catskills were visible, and according to the dust jacket copy for *My Moby Dick*, there is a trout stream nearby which "he will only call 'Bill's Brook.'" Humphrey took an interest in conservation efforts along the Hudson and eventually joined an organization of celebrities called The Scenic Hudson Committee on the Arts, which included Angela Lansbury, Helen Hayes, Woody Allen, and Jessica Tandy.

In a letter to Katherine Anne Porter (10 January 1967) he describes the Hudson River Valley. She had sent a Christmas card with a picture of Ploestenkill, New York, 1850, inquiring if upstate New York still looked like that. Humphrey's charming reply is rueful:

Alas, no, I'm afraid upper New York State doesn't look quite like that any more. I don't know Ploestenkill, N.Y. But I don't need to in order to visualize some of the changes that have overtaken it since 1850 when the artist sat on his hill and painted his postcard view. You have heard of that fabled valley where ailing elephants betake themselves to die— well all old sick autos seem to turn instinctively to the Hudson Valley when their headlights grow blear and their crankshafts stiffen and their shock absorbers won't absorb the shocks any more and hardening of the fuel line overtakes them, and this happy rural seat is now littered with their rotting carcasses and skeletal remains, and I fear that if my neighbors have their way there will be a Republican administration again in power before Lady Bird's highway beautification campaign sweeps any of them out of sight. But, once you're past the nearby trailer camp, or mobile home estate as it calls itself, and onto our 165 acres you're about as safe as I guess you can get in the eastern [part] of these United States of ours nowadays and still get the *NY Times* the same day.

William and Dorothy shopped in the area for

antiques to furnish the house and spent part of the summer of 1965 remodeling. According to his long-time friend, Andy Dupee, the furnishings were extraordinary. Then they rented a house in Cambridge, Massachusetts, so that Humphrey could teach at MIT, and they visited the country house monthly until the job was over. For a while in the mid-seventies they apparently wanted to sell it, and Humphrey referred to it in a letter to the Dupees as a "white elephant."

Humphrey told Katherine Anne Porter (24 May 1965) that he took the job at MIT both for the money, which was very good, and as a way to give focus to his reading. He had only one course to teach and was permitted to choose his subject. He decided to give a course on the development of the English novel. His lecture notes survive at the University of Texas. His particular slant is interesting: he spent much of his time on the analysis of prose style, and he complained in an aside that contemporary novelists write simply and leave style to the journalists. His perfectionist attitude comes through in such comments.

He entertained Porter with a letter (7 January 1966) about the very odd Christmas they had just spent with Robert Lowell during the MIT period. Lowell was teaching at Boston University, but had suffered a breakdown and would be spending Christmas in the mental ward. Although they didn't know him, the Humphreys generously arranged for him to have Christmas dinner with them. Dorothy Humphrey worked hard cooking a big dinner, and Humphrey went to the hospital to collect his guest. Everyone, including Lowell, was astonished: it was, in fact, December 24th. Finally Lowell was given permission to leave with Humphrey, and once they were out of the hospital remarked how strange it was to spend Christmas dinner with the only people alive who didn't know when Christmas comes. The Humphreys had no confusions in entertaining another guest, an old friend, Leonard Woolf, who was visiting America for the first time in the company of another friend, Trekkie Parsons. Woolf and Parsons came to see them on 29 April 1966.

The first extended critical study of his work appeared in 1967. James Ward Lee sent a letter asking for biographical information for a pamphlet on Humphrey in the Southwest Writers Series. Humphrey's reply, dated 29 January 1967, stated:

> I was brought up to believe that it's bad manners to talk about yourself, and the more I see of this age of self-advertisement the truer that teaching seems to me. I try not to raise the noise level. Besides, even if I wanted to I could never provide you with enough biographical information for you to make eight or ten pages out of it. Writing and earning a

> living have not left me time enough to do all
> that much. My career has been pretty much
> creating what's inside those books and if the
> personal information on the dust jackets
> seem to you meager, there's a reason. As for
> *Who's Who*, I don't approve of it and don't
> answer their letter.

His reluctance to make himself a public figure may
have contributed to his relative obscurity, as Stephen
Cooper has said: "He has largely avoided the New
York literary scene and gone his own way. His quiet
life and low profile may account in part for the lack of
attention his later books have received" (236). His
reluctance to give interviews (and a book tour would
doubtless be even worse, not to mention talk shows)
did not help to keep him before the public.

During this period Humphrey struggled with his
novel about the Renshaw family. The material proved
extremely frustrating, so he decided to finish his other
project, the collection of stories he had been working
on during his stay in Europe. In that long and arrogant letter to Alfred A. Knopf from Italy in 1961, he
described his Ordway family project first, then said
this about the stories:

> but none of them finished (though two of
> them I have now thirty pages each) and all

this too done since coming to Rome in June (most of the spring in Sienna I was plagued with kidney stone trouble). These stories are all on a related theme, the discovery of oil in my part of Texas and Oklahoma in 1935–6, and the changes it made in the lives of the dirt farmers and the Indians on whose land it was found. Of this book of short stories I have about 100 pages, some of it the best writing I have ever done.

He described the project to Annie Laurie Williams as a kind of detour in the writing of *The Ordways*:

Meanwhile, I got detoured. After ten years of not one idea for a short story, I suddenly got started on ten all at once! They're all on a related theme: the discovery of oil in my parts of Texas-Oklahoma when I was a boy, and the effects (disastrous) that this sudden wealth had on the poor-whites and Indians whose land it was found on. I got a little weary of those Horatio Alger of Petroleum stories about H. L. Hunt and Dad Humble and Sid Richardson, and decided I'd tell how it really was. One of them, of thirty-five pages, is finished, the others about half-finished. They're probably the best thing I've done. But

meanwhile, I've laid them aside again and
gone back to the big book. (24 January 1962)

The stories were finally finished in London in 1965,
with one story written in four days to meet the
publisher's 15 March deadline. In a letter written on
10 March, Humphrey told his friend, the publisher/
editor Seymour Lawrence, that he had been working
ten hours a day and then collapsing at night over a
bottle. In spite of the deadline, the book did not appear from Knopf until 1968.

For a time the work was to be called "Red River
Valley," this being the region of Texas and Oklahoma
that he wanted to deal with. A reference to a sentimental cowboy ballad might have been a mistake. The
final title makes it clear that Humphrey wants to fix
a particular locale at a significant moment in its history, and he does a superb job of that. The area gener-
ated some extraordinary events and legends during
the 1930s, the period of the Dust Bowl so well known
in folk songs—and in John Steinbeck's *The Grapes of
Wrath*. At the same time that an area knocked down
by the Depression was being knocked out by the erod-
ing winds, oil discoveries brought enormous wealth
to a minority on both sides of the state borders, though
the biggest discoveries were in Oklahoma. Stories
abounded: about farmers who became rich overnight
and competed to buy enormous cars so that hearses

became a favorite vehicle; about Indians whose formerly worthless lands made them rich too; about outlaws like Bonnie and Clyde and Pretty Boy Floyd who served as Robin Hoods on behalf of the poor. The stories were in fact true, except for the nobility of the bank robbers.

William Humphrey, the destroyer of myth, had much to work with. The opening story of his collection, "The Ballad of Jesse Neighbours," is one of his best. Jesse's life is a travesty of several sentimental plot motifs: the poor boy who sets out to make a better life for himself and his impoverished intended; the rich young woman who scorns the poor boy; the outlaw who turns to crime over lost love or social injustice; the pathetic parents coming to pick up the body of their executed son. And along with these familiar elements—familiar in folklore, in country music—the myths of Texas and the oil strike permeate the work. The stories were most recently published in Humphrey's *Collected Stories*, and citations will be made to that text.

Jesse's impoverished intended and the scornful young woman are one and the same. Jessie dedicates himself to improving his Oklahoma farm for the sake of Naomi, his beloved, a young woman who prizes him. Nights he plays the guitar and sings to make a little extra money. But in the midst of his plans, Naomi's worthless father, Bull Childress, becomes a rich man

when oil is found on his land. This is the stuff of legends, or at least anecdotes:

> The story told was that the well blew in
> while old Bull was in the outhouse looking
> at the pictures in the unused pages of the
> mail-order catalogue, and that when she let
> go he shot off the hole and out the door with
> his flap hanging open and his britches down
> around his knees, tripped and sprawled flat
> on his face, rolled over, looked up, and then
> lay there moaning with joy and letting the
> slimy, thick, foul-smelling black rain spatter
> in his face and into his open mouth like sweet
> California wine. (207)

The ominous side of oil is hinted at by the transformation of the farm into a kind of wasteland by the
gushing well. Nothing will ever grow again, Bull's wife
complains; that's fine with him. He's rich now and
would be happy for it to gush for a biblical (and therefore even more ominous) forty days and nights.

Humphrey's description of the sojourn the
Childress family spends in Dallas shopping at the
Neiman-Marcus store is wonderfully lavish. Naomi
is transformed by the skills of the clerks and the
beauty operators into a kind of princess, one who will
scorn her deserving young lover. In life the virtuous

man is not very likely to get the princess, and when the Childress family returns, driving one new Packard home and towing another—two being needed to carry all their purchases—Naomi is no longer interested in Jesse. The interlude in Dallas carries the mystique of Texas wealth to such an extreme that it becomes comic, so that it almost deflates itself, though not quite. The reader can savor the Arabian Nights atmosphere of the famous Neiman-Marcus store: Humphrey does not savage it. His real demolition is on the Bonnie and Clyde legend.

As he mentions in his autobiography, *Farther Off from Heaven*, young Humphrey heard stories about Clyde Barrow and Bonnie Parker, who robbed banks in his region until they were cut down in an ambush (177). Pretty Boy Floyd was another real-life legend: a bank robber who was said to help the poor with his loot. Jesse responds to his loss of love by deciding to rob a bank. He is not surprised by Naomi's treachery: "The lore of his class, the songs he sang, were rich in cynical commentaries on such situations as his" (212). Part of the lore of his society is the myth of the outlaw, and the story digresses to tell the stories of Bonnie and Clyde (recently ambushed in Louisiana) and Pretty Boy Floyd, still at large.

Jesse decides that anything beats the life of a dirt farmer, so he sets out to rob a bank across the river in Clarksville, Texas. He chooses Texas because he doesn't want to inadvertently rob a bank containing some of his beloved's money. This misguided chivalry will prove fatal. Not long before, three robbers were shot dead by snipers when they tried to rob the Clarksville bank, and "swollen with self-conceit," Jesse imagined that the authorities would not expect another robbery. He manages to do everything wrong, panics, and is knocked unconscious by a bank guard. The conceited young emulator of Pretty Boy Floyd learns from his lawyer that bank robbery is a capital offense in Texas. As an Oklahoman, he is an excellent person to make an example of, and he is sentenced to die in the electric chair in Huntsville, far from Oklahoma. The action moves rather quickly in this story: it has the focus on dramatic scenes typical of the ballad tradition, and by the next page Jesse is dead and his body has been collected by his parents. The ending is deliberately sentimental in its evocation of their journey back home: "And still though they sat, in four hundred and fifty miles it happened now and again that one or the other would brush the strings, drawing from them a low chord like a sob" (222). This mournful sound is the true ballad of Jesse Neighbours.

In 1967, before the whole collection was available, James Ward Lee considered it Humphrey's best (*William Humphrey* 17), and certainly it is better than any story in *The Last Husband*, with the possible exception of "The Hardys." Lee admires the economy of the story—its quick reversal of fortune—and the regional descriptions. He also admires the social theme: Jesse has not gained a cent from his bank robbery; he is persuaded to rob it simply because of the Bonnie and Clyde fever; yet he pays with his life for being a "poreboy" (18). Mark Winchell, one of Humphrey's severest critics, also admires the story, although he does not like the shift to the parents at the end, feeling that we should see the effect on Naomi Childress (*William Humphrey* 31). But she, unlike the baffled parents, has been transfigured by Neiman-Marcus and lives in another sphere. Jesse is where he belongs, accompanied by his parents.

Winchell notes that there is a naturalistic atmosphere in the story: "The moral vision of this story is deterministic, almost in the manner of Theodore Dreiser" (31). The observation is accurate: the Depression era crushed so many individuals, especially the poor, through economic forces. In parts of Texas and Oklahoma, nature, represented by the Dust Bowl, ground the poor down even further. There is a dark tonality in the satire of *A Time and a Place*. Elizabeth Tebeaux calls Humphrey's universe grim and Godless: "Bound by circumstances they cannot control, Humphrey's characters make inevitably wrong choices" (333). In one of his interviews with Ashby Crowder, Humphrey says: "A friend of mine, a writer, a professor, a serious-minded man, once said to me, 'American literature is too grim.' I would say that most literature, beginning with *The Iliad*, is grim, reflecting the grimness of life" (34).

One of the grimmest themes in *A Time and a Place* is the destructive character of wealth. The sudden wealth brought by oil may ruin human happiness. The Childress family's oil wrecks Jesse Neighbours's noble and humble plans for his life. In "The Pump," Jordan Terry seems reasonably happy and sane with his new oil money and enjoys listening to the sound of the pump on his well, until he discovers that his neighbor, Clarence Bywaters, is drawing on the same pool as his own. He then becomes obsessed, fearing that his oil is being sucked up by the neighbor's pump. Greed makes him wretched, and when his pump breaks down, he sits drinking and rocking nervously on his porch. Suddenly the rocker, a kind of parody of the action of the pump, stops; Jordan Terry's own pump, his heart, has malfunctioned. The man has been turned into a parody of human life by his own greed, an idea which Humphrey expresses succinctly: "He was still warm when they got to him but it was as if rigor mortis had set in while he was still alive. They had to pry him loose from that chair, and getting him into his coffin was like straightening a bent nail" (321).

The cynicism of the narrator of "A Good Indian"

is so corrosive that readers are repelled rather than edified. The storyteller is an Oklahoma car dealer who once thought Indians were glamorous, especially when he discovered that he had Indian ancestry. Here the story is a little like the final story, "The Last of the Caddoes." But unlike the boy in that work, the narrator comes to despise Indians, and he enjoys telling about the day that an Indian named John came with a bundle of money from the sale of his land and bought a yellow Cadillac. John wrecks it almost immediately and wants another, which the narrator sells to him for his remaining cash, plus his wagon and team and the wrecked car. A second wreck naturally ensues, since John cannot drive, and this one is fatal. The narrator feels no guilt, and when John's widow arrives, he lends her the wagon and team to carry away the body. His callous inhumanity lacks the bizarre verbal inventiveness of Faulkner's Jason Compson and Flannery O'Connor's Misfit; the character is simply repulsive and his wise-cracking attitude has no subtlety in it. The story reinforces Humphrey's theme that wealth can destroy as surely as poverty, but nothing about the characterization or the style seems memorable.

Much more powerful is "A Job of the Plains," a reversal of the biblical story: Humphrey's modern Job, Dobbs, is ruined by good fortune, not by loss. Dobbs at first suffers financial misfortune, unlike the biblical character, who begins in prosperity. He talks to his "comforters' on the town square, lamenting his bad luck and complaining that he has never been a sinner. One friend suggests that maybe oil will be found on his land. Shortly after, a cyclone destroys his house. He appears to be at the nadir of his luck, but his friends pitch in and help him. True misfortune comes when oil (as prophesied on the town square) is discovered on his land, and he loses his former happiness. His children are corrupted, many of his friends ("foul-weather friends") who helped him after the cyclone avoid him now, feeling inferior. He spends his life in boredom, condescended to by his children, who all make bad marriages. He accumulates livestock, like the original Job, and dies, having "had his fill of days," a significant variation on the original, in which the character dies "full of days." As Sylvia Grider and Elizabeth Tebeaux say in their excellent study of the story, the conclusion is "a line by line parody of the final six verses of Chapter 42 of Job" (302). A mark of Humphrey's skill as a stylist is his ability to parody the Bible throughout the story without becoming ludicrous: he shows literary tact in deciding just how closely to echo his great original.

Grider and Tebeaux suggest that this story sets the naturalistic tone for the work as a whole, an astute comment. This is the story with the greatest philosophical reach, but Dobbs, they point out, has no developing view of God, no view of God at all. He is a passive character with no understanding of what has happened to him, making him neither tragic (that requires insight) nor patient. The crux of the story, they say, lies in the absence of God: there is no meaning in life for Dobbs. Humphrey himself lost his faith when his father died, an event that seemed without meaning or justice. The other stories generally present us with characters in less metaphysical situations, but it is the same arid, arbitrary world in which wealth and poverty come to people by chance. In their words, "the stories become a catalogue of human failure" (305).

This bitter vision becomes interesting for two reasons, one philosophical, one aesthetic. It is truly a vision, relentlessly grim as it is, just as Humphrey's beloved Hardy has a vision. Of course, Hardy is more obviously compassionate toward his characters. And the working out of the vision through irony and brilliant naturalistic detail makes the stories pleasurable, whatever the aftertaste. The irony helps demolish certain myths: dreams of wealth, fantasies about the outlaw, fantasies which help console those victimized by crushing social and natural forces.

One of the most interesting stories, one not discussed much by the critics, is "A Home Away from Home," a work in which a character manages—for once in the book—to have some understanding of her situation. An oil company decides to drill on the farm where Elgin Floyd, his wife Sibyl, and their daughter Geraldine live. Elgin is captivated by dreams of wealth, while his wife, a much more sensible person, immediately plants a garden for fresh vegetables and prepares the house to offer board to the oil workers, figuring that their money will be a sure thing. She grows vegetables to feed the guests; her husband abandons farming. Eventually the drillers strike gas, not oil, and in the 1930s gas was useless. The well blazes like the fires of hell, and it has to be put out until a flare can be prepared in a nearby field. The man who comes on a motorcycle to prepare the explosives is a grotesque vision of technological glamour:

> He looked like a man-sized bug, shiny black, with big yellow bug's eyes sticking out beyond the side of his head. He wore an aviator's black leather helmet strapped underneath the chin, the immense wraparound goggles, seated on sponge-rubber padding, made of amber glass, reflecting the light like the multicellular eyes of a fly seen under a microscope. He wore a black leather bow tie and a leather jacket with, counting those on the elbows, a dozen zipper pockets, fringed leather gauntlets, black pants as tight as a coat of lacquer, and knee-high black puttees

with chrome buckles. Dividing his thorax
from his abdomen was a waist no bigger
around than a dirtdauber's enclosed in a
black kidney belt studded with cats'-eyes, in
hearts, diamonds, clubs, and spades. (280)

This individual, nicknamed Speed, appears age-
less, but he is actually twenty-five, but not expected
to live to thirty because of the extreme danger of his
profession. He is, in fact, a kind of early prototype of
the legendary Red Adair, the Texan greatly admired
for extinguishing oil field fires. When he takes off his
helmet, the cost of technology becomes visible:

He removed the helmet, disclosing a head
as hairless as a hard-boiled egg and of the
same whiteness. He had neither eyebrows nor
lashes nor trace of beard: all had been burnt
away. His features were fixed, rigid, expres-
sionless; only the eyes, beneath their lashless
lids, moved. A weathered china doll decorat-
ing the grave of a long-dead child was what
he reminded Geraldine of. (280)

He performs his heroics with the gas well, causing
both the mother, Sibyl, and the daughter, Geraldine,
to faint as they watch him crawl toward the fire in
his white asbestos suit, a suit which makes him look

more like a bug than did his black motorcycle gear.

The drillers continue, but finally have to give up, leaving Mr. Floyd to poverty: he has failed to plant crops. Even his sensible wife has failed to make money out of her boardinghouse, having spent too much feeding the glamorous drillers. Worst of all, Geraldine runs off with Speed, in a scene that mingles sexuality and machinery: "'Mama, you'll just have to manage the best you can without me,' said Geraldine, straddling the saddle seat, her skirt three quarters of the way up her thighs, her arms hugging that narrow waist encased in its jeweled kidney belt" (282). The Floyds have a souvenir, a gas flare that may burn for forty years (a biblical number), a flaming sword, Humphrey says, "like the one set to guard the east gate of Eden." Their lives were not paradisal before, but they were much better than before the drilling began.

Not every story deals with oil, but fantasies and delusions run through most of them. In "The Human Fly," one of Humphrey's finest stories, the Depression era craving for escape is explored. The masses want vicarious excitement, and the fad of the human fly, a daredevil who would scale skyscrapers, fed that craving. As explained by the narrator, a sarcastic newspaperman (a common American literary and cinematic type), "Grippo, the Human Fly," advertises his plan to scale the eight-story courthouse of a little Texas town called—the irony is too obvious—New

Jerusalem. The courthouse and its chiming clock tower suggest William Humphrey's own Clarksville. The Chamber of Commerce has sponsored this stunt, with a prize of a thousand dollars, realizing that the victims of the Dust Bowl need some amusement.

A great crowd gathers. No one wants to miss the event, except "California" Stan Reynolds, a thirty-year-old man who has always dreamed of flight from New Jerusalem to California but has never escaped farther than Paris, Texas, forty-seven miles to the east. Stan, as Mark Royden Winchell points out, manifests "a Western theme which is not found elsewhere in [Humphrey's] work—the dream of California" (*William Humphrey* 32). The dream was common in the Dust Bowl, and is common enough today. As any skilled reader would foresee, Stan avoids appearing at the Courthouse because he is the Human Fly. He will cater to the fantasies of the thrill-crazed crowd in order to finance the fulfillment of his own fantasy. Humphrey reveals something about the delusions of dreamers when he describes the reaction of the crowd when Stan's helmet comes off after a short fall during the climb: immediately the crowd feels duped and takes on the emotional quality of a mob. Somehow the feat is meaningless if performed by one of them: delusive thinking. But Stan continues to climb, in spite of his wife's entreaties: he can't give up his prize, his dream. Humphrey can evoke physical action brilliantly, and the reader is drawn into the suspense of Stan's ordeal, almost inch by inch. He is finally defeated by the task, reaches for a rescue rope, and falls. He lives out his life, another thirty years, paralyzed and even more embittered, a helpless ward of the town. The conclusion is a dark epitaph for his dream: "Some readers may, like ourself, be intrigued to know how many times the town clock chimed over that period. 10,571,358" (346).

The masterpiece of hope and delusion in the book is "The Rainmaker," the hilarious story of Orville Simms, whose pathetic truck bears the sign, "The 1 & OnLY ProF. ORViLLe SiMMs." Simms is a confidence man, a spiritual descendant of characters like the King and the Duke in *Huckleberry Finn*. But he is not a very good one: at the beginning of the story he is on the Oklahoma side of the Red River, fleeing the mob which has tarred and feathered him, the fate met by Twain's con men. He makes it to the ferry and leaves the mob behind. A reader curious about how a victim of tarring and feathering cleans himself up will learn from Humphrey's meticulous description. The story is told in a leisurely way. We eventually learn that Simms had been a poor farmer in Arkansas. His first attempt to peddle dreams rested on the fact that Arkansas is the only state in the Continental U.S. to have diamonds. Simms erects a sign:

TRy yOUR LUCk
HUNt fOR OZARk DiMoNds
Big 1s HAVe BeNN FOUNd
1$ peR. HR.

Only one man ever stopped, and only after the price
was cut in half, but he was a wiseacre who looked
closely at Simms "and then said on second thought
he believed he wouldn't after all, because he could
tell by looking that he, Simms, had done already found
all the real big ones" (298). In folklore, the poor man
who sells his farm is likely to discover that it has
treasure on it that the farmer cannot identify, and
this is the case with Simms, who sells his land to a
man who knows that the bat cave on it is full of valuable guano. No wonder Simms sets up as a con man.

A flashback explains why Simms was tarred and
feathered by the people of Arrowhead, Oklahoma.
They were, in fact, the most trusting people Simms
had ever met. He performed his act for them, a mixture of pseudo-scientific patter and stage props like
dynamite, balloons, and rockets. He recognizes that
he offers entertainment to the desperate (spectacle
is another form of escape fantasy) as well as hope of
rain. The final touch in his act was to climb a wind-
mill to draw down rain clouds. In a wonderful comic
moment, the big black clouds do appear and even the
con man is taken in: "There! That ought to satisfy

you." But the rain clouds are in fact the black winds, the dirt-bearing scourge of the Depression, and Simms is almost blown off the tower. When the hideous storm is over, he finds a group of men waiting for him at the base of the tower, wearing bandannas against the wind, which makes them look particularly sinister.

On the Texas side of the Red River, Simms encounters a new situation, people who have plenty of money, because of oil wells, but even less water than the rest of the region: no water is available to wash the Pierce Arrows, Packards, and Cadillacs that the inhabitants have bought. The rainmaker directs his efforts at rain-making from the top of the eleven-story courthouse this time. The story is like a joke with a second punch line: what could go wrong this time? For one thing, real rain begins before his act can really get underway. He expects to be asked for a refund of their money, but these people are so trusting that they assume that he has brought the rain without effort. This, we are told, is a moment of profound insight for the protagonist: "'Orville, my friend,' he said to himself in an awestruck whisper, 'if you had half the faith in yourself these folks have in you, you could be governor of the state'" (136). But this moment is not the climax: after three days of torrential rain, those who trusted him to start it come to ask him to turn it off, and of course he cannot. The desperate rainmaker thinks to himself again, this time echoing a famous saying by Abraham Lincoln:

> Dear Lord, listen to a con man's prayer.
> Looking to the future—if I am allowed any—
> please show me the way to some other part
> of your creation where you distributed a little
> bit more sense. Some place where—how does
> it go?—where you can fool some of the people
> all of the time and all of the people some of
> the time, but deliver me, Lord, from a place
> where you can fool all of the people all of the
> time. (312–13)

The story ends as it began, at the ferry on the Oklahoma side of the Red River, with the ferryman, who will not even attempt river crossings when much of the world is being washed away—buildings, trees, livestock. He sees a truck over on the Texas side, with the driver "honking as if his life depended on it" (313). The second point of this tall tale is that too much rain can be as dangerous for the miracle-worker as no rain at all.

The story is amusing, certainly, and it contributes to Humphrey's exploration of self-delusion as well as giving a powerful picture of the drought and winds. The miseries of the Dust Bowl made people credulous and eager for marvels. A bit of fantasy forms the subject of a much quieter story, "A Voice from the

Woods." The narrator's mother is visiting him and his
northern wife in their New England home one spring,
and the sound of a mourning dove—unusual in the
area but very common in Texas—reminds mother and
son of the South they both have left. The mother tells
her daughter-in-law about Pretty Boy Floyd, and this
leads her to remember the bank robbery in Blossom
Prairie, one of Humphrey's names for Clarksville.
("Blossom Prairie" in the story even had a College
Avenue without a College, just like Clarksville.) The
bank robbery is clearly the Clarksville robbery described in "The Ballad of Jesse Neighbours." In a draft
of a letter to James Ward Lee from 1967, Humphrey
said that the robbery in "A Voice from the Woods" was
based on one that occurred in Clarksville during his
childhood, but he could no longer be sure what he
remembered and what he had invented.

The mother tells how the three men were betrayed by their confederate and shot dead by snipers
as they left the bank. The curious part of her story
lies in her nostalgia about the ringleader, Travis (a
typical Texas name), who had courted her briefly, and
was clearly an unsuitable match. Still, she envies the
red-haired woman who took part in the preparations
for the robbery and who was sent to prison for eighteen years. A bit of humor is added by the redhaired
woman's cuckolded husband, who adores his wife
Mildred (a rather unfashionable name), and stands

up in the courtroom to say, "Mildred! I'll be waiting for you!" Her reply is, "You'll wait a lot longer than any eighteen years!" (328). The mother in the story describes her brief jealousy at the trial when the dead man's lover was taken off to prison, a curious thought to express to a son, but made entirely credible in Humphrey's story. Her memory of the moment of jealousy has been triggered by the melancholy sound of the mourning dove. In their eagerness to see the story as another example of Humphrey showing the meaninglessness of life, Grider and Tebeaux misread it, seeing it as "the passionless, pointless conversation between three nameless, faceless people" (306). The mother emerges as a strong personality, and her conversation is by no means nameless. She has pointed to an irony of life, certainly, a "satire of circumstance," to use Hardy's term. She had a good marriage and a child, but she could still regret (a very Hardyesque word) never experiencing the deluded passion of the redhaired woman. She understands the foolishness of that regret, but it is a natural emotion and she registers both it and its apparent oddity. She has missed some element of life, and she knows it. Humphrey skillfully uses the triggering incident of the dove and the presence of the narrator's wife, an outsider to the region where the remembered events took place, to tell his story.

The remaining stories, "Mouth of Brass" and "The

Last of the Caddoes," deal with race. In "Mouth of Brass" the friendship of the boy narrator with a black man is a means for exploring southern racism in a time before the Civil Rights movement. The black man, Finus, is a street peddler of tamales, and he has a remarkable bass voice, which makes life in Blossom Prairie precarious for him: in a racist society where blacks are supposed to be self-effacing to the point of invisibility, Finus often makes white men angry. They accuse him of talking back to them and on one occasion a sailor knocked him down. And yet as a street vendor he must call out the name of his product, "MOLLY OT! Hot tamales!" (258). The narrator says that Finus a simplified spelling of the Hebrew name, Phineas, which means "mouth of brass," a bit of far-fetched symbolism explained by the theory that someone hearing the infant cry chose the name to fit the voice.

The story has a conventional pattern. As Mark Royden Winchell notes, "the relationship of mentor and protégé that develops between the black man and the white boy belongs to a tradition that goes back through Faulkner's Sam Fathers and Ike McCaslin to Twain's Huck and Jim" (*William Humphrey* 31). But unlike Huck Finn, the narrator has no chance to rescue his black friend. The details of the friendship are vividly conveyed. The boy wants to accompany Finus on his rounds, and we follow him into Finus's one-room house, where he helps roll tamales in corn shucks. They make the rounds of the town, giving the boy his first sense of how the town is organized, and they meet all the interesting people, the spice-loving ones.

This is a common strategy in children's books: the child learns about life through a mentor who is a social outsider, thereby broadening the young reader's awareness of diversity and encouraging tolerance. But this is not a children's story, and Finus is murdered in a meaningless incident on the town square one Saturday. Jewell Purdom, a surly drunk, sends his son Gilbert to buy a dozen tamales. Gilbert eats five of the baker's dozen he is given, and his father thinks he's been cheated. Finus in a panic calls out his "Molly ot! Hot tamales!" and Purdom kills him with a knife, thinking that the man is taunting or defying him. The narrator doesn't witness the killing, but he is on the square and sees the pool of blood, in which (and here the symbolism is much too obvious) the statue of the Confederate soldier and the steeple of the Methodist church are reflected. Naturally no one will tell the town constable what happened; no one saw anything. The racist code of the South has been upheld.

The story is powerful within its limitations, especially when the boy's parents, who are uneasy racists themselves, try to cope with his feelings. But it has a contrived quality, and a dated air: Humphrey is

writing about the Clarksville of his childhood, but
even in 1968 the world of Huck Finn and Jim seemed
a simplification. Humphrey is a man of racial good-
will, but his Finus is a rather simple man and we
don't learn much of the experience of racism as he
would feel it. In the notebooks of *Proud Flesh*,
Humphrey contemplated ways of making his black
characters respond to the Civil Rights movement, but
was unable to do it. Leaving the South in 1944 left a
gap in his understanding of the evolving racial issue.

Race is the subject in "The Last of the Caddoes,"
another work with a character deluded by fantasy.
Humphrey considered this one of his finest stories.
When Harold Hayes at *Esquire* accepted it on 20 May
1968, he told Humphrey that it was every bit as good
as he had said. The story deals with Jimmy Hawkins,
who grows up on the shores of the Red River. When
he learns that he is part Indian, he begins a process
of change which estranges him from his mother and
may lead him to matricide. The Indian ancestry is
real, his grandfather being half Indian, but his obsession has delusional elements. His grandfather
knows nothing about his father's background, not
even the name of the tribe, so Jimmy decides that he
must have been one of the vanished Caddoes, which
makes Jimmy (not counting his father and grandfather) the last of the Caddoes.

The boy's alienation from his family, especially

from his mother, who has no Indian blood, grows
steadily. He excavates an Indian mound on his
grandfather's farm with great care. In writing about
his own story in a notebook, Humphrey thought that
it might represent the destruction of the American
Indian, the eradication of their presence. In the story,
the mother smashes one of the son's excavated artifacts on his thirteenth birthday and tells him that he
has become a snake in her bosom, which leads him to
rename himself "Snake-in-His-Mother's Bosom."
And he takes very seriously her outburst, "You will
be the death of me." The snake image undoubtedly
comes from Aeschylus's play, *The Libation Bearers*,
the second work in the *Oresteia* trilogy. Humphrey
had been using the play as a source of symbols for his
novel *Proud Flesh*, and it is a key symbol:
Clytemnestra dreams of giving birth to a snake who
bites her bosom, and her son, Orestes, who has come
to Thebes to kill her, recognizes that he is the snake.
And Clytemnestra uses the same image at the end
when Orestes is about to kill her. The boy in Humphrey's story runs away from home, and in a finely-
written scene witnesses a snake discarding its skin.
He, after all, has discarded his white skin. His mother
catches him, and he goes home with her, but the story
ends with the boy feeling that eventually he will receive a message from ancestors instructing him to
kill his mother (371).

Humphrey and Harold Hayes both admired the story, and the critic hesitates to argue with both the author and a distinguished fiction editor. It caught the attention of a Texas director, Ken Harrison, who made it into a short film. The story was doubtless important to Humphrey, who himself had Indian ancestry, and who, like the boy in the story, could get no details from his grandfather. The story is well thought out—Humphrey is always a careful craftsman—but lacks the verbal exuberance of the best stories in his collection, like the magical description of Neiman-Marcus in "The Ballad of Jesse Neighbours," or the marvelous description of Speed the well-dynamiter in "Home Away from Home." In a workbook for *Proud Flesh*, Humphrey mentions similarities between "The Last of the Caddoes" and Lawrence's "The Woman Who Rode Away," but the Englishman's story engages the reader more imaginatively through its fable and sun-moon symbolism and puts the case for the Indian world view more powerfully than Humphrey can through a few artifacts dug up in a mound. It seems more a study of the onset of schizophrenia in adolescence than a profound exploration of cultural difference.

The boy is the last in a series of characters who delude themselves in *A Time and a Place*. The people of the Red River Valley respond to their impoverished lives by dreaming of wealth, by imagining themselves as outlaws, by climbing buildings to win impossible prizes, by watching credulously as a rainmaker offers them magical performances to end the drought. Unfortunately, even those who gain wealth, like Dobbs in "A Job of the Plains" and Jordan Terry in "The Pump," may find that it brings them no happiness. They come up against the flaws in human nature. In Humphrey's grim Dust Bowl world, the grimmest facts are not the facts of nature and economics but the truths of human nature. He creates a consistent human world to demonstrate these truths, a world as unified as Hardy's Wessex. The whole of Red River Valley in the 1930s is as barren as one part of Hardy's world: Egdon Heath. Fortunately, the bleakness is relieved by the brilliance of language and the skill of his plot and characterization.

6

Humphrey's *Oresteia*:
Proud Flesh

The Humphreys spent the early part of 1969 in France, returning to the U.S. in early May so that William could receive an honorary degree from Southern Methodist University in Dallas. This was Humphrey's first trip back to Texas in many years, and he took the opportunity to revisit Clarksville for the first time since 1937. The visit would make possible his memoir, *Farther Off from Heaven*.

Annie Laurie Williams told him on 10 December 1968 that Universal Pictures was about to make a staggering offer for *A Time and a Place*. His response, recorded in one of his notebooks, was skeptical: "What on earth are they thinking of? She plans to ask $150,000. Called to ask would I allow her to take as little as $100,000!!!" Nothing came of this situation. Hollywood offered hope but no fulfillment during the rest of Humphrey's career: in a letter to Fred and Andy Dupee (7 January 1973) he spoke of reading the proofs of *Proud Flesh* and "waiting hopefully for the phone to ring and find Hollywood on the other end of the line."

In the late 1960s he was still struggling with his third novel, and the agony went on for years. He had sent a fragment of it to Alfred A. Knopf and to Lemay Harding, his editor, in 1963, and both were not sure what to make of it. After *The Ordways* in 1965, he gave full attention to the work. In the summer of 1964 he wrote his agent an optimistic letter from Sussex about it: "My work on the new novel has gone quite well, and I should say the book is now about 2/3rds finished—although the third remaining to be done is, as always the hardest" (31 August 1964).

The 1960s were years of increasing social unrest, first over civil rights for blacks and then over the war in Vietnam. Humphrey was deeply touched by these events. His disgust over the heavily-televised war would probably influence the bleak depiction of society in the concluding section of *Proud Flesh*, in which Amy's suffering becomes a television pastime. Humphrey took part in the march on the Pentagon in 1971 and agonized over the Pentagon papers and Watergate as he struggled with his apparently unfinishable novel. Vietnam impinged on his writing career very briefly in 1970, when Harold Hayes, the editor of *Esquire*, asked him if he would consider writing the "as-told-to" story of Lieutenant William Calley, who was prosecuted for the My Lai massacre. The work would be published in part in the magazine and then issued as a book by Viking. Humphrey considered this only briefly, feeling that he would become an advocate for Calley rather than a seeker of the truth. The project went to John Craft instead. One project that kept him busy as a writer was his small comic masterpiece about salmon fishing in Britain, *The Spawning Run*, which will be discussed in Chapter 9.

The period around 1969–1970 was probably the worst time of Humphrey's adult life. He began to drink heavily while trying to give up smoking, he told Katherine Anne Porter (14 July 1969): "So as not to climb the walls from tobacco withdrawal anxiety, I drink myself into a stupor every night and come out of my hangover about noon—another reason I haven't written." On 5 January 1970, he was steadying the ladder for a workman who was breaking up the masses of ice on the roof of High Meadow, and he suffered a concussion when a chunk ("about fifteen cents worth it would have been in Clarksville, Texas") hit his head. By February he was wondering if he was having a nervous breakdown, according to one of his notebooks. In an entry dated Sunday morning, February 9, he engaged in "A little self-communion," as he called it:

> I am really disintegrating. God, even my handwriting shows it. Dead drunk every night. Sick, hungover. Shaky half the next day, recovering in time to start drinking again. A crack-up. That's what I have had— or am having. The worst may be yet to come. It certainly will be unless I begin to put up a little resistance. For one thing I must cut down on the drinking. And I must somewhere find the strength and the courage to get back into the novel.

On May 25 he wrote in a notebook: "I'm dissatisfied with myself. I drink too much. Read too little. I'm drifting into stagnation." A later entry (30 October 1970) says: "Too much wine. Too much beer, too much narcotics—I'm substituting, not quitting. Must not go on." He was still drinking in the summer of 1971, when he wrote Katherine Anne Porter about an accident that took place when he was playing ball with the children of friends. He broke a toe and sprained an ankle on his right foot. He said jokingly: "Well, I always knew I had a hollow leg, now I know it's the right one, because although I try every night to fill it with Virginia Gentleman, I haven't succeeded yet" (10 July 1971). This period of unhappiness would help him create the character of Ben Curtis in *Hostages to Fortune*.

Eventually a *deus ex machina* would give him the key to finishing the book, which he finally managed to do on 8 April 1972, while living in the London house where George Eliot died. *Deus ex machina*, a term from classical tragedy, describes what happened very well: he read *The Oresteia* of Aeschylus and related plays by Sophocles and Euripides and came to a new understanding of what his novel meant and how it should end. He found new insights into the social issues from *The Libation Bearers*, the second play of *The Oresteia*, while his understanding of the matriarch of the Renshaw clan, Edwina, was deepened by the figure of Clytemnestra in both *Agamemnon* and *The Libation Bearers*. And he thought that the parallels between the protagonist of Sophocles's *Electra* and his other important female character, her daughter, were uncanny. The great practitioner of the *deus ex machina* is Euripides, and his use of the device has often caused dissatisfaction by imposing arbitrary endings on a plot.

Humphrey's long letter to Alfred A. Knopf, Jr., (26 October 1961) reveals some of his original conception:

The short novel concerns the death of a southern matriarch, the assembly of her large and violent clan (ten children) and the efforts of a couple of these rural Eumenides to track down and bring home for the burial (while the rest of them keep the old lady's remains in the town ice house) the renegade youngest son in New York City.

The projected short novel became Humphrey's longest work. His matriarch has six sons, Clifford, Clyde, Ross, Lester, Ballard, and Kyle, and four daughters, Amy, Gladys, Hazel, and Lois. Her husband, Alonzo, known to his face as Lonzo and behind his back as "Old Dot and Carry" because of a limp from a broken and twisted toe, faded from the family's life before he even died. It is a matriarchy that the clan lives under, and Edwina's law is supreme. The clannishness of the family is notorious even for the South, and they are capable of violence when the family honor or interests are threatened. They are major landowners, cotton growers, in their part of Texas, an area much like Red River County.

However, one child is a rebel against the rule of *Mutterrecht*, as the Swiss anthropologist Johann Jakob Bachofen called it: Kyle, the youngest, most-loved, and most rebellious. Kyle hates his family. Humphrey thought of using the famous opening sentence of Tolstoy's *Anna Karenina* as the epigraph of his novel: "Happy families are all alike; every unhappy family is unhappy in its own way," which would have emphasized the centrality of family dysfunction. At a family reunion Kyle once explained the term "xenophobia" to his family and declared that "It's what you've all got. Our whole tribe has got it. All but me." His sister Amy retorts that he has "kinophobia," and he replies, "Yes, I can get along well enough with most anybody as long as they're not related to me" (231). He is paradoxically the consummate Renshaw in his willful, stubborn ways: "He was the final print of which they were the trial proofs." Kyle carries their self-obsessed contrariness to the point of rejecting them, and he leaves home for unknown parts. His mother is unable to die in peace without him present, and the remaining children become obsessed with finding him before their mother dies, and then when she does die, with finding him before the funeral. They commandeer the local ice house and store their mother in it while two sons, Lester and Ballard, go on a hopeless search.

This matriarchal household has a number of black servants, as well as seasonal black workers. Eulalie is a matriarchal figure in her own right. Her daughter, Rowena, has two children: a son, Archie, and Shug, the involuntary mistress of Clyde Renshaw. Shug has been married off to an alcoholic nicknamed

Jug as a cover for her relationship with Clyde. The subordination of the blacks in a racist world is symbolized by Eulalie's toy wagon, which infantilizes her. But paradoxically Edwina and her daughter Amy are shown to be dependents themselves by the little wagon that Eulalie takes everywhere: in crises during the novel each has to be carried in by the servant. Humphrey worried about the influence of Faulkner as he worked on this novel and admonished himself not to make Eulalie too much like Dilsey, the patient, saintly black woman in *The Sound and the Fury*, the character who keeps the Compson family going. In his drafts he first called Jug "Tip" and on a few occasions "T. P." He must have realized that one member of the black household in Faulkner's novel was, in fact, named T. P. One of the anxieties of influence must be its tendency to operate unconsciously.

The novel simply did not come into focus for Humphrey for years, and one sign of his uncertainty was his inability to give it a defining title. Titles were never easy for Humphrey, and he actually felt uneasy when he was able to name his next novel, *Hostages to Fortune*, from the start, as if giving it a title would predetermine what he wrote. *Proud Flesh* was the hardest novel to name: his notebooks for the book have lists of prospective titles. At one point, early in his *Oresteia* notebook, he had two lists. One was of fifteen titles referring mostly to the Bible or Greek

mythology (all with allusions to mourning or the Furies); the other had eleven titles drawn from *Hamlet*,
another celebrated work about mourning. The final
choice, *Proud Flesh*, was brilliant, as it alludes to pride
in one's kin and to festering conflict. The quarrels of
Edwina and Kyle are described this way: "Over the
lacerations they inflicted upon each other, tissue
formed like proud flesh over festering wounds" (233).

He had difficulties naming Edwina's eldest child,
Amy, as well. She was long called "Hallie," a good
southern name. But he disliked it and kept reminding himself to find another. For a while she was
"Sara," but he didn't like that name either. Finally
he discovered the perfect name, one that implies love.
But Amy is in truth not loving at all, as the book reveals. She is in fact the counterpart of Kyle, who is
the Orestes to Amy's Electra, though she has denied
it all her life. Along with uncertainty about naming
her, Humphrey worried about her characterization
and about her fate in the novel, one that turns out to
be, as critic Gary Davenport has astutely called it,
"hyper-realism" (500). One of his notebooks for *Proud
Flesh* has an inscription instructing a friend to destroy all the workbooks for the novel if he should die.
The reason given:

> . . . because it isn't really a novel. There is too
> much agreement that an altogether differ-

ent kind of book—examples? *The Brother's Karamazov*, *Moll Flanders*, *Proust*—should be called novels. Why isn't this one. It has even less to do with critical realism than Dostoyevsky's or Proust's works.

Humphrey's archives at the University of Texas contain six notebooks for *Proud Flesh*, and the sheer number indicates the trouble he had with the book. The most important notebook is a hard-covered one with the notation, "Poughkeepsie, June, 1965." He had finished *A Time and a Place* in London on March 11 of that year, and now he was back in the United States, house-hunting in the Hudson area. The notebook was entitled "Proud Flesh / or /A Time to Mourn." On the first page he has written, "Notes on the *Oresteia* read in connection with a novel in Progress tentatively entitled The Renshaws by William Humphrey." In the middle of his uncertainties about his novel he read the complete *Oresteia* of Aeschylus for the first time, in Richmond Lattimore's translation. Before he had only known the *Agamemnon*. He was overcome with excitement and quickly read several translations of the work (most important: Philip Vellacott's Penguin Classics version) as well as Euripides's *Orestes* (as translated by William Arrowsmith) and Sophocles's *Electra* (in David Grene's version). He found that the Greek myths provided him with a special understanding of his themes and characters. There is much material on his reading and ways that might be applied to the novel. Some of the paths were dead ends, but several roads are worth pursuing. The important ones involve the justice theme, the nature of the characters, and the bizarre conclusion of the novel.

The most important play in *The Oresteia* for Humphrey is the second one, *The Libation Bearers*. In the first play, *Agamemnon*, Clytemnestra and her lover Aegisthus murder her husband on his return from Troy. This story has only minor interest for Humphrey, though we shall see that his Clytemnestra, Edwina Renshaw, has eliminated her husband through indifference. The chorus of *The Libation Bearers* is made up of foreign serving women: slaves, in fact. The play helped Humphrey think about the question of racial justice, an issue which was on everyone's mind while he was writing the novel. He also represents the white community through the male neighbors who gather at the pear tree outside the Renshaw house and the local housewives who sit in the kitchen. They all comment in a choral fashion on the family and its doings, particularly on their pride, so the work really has three choruses. The housewives who bring pies and other food for the distressed family are actually called "a chorus of voices" (112). The pear tree where the gossiping men stand clearly represents the dying mother: in its decay, it can't hold its fruit, which tumbles to the ground prematurely.

Humphrey's libation bearers are the black servants in the Renshaw household, who have been living under the autocratic rule of Edwina Renshaw. They are in a sense part of the family. With Edwina's death, some change in the social order seems likely, and the novel is set in a time when the civil rights movement is taking place. In his Oresteia notebook he puzzles over just what the blacks might gain from the situation. He considers for a while the possibility of bringing the civil rights movement into the work, and wonders if he could find a Nat Turner, but this seems unlikely in the Renshaw household. He contemplates having one of the servants take part in a demonstration, where he would be faced down by Edwina. Obviously, he conceives of Edwina as so powerful that no black employee could stand up to her. But he decides against such a political situation: "Well, merely to bring Faulkner up to date is certainly not what I want to do. And to an extent that's what this notion sounds like," he concludes.

He settles for a symbolic approach to the justice issue: after Edwina's death, her daughter Amy locks herself in the storm cellar in a fit of penance and becomes a media celebrity. Archie and Jug work as parking lot attendants for the hordes of people who come to confess their sins and crimes down the air outlet.

Humphrey thought of having the blacks operate concession stands offering iced tea, a symbolic form of "libation bearing," but this would have made them appear to be mercenary spirits capitalizing on the family's grief. They remain choral figures, bystanders to the actions of the white characters, except for Shug, Clyde's black mistress, who is not a bystander, though she hates her role. At one time Humphrey had considered making one of the black characters a half sibling, fathered by Lonzo Renshaw, but this seemed indeed too Faulknerian, as he observed in one of his notebooks.

One consequence of Humphrey's long absence from the South is his inability to imagine black characters in ways that go beyond his models. The chief influences are Katherine Anne Porter's *The Old Order* and, of course, William Faulkner's novels. Humphrey is unable to create complex black characters who respond to the social forces of the 1960s. The black cook and head of the servant family, Eulalie, is, as Humphrey feared, a little too much like Faulkner's Dilsey, though without Dilsey's intense spirituality and knowledge of human nature. None of the males has the spiky individuality of a character in Faulkner's *Go Down, Moses* like Lucas Beauchamp or the resourcefulness of "Tommys Turl" in the same book. For all his concern about social justice, Humphrey manages to patronize his black characters. They are described as having a "third eyelid," a transparent one like a nictitating membrane, a way of saying that they become distant (we speak of "eyes glazing over") when they wish to evade a subject. This is traditional behavior of the powerless, but the problem is that it doesn't fit the outburst of black pride in the 1960s.

The most interesting angle on black-white relationships comes from the white side: Clyde, who runs the farm, is obsessed with a romantic image of blacks acquired by observing the lives of the migrant workers, who live chaotic lives. Every one of the stereotypes about blacks appeals to him: the reputed gambling, drinking, and sexual license . He even carries a razor on a string around his neck like the black man in Faulkner's "Pantaloon in Black" from *Go Down, Moses*. Doc Metcalf, the family physician, observes that he actually shaves with an electric razor. The razor, a traditional weapon among southern blacks, is used by Clyde in a half-hearted attempted to unman himself after his mother's death.

The relationship of Clyde and Shug is Humphrey's way of exploring black and white relationships. Clyde forced himself on her when she was still in school. The relationship is sterile, emotionally and literally: after their first encounter, which takes place outdoors (part of Clyde's primitivism), Shug sees a discarded condom on the ground. Humphrey wisely

avoided the traditional machinery of miscegenation,
unacknowledged siblings and tragic mulattos so common in southern fiction, though he did consider these
possibilities as a way of stressing that the black characters are intimate parts of the matriarchal household. Clyde's problem is that he cannot admit to
himself that his passion for Shug is anything but
physical. He wants to crave her like an animal because this is how he imagines black sexuality to be.
What he represses is the emotion of love. He can never
bring himself to kiss her. Her response is rather traditional: she knows that he is obsessively jealous, and
she "betrays" him with every available black male on
the place, except her drunken husband, who is the
hated decoy for her relationship with Clyde. The relationship of Clyde and Shug has something archaic
about it, even if the worst "sex on the plantation" cli-
ches are avoided.

In Humphrey's South, the love that dares not
speak its name is not homosexuality but sex between
the races. Clyde's wife Eunice is aware of his relationship with Shug and even thinks of exposing him,
of ruining him forever by taking the unheard-of measure of asking for a divorce with Shug as correspondent. For some time the novelist contemplated having
her expose him in the most literal way: by spying on
him and making a film of him in sexual embrace with
Shug. It is fascinating to see Humphrey working out

possible scenarios—where would she get the camera? would she show it to the lawyer or to the whole Renshaw family?—and abandoning them. This complication was clearly too contrived, too melodramatic, and in the published text he confines himself to having Eunice imagine going to a lawyer and having her revenge by telling the story. But fantasy has a limit, and she knows that the lawyer would find her claims literally unthinkable.

Clyde suffers from a division in his erotic life which was described by Freud in an important paper "Contributions to the Psychology of Love: On the Most Prevalent Degradation in Erotic Life." While Clyde does not appear especially attached to his mother, he has divided womankind into two groups, a consequence of the Oedipus complex. There are respectable women, like his mother and his wife, and degraded women, like Shug, and he functions sexually with Shug while refusing to sleep with his wife. The wife, of course, is a symbolic version of his mother in the Freudian scheme of things. The Renshaw family are "motherlovers," as Doc Metcalf calls them. A male denying his incestuous desires toward his mother chooses a love object that he considers degraded. As Freud puts it:

> The man almost always feels his sexual activity hampered by his respect for the woman

> and only develops full sexual potency when
> he finds himself in the presence of a lower
> type of sexual object. . . . Full sexual satis-
> faction only comes when he can give himself
> up wholeheartedly to enjoyment, which with
> his well-brought-up wife, for instance, he
> does not venture to do. Hence comes his need
> for a less exalted sexual object, a woman ethi-
> cally inferior, to whom he needs ascribe no
> aesthetic misgiving, and who does not know
> the rest of his life and cannot criticize him.
> (210)

The tensions of this situation, aggravated by the death
of his mother, are almost intolerable, and he even tries
to castrate himself, twice; once with a razor, once with
a scheme to take saltpeter, the legendary anaphrodi-
siac. To admit that he loves Shug would put her on
the same level as respectable women. Freud's patients
often managed tremendous feats of sexual prowess
with the shameful woman, while finding themselves
unwilling or unable to perform with "respectable
women." Castration is the fate feared and craved by
the Oedipal personality, which develops a need for
punishment for desiring the mother and hating the
father. During the writing of the novel, Humphrey
was definitely consulting another important paper by
Freud, "Dostoyevsky and Parricide," which, as we

shall see, discusses guilt and castration anxiety.

Clyde lives in a world in which "niggerlover" is the ultimate insult for a white man. Ironically, the Renshaws are what Doc Metcalf thinks of as that "crew of motherlovers," which implies a desire to violate a universal taboo. To be a secret "niggerlover" is preferable to being a "motherlover." They also violate the rules of the human community, what the Greeks would call the polis, through their commitment to clan over society. They are willing to commit murder: they avenge the killing of a cousin, Claude Renshaw, by terrifying his killer, who jumps out of a window. They kidnap Ben Metcalf, the town doctor, and hold him captive to watch over their dying mother—and later her corpse—depriving the town of its beloved physician. They take over the ice house, something needed by the whole community in a hot Texas summer, to preserve her body until Kyle can be found. And two of them, acting on a rumor that Kyle may be in New York City, set out like bumbling southern Furies to find the errant brother and bring him to their own kind of clan justice. Perhaps the ultimate defiance of the polis is the family's refusal to let the Military Police haul away a Renshaw grandson, Derwent, who has gone AWOL to attend Edwina on her deathbed, and who refuses to leave until her funeral.

In his *Oresteia* notebook, Humphrey says that retribution and justice have always been his theme, and he is struck by the importance of justice in the various introductions to the trilogy. In *Home from the Hill*, Wade suffers retribution, though not for his actual sins. And in *The Ordways*, Sam learns to transcend the primitive revenge code of the West and accept a higher moral principle of forgiveness. The third play in Aeschylus's trilogy, *Eumenides*, deals with the establishment of a court in Athens, the Aereopaga, one in which the archaic spirit of revenge represented by the Furies is sublimated into a superior concept of justice in the polis. At the end of *Proud Flesh*, the three younger sisters, Lois, Gladys, and Hazel, who sit brooding in the kitchen like Eumenides, have dispatched Lester and Ballard as their emissaries to find their younger brother: the tribal code says that he must be confronted for his desertion of his mother. The confrontation of the family back in Texas with civil society has not been resolved at this point. The power to the ice house has been cut off, so the primitive attempt to preserve her body at all costs till Kyle's return must fail. Mother right, kinship law: these archaic ideas will thaw out and spoil, so to speak. Humphrey is not sure in his notes for the novel if any of the reforms underway in 1965 (the Civil Rights Bill) will actually relieve the suffering of southern blacks.

The novelist has not found adequate terms for discussing justice in the work. He began it before the civil rights movement, before the war in Vietnam, and lived through those events as he wrote. The novel has a period flavor much of the time: the conflict of a clan with the civil society of a small town (represented by the doctor and the sheriff who would like to prosecute the Renshaws for their arbitrary behavior) seems dated. The Renshaws live in a world like the world of *Home from the Hill*, a kind of 1930s world, although the novel is set in the 1960s. Humphrey's occasional allusions to television and long-haired demonstrators are actually jarring. He has no real insights to convey about the civil rights crisis, for Clyde and Shug operate on the level of plantation overseer and beautiful slave, rather archaic figures. Indeed, Humphrey feared that there would be no social justice for blacks at all and no economic gains. The cotton growers of the area are interested in the new cotton-picking machines, and one says, "Seen the mule go, and now the nigger'll go the way of the mule. It's just a matter of time" (69). Humphrey at one time contemplated having Clyde replace the black farm laborers with a machine. His note about this possibility says, "He signed the contract today. Exterminate the brutes." Humphrey clearly saw Clyde as a bit like Kurtz from *Heart of Darkness*, a white man who goes native and goes mad and finally repudiates the black people he has manipulated, economically and sexually.

Humphrey believed that Aeschylus gave him a better understanding of his characters and their conflicts. He thought his Edwina was very similar to Clytemnestra, a "man-hater," a woman with a man's will. Edwina did not murder her late husband, Alonzo, but she got rid of him by more subtle means, denigrating his importance (always speaking as if the children were hers alone). His lameness probably represents some psychic crippling. His injury occurred when he kicked a calf that was trying to suckle at its mother when he himself was trying to milk it. Humphrey was particularly struck by a verbal parallel between his novel and *The Libation Bearers*: Aeschylus has Electra say of her father, "For he that is dead is earth and is nothing," while *Proud Flesh* says of Alonzo that he has been "ashes and a handful of anecdotes for a quarter century now." The Greek king, Agamemnon, was killed by his wife's lover, Aegisthus, who was also his nephew. Alonzo is driven from his wife's bed by threats from his eldest son, Clifford, who says that he will kill him if he makes sexual overtures to the mother again, which enacts a common infantile fantasy of driving the father away from the mother's bed. Clifford never marries until he is tricked into it by the Widow Shumlin, who pretends to be his mother, or at least imitates her voice, and suggests that what he needs is to marry someone like . . . the Widow. In his *Oresteia* notebook,

Humphrey says that Clifford, the nominal head of the family, and Clyde, who actually runs the farm while Clifford hunts and drinks, together constitute Aegisthus, the supplanter of Agamemnon. Their alliterative names show an affinity between them. Kyle, whose name is a kind of anagram of "Clyde," is antithetical to both brothers.

The novelist was struck by some details in the *Electra* of Sophocles that seemed appropriate to Amy: she notes the "bird of mourning" in one of her soliloquies; Humphrey has a motif of the mourning dove. Electra is childless, and has "no loving husband for companion"; Amy has no children and her relationship with her husband is a nominal one. Humphrey modeled Amy on an aunt of his who was said to have had a number of abortions because children would have impeded her career, and Amy is presented as a character entirely focused on her work as a nurse. Amy loves fine clothes, which is a dramatic difference from Electra, who is a Cinderella-like figure in her mother's household. Humphrey felt that he had accidentally honored the myth by reversing that detail. Amy, like Humphrey's aunt, loves Neiman-Marcus clothes. Another reversal: the Electra of Sophocles rebels against authority, while Amy is so subservient to it that the reader's suspicions are likely to be aroused about what she is suppressing. Down deep she knows that authority is weak: as a girl, she was shattered by the revelation that the answer to a math question in the back of her textbook was wrong. The teacher said that this was an important lesson: "The lesson is, it is not enough to be right; you must know that you are" (182). But Amy is left uncertain about whether or not she is right, about who she is, hence her fear of mirrors, of her own shadow. She knows that somehow she is not what she appears to be. She nurses an unconscious hatred for her mother, something the reader can sense if not understand. Edwina hates and fears Amy, as if she knows intuitively what others do not, and the reader gives weight to that.

After reading the Greek plays, Humphrey decided that her hatred for her mother can be explained by her similarity to her. She too has no use for men. What she wants is to supplant her mother, and Edwina complains that Amy has tried to take her place, to act as mother to the siblings. Amy dislikes the idea of childbearing, having been repelled by the sight of a black servant burying the bloody sheet after the birth of her brother Kyle: the sexuality and fecundity of the mother repels her just as it repels the sons. Amy is the eldest child; Kyle is the youngest. They appear opposites in their feelings about their mother, but in fact they are not. Humphrey's characterization of Amy was profoundly affected by the works of Aeschylus and Euripides, for the character became clear to him at last. He decided to plan for a dramatic reversal in Amy, to make her kill her mother by terrifying her, by focusing her suppressed hatred and rage on the fragile woman.

When Humphrey read Philip Vellacott's introduction to his version of *The Oresteia*, he was struck by one idea about the theme of social justice: Vellacott points out that women in Athenian society were relatively powerless. The novelist felt this was very applicable to his novel, full of suggestion: southern women were in bondage in a similar way, so the Clytemnestra in *Proud Flesh* has responded by supplanting her husband and asserting all the rights over the family for herself. Readers are unlikely to follow him very far in seeing a feminist theme in the novel: while Edwina and Amy may be reacting to a patriarchal society, a traditional man-hating matriarch and a barren career woman are too close to anti-feminist stereotypes. As with "The Fauve," Humphrey has difficulties making his intentions clear when sexual politics are involved.

In thinking about Amy and her dramatic change of character, Humphrey went back to two of his favorite novelists, Joseph Conrad and Fyodor Dostoyevsky. He saw Conrad's *Lord Jim* as an important model: Jim thinks of himself as a hero but is in fact a coward, as the plot reveals. Humphrey seems to think that the reader will be surprised by Amy's change, but there are in fact too many hints that she has another self, a shadow self, a different identity from the one presenting itself in the mirror every day. No one is likely to be shocked by Amy's transformation.

While working on Amy's characterization, Humphrey reread Dorothy Van Ghent's brilliant study of *Lord Jim* and took comfort from her idea that Jim is one of the simplest characters in the history of the novel, but still one of the most memorable. The dramatic reversal in his character is powerful, a moment of epiphany. Van Ghent notes that Conrad works through epiphanies, moments when the dark side of a character emerges. She notes that "the impossibility of escape from the dark companion within leaves a man more perfectly alone in this world because he has that companion—who is always and only himself" (235). Conrad likes to present the moment of revelation, of reversal, as it is perceived by another character, and Doc Metcalf is that character for Humphrey. The free-ranging point of view in the long opening section of the novel—sometimes omniscient, sometimes focused on Clyde—narrows to narration by the doctor, who recounts the death of Edwina on a tape made when he is being questioned by the sheriff after his escape from the Renshaw house. He describes how he and Amy attended the unconscious Edwina, and how he began to see his nurse making error after error. If he had not intervened, they would have been fatal. He also describes being there for the moment when Edwina became conscious and was "frightened to death" by the hatred in the gaze of her supposedly loving daughter. He had also witnessed her profound realization that she is a matricide, in spirit if not in law. When her mother appeared to have died, Amy reacted by abasing herself: she smeared cow-dung on her bare breasts and stuffs her mouth with it, atavistic behavior anticipating her fit of guilt when her mother does die. The doctor tells us how Eulalie found her in the garden and carried her back in the toy wagon.

It is not surprising that a novelist would look to a predecessor like Conrad for ideas about the handling of his material. But it is interesting to see Humphrey relying on a literary critic, Van Ghent. He had those years of teaching fiction at Bard, and he had recently taught the history of the novel at MIT. He must have been especially interested in Van Ghent's discussion of tragedy, ancient and modern, although he does not cite it in his *Oresteia* notebook. She believes that Aeschylus and Sophocles could place tragedy in a social context, but tragedy in the classical sense is impossible for writers like Conrad because humanity is now too isolated: "What intervenes between Conrad's ambivalent attitude toward Jim's story and the attitudes of Aeschylus and Sophocles toward their subjects is modern man's spiritual isolation from his fellows" (232). Kyle has already "killed" his mother by deserting the family, and he has exiled himself before her death, before the Eumenides (his young sisters) can send Lester and Ballard to find him. Rumor says he may be in New York, a notoriously isolating city. Amy chooses, as we shall see, to cut herself off from society as completely as anyone can short of suicide, though society decides that it needs her, just as Athens eventually sought out Oedipus, of all people, for a blessing.

In killing her mother, Amy acts in complicity with the absent brother. In the Greek myths, Orestes returns from exile and is recognized by Electra at the tomb of their father. Kyle does not return literally: Humphrey sees him as a kind of mirror for his sisters, a mirror which need not be brought to life; hence he will never be found. He represents their shadow sides, the unthinkable rebellion against their mother. Amy fears mirrors and rarely sees her shadow: it is ominous that she sees it in the novel after Edwina falls ill, for her shadow self is constituted by her hatred of her mother—and Kyle represents her shadow too. The most important recognition scene in Greek drama, the one singled out for praise by Aristotle—is the scene between Orestes and Electra. Amy's equivalent is a long contemplation of the day of Kyle's birth, the day that Edwina made it most clear that she rejected Amy, the trained nurse who wanted to attend her (162): "You get out of here! Get her out of here! Get her out of here!" Together Kyle and Amy have killed Edwina, one by neglect, one by an obsessive care that unmasks itself as envy and hatred.

Humphrey considered Dostoyevsky's *The Brothers Karamazov* as a parallel for his own work. In that novel, he observes in his *Oresteia* notebook, the Oedipus story is retold. Old Father Karamazov and his son Dmitri share a mistress, creating a kind of incestuous rivalry between them. The father is not murdered by Dmitri, but by the shadow self of the brothers, the illegitimate half-brother, Smerdyakov, who carries out their hostility to the father. Near the end of the novel, Ivan is told by Smerdyakov that he has carried out Ivan's wishes, a profoundly disturbing claim, all the more disturbing because it is true not in the police court sense but in a psychological sense. Humphrey was unsure how to have Amy learn what she has done, and for a while he thought of having her look into a mirror. But he decided that the best mirror would be a figurative one: Edwina's face, on which she sees a look of horror that lets her infer her own hatred and aggression.

In one of his notebooks for this novel, Humphrey mentions consulting Freud's essay, "Dostoyevsky and Parricide." This paper of 1928 was probably the source for Clyde's flirtation with castrating himself, an act intimately connected to the ambivalence and guilt feelings of the Oedipal situation. Anxiety about castration by a jealous and hated father is internalized as guilt: the individual feels an urge to punish himself. More important is the relevance of the Oedipal situation to the character of Amy. Freud's discussion of Dostoyevsky's psyche and his interest in parricide in *The Brothers Karamazov* surely contributed to *Proud Flesh*. Freud notes that Dostoyevsky's personality was masochistic: his repressed sadism led him to become the "mildest, kindliest, most helpful person possible" (224). This sums up Amy rather well. Another detail in her characterization grows from Freud's explanation of Dostoyevsky's epilepsy, which Freud believed was neurotic rather than physiological. Dostoyevsky's father was a brutal man, murdered by his own serfs, and Freud suggests that Dostoyevsky's epilepsy resulted from his guilty feelings about a murder that he must have secretly craved. Amy's behavior once she isolates herself in the storm cellar suggests an epileptic fit: "Hollow groans, strangled cries, hoarse guttural growls as though she were gagging on self-disgust, whimpers and grunts as of a wounded animal in its lair biting itself to allay a great pain: these were all they could get out of her" (258). According to Jose Yglesias, Humphrey claims that he "is interested in the passions of normal people, not in abnormal psychology" (64), but the Renshaw family seems remarkably abnormal.

The writings of Aeschylus and Sophocles would help Humphrey bring his novel to an end by hinting at a fate for her and for Kyle. But there are other matters worth considering before the rather surprising conclusion is discussed. The echoes of other writers, like Conrad, Faulkner, and Shakespeare, are important intertextual resonances in the novel, as is the Bible. Doc Metcalf is a key reflector of the action: in a way he is the equivalent of Marlow in *Lord Jim*. The astounding hysteria of the Renshaws is witnessed by him, along with their reluctance to admit that she is dead. He fears that they want him to bring her back to life. He reports Amy's dung-eating paroxysm, and he tells us about Clyde's half-hearted attempt to emasculate himself with the razor that he has been carrying (Chekhov's rule, that a gun on the wall in a work must go off before the conclusion, is fulfilled here). He can witness all this because he is the putative prisoner of the Renshaw family, and his account is given to the sheriff on a recording. He is the one who informs the community that Edwina has been dead for five days. She has not been buried, first because of her well-known fear of being buried alive, second because the funeral must be deferred for Kyle.

To the despair of the authorities, he can give no evidence that a court would accept about his confinement by the Renshaws. Nothing was said, and he was never restrained by force. The power of the family's obsessions is so great that he simply understands that he is a prisoner. He finally escapes and is found wandering in a field, incoherent and tattered. Humphrey observes in several of his notebooks that Doc is a King Lear figure: an old man treated miserably and with ingratitude, suffering from exposure, and found wandering in the fields. He speaks a mixture of sense and nonsense, like Lear in the aftermath of his madness. He rather improbably cites Ecclesiasticus 38:1 to the authorities, a rather obscure passage from the Apocryphal books of the Bible which declares: "Honor the physician," something the Renshaws have clearly failed to do.

Doc, a reliable, compassionate man, is an excellent reflector of the Renshaw madness. As a doctor he has known the family, and he also knows about pathological states of mind. He therefore serves as a measure of their folly. He registers that sense of outrage at the scandal of existence which, as we have seen, is something Humphrey seems to have picked up as a theme and effect from Faulkner. André Bleikasten observes that Faulkner's characters are frequently in a state of astonishment—a reaction to outrage, which he defines as a "violation of common decency"—and one of his prime examples is the failure to bury Addie Bundren in *As I Lay Dying* (130). Humphrey's novel has an abundance of astonished characters who confront the indecent behavior of the family. At least the Renshaws have an ice house in which to store their mother's body, though the reaction of the townspeople is to wonder if anyone will want to eat the other food stored in it. Other reactions of the Renshaws to their mother's death are excessive as well: the women tear at their flesh with their nails and pull out their hair, and Clifford, the inarticulate eldest brother, expresses his grief by silencing all the barking dogs in the area. Dogs traditionally howl because they sense death. Clifford can't endure that indication of his mother's mortality, so he cuts their throats, those of his own dogs first, later the neighbors'—another rejection of the community in favor of clan feeling.

After Amy secludes herself from the world in Part Three of the novel, a preacher who comes to advise her quotes from Chapter 38 of the Apocryphal Ecclesiasticus on mourning. Humphrey cites a bit of the preacher's text: "Let tears fall down over the dead . . . but just for a day or two . . . and then comfort thyself for thy heaviness. For of heaviness cometh death, and the heaviness of the heart betokenth strength" (293–94). At the start of his *Oresteia* notebook, Humphrey quoted more fully from this chapter, one of his favorites, cited again in "The Parishioner," a story in *September Song*. The chapter is the very one referred to by the doctor ("Honor the physician"). Humphrey wrote out a long passage as if to explain his theme to himself:

> My son, let tears fall down over the dead and
> begin to lament, as if thou hadst suffered
> great harm thyself; and then cover his body
> according to the custom, and neglect not his
> burial. Weep bitterly, and make great moan,
> and use lamentation, as he is worthy, and
> that a day or two, lest thou be evil spoken of:
> and then comfort thyself of thy heaviness. For
> of heaviness cometh death, and the heaviness
> of the heart breaketh strength. In affliction
> also sorrow remaineth and the life of the poor
> is the curse of the heart. Take no heaviness
> to heart: drive it away, and remember the last
> end. Forget it not, for there is no turning
> again: thou shalt not do him good but hurt
> thyself. Remember my judgment: for thine
> also shall be so; yesterday for me and today
> for thee. When the dead is at rest, let his re-
> membrance rest; and be comforted for him,
> when his Spirit is departed from him.

Prospective titles of *Proud Flesh* from this text included "According to the Custom," "Let Tears Fall
Down," "Let Remembrance Rest" and "Yesterday for
Me." The passage advocates a sane approach to mourning, one that the Renshaws cannot comprehend.

Along with the grotesque grieving, there is slapstick comedy in the novel, as if Humphrey wanted a Shakespearean range of style. In fact, he cautions himself in one notebook entry to restrain the comedy. Jug serves as his rustic clown: the old alcoholic hides his wages from himself so that he won't spend the money on bootleg wine, and then spends much of his time frantically searching for it (137) so that he can buy more of "Bing's Tea," a watered-down wine supplied by the local bootlegger, Ed Bing.

The major slapstick subplot, one interspersed with more serious matters, is the chronicle of poor Hugo Mattox and Mrs. Shumlin's cow, a kind of southern folk narrative. Mattox is carrying a load of cotton to town in a borrowed truck, accompanied by his wife and little boys. He has a series of complicated misadventures involving flat tires before he is run off the road by Lester Renshaw, who is driving frantically to his mother's deathbed. Mattox winds up injuring Mrs. Shumlin's cow very slightly: it loses the tip of its tail. He loses his cotton, not to mention the truck (79–80). The hapless Renshaw's collision with the cow is strongly reminiscent of the collision of a spotted horse with the Tull family and their wagon in Faulkner's *The Hamlet*. The story is very funny, but highly derivative. Humphrey was very nervous that the initial refusal of the family to accept that their mother might be dead would be too Faulknerian, reminding readers of "A Rose for Emily," in which Emily refuses to acknowledge that her father is dead. But the cow episode is obviously just as Faulknerian.

The episode has an aftermath. Mrs. Shumlin's loss is greater than might appear, for the cow is her livelihood and it will never give milk again: having lost the tip of its tail it will be driven to distraction by the flies that it can no longer flick away. The owner, seeking justice, goes to the Renshaw house and gets far more than she expected. She fits into the type of the crafty, husband-hunting widow, and she tricks Clifford into marrying her by tricking him into thinking that he is hearing his mother's spirit in the barn, where, appropriately enough, he is milking a cow. This preposterous denouement to the story of Mrs. Shumlin's cow is exactly the kind of humor that Humphrey was warning himself against.

On the subject of denouement, the Greek plays offered Humphrey a conclusion to the novel he struggled with for so many years. In *The Oresteia*, Orestes wanders away after killing his mother, pursued by the Furies until he can establish his freedom from guilt in a trial before Athena and the Athenians. Oedipus becomes a wanderer over the earth after killing his mother. Kyle has already gone into exile: his absence has been one of the causes of his mother's fate. But Humphrey had to decide what to do with Amy. He found a brief passage in the Electra of

Sophocles. Chrysothemis, the obedient sister of
Electra, comes to talk to her and warns her that if
she does not give up her inordinate grief for her father, she will be locked away. In his *Oresteia* notebook, Humphrey cites this passage, misattributing
David Grene's translation to Richmond Lattimore:

> From what I learned—and if you don't give
>   over
> Your present mourning—they will send you
>   where
> never a gleam of sun shall visit you.
> You shall live out your life in an underground
>   cave
> and there bewail the sorrows of the world
>   outside. (140)

Burial alive is a fate traditionally reserved for extraordinary offenders against gods or humanity: for
parricides and blasphemers, individuals who are
thought to be unworthy of sharing the upper world
with decent human beings. This particularly terrible
exile Amy imposes on herself in the third section of
the novel. She intends to live out her life in the dark,
and she will accept only bread and water. After con-
veying a last message to this effect through Jug (she
"adds insult to injury" by choosing another pariah to
convey the message), she gives up human utterance,

limiting herself to moans. Food is brought to her by
Eulalie in the same toy wagon she used to haul
Edwina in from outside when she collapsed early in
the novel. Edwina Renshaw feared being buried alive,
and her daughter has appropriately chosen this fate
for herself.

But just as Oedipus, the incomparable transgres-
sor against gods and humanity, becomes blessed in
his wanderings, as he is presented in Sophocles's
Oedipus at Colonus, Amy becomes a magnet for all
those with shameful secrets, and the Renshaw home-
stead turns into a shrine in an extravagant conclusion that surprised the author: twice in his notebooks
he refers to the last sections as "wild," saying, for example: "The idea of this thing is already so wild that
to get timid now is too late." One of his problems is
that he does not break with realism as dramatically
as writers would in the years to come: *Proud Flesh* is
not quite postmodern. It is not magic realism but a
kind of exaggerated realism with a mythical structure that only the author perceived.

Soon a parking lot is needed and Amy's pilgrims
are covered on television. They leave revolvers and
drug syringes and whisky bottles and other symbols
of their sins. The narrative focus of this section is
Clyde, the most articulate of the family, and the character we know best thanks to his brooding over race
in Part One. He himself feels outrage over the intru-

sion of the outside world into the private world of the clan, and outrage and despair permeate his story.

Here Humphrey uncannily anticipates the 1990s and the rise of confessions on television: Amy attracts an enormous following of those who wish to tell their stories to her down the air intake pipe of her living tomb. What they get in response is a series of emotive wails without words, but they take these sounds to be meaningful and interpret them. Humphrey's intention, as revealed in his notebooks, is to turn her into a Sibyl by virtue of her suffering, which is elevated in the listeners' minds to be suffering for everyone. She turns, in effect, into a parody of Christ, offering the consolation of no hope at all: "A faith for our times: confession without absolution. Group guilt. Nobody believes in absolution any more but everybody had more of an urge to confess than ever—maybe that was the reason" (315). Hence the "deified sister" offers release from hope to those who cherish their guilt: "Their sins were the only things that made them interesting to themselves. Absolve them and they would have nothing left" (315).

Of course, television confessions in the 1990s would offer not absolution but therapy, guidance by experts, and approval by the studio audience. The sinners in *Proud Flesh* simply spew their words like vomit down the air intake. Some of those words are captured by the television crew. For a moment Clyde thinks that one man caught on the news is himself, confessing that he loves a black woman. But he has not made this confession: he has heard the other man and taken it to be himself, caught himself in the mirror of the television footage. What shocks him is the realization that this is his deepest emotion, previously denied.

Humphrey's notebooks from this period express his admiration for Flannery O'Connor's extremist characters, and the parody of religion in Amy's sybilline role may owe something to O'Connor's bizarre heretics in *Wise Blood* and "A Good Man Is Hard to Find." As Charlotte Wright has observed, the title *Proud Flesh* may echo *Wise Blood*. Amy has no peculiar doctrine to offer: she, like Oedipus at Colonus, has taken on a role that she never sought. Her response to the pilgrims is wordless, and they reply in the same way. In this "gospelless church" (something like the Church without Christ in *Wise Blood*) she howls through the intake in a scene reported as a television program—because Clyde is watching it on television:

> It began low, like wind sweeping over a waste. ooooooooooooooh. Then like a wind it quickened: oooooooOOOOOOH. Like a wind over some desolate waste it rose to a howl, a shriek: aaaaaaaAAAAEEEEEEEEH. It fell

away only in a series of dying gasps: AAAH aaah aah ah a. . . Only to rise again. And again. And again. (318)

The response of the "congregation" is rendered in a similar way. Originally Humphrey had planned to write a lament for Amy, worthy of Jeremiah or Ecclesiastes, drawing on the resources of southern evangelism, a tradition of eloquence still alive in Texas. Instead he provides a scene like something out of regression therapy: language is abandoned for expressive cries. Clyde is left feeling desolate, self-exiled: he goes to the window of the house after the television footage fades out and feels excluded from humanity: "He had admitted the inadmissible. He had condemned himself, he had exiled himself. Of all degradations, what more shameful than a forbidden love?" (320). The reader will perceive the irony intended here, that Clyde feels shame for what is in fact a potential enlargement of his bigoted identity. In his notes for the novel, Humphrey states that Clyde will be somewhat pitiable but not lovable. His fate, by his own standards, is a horrible one. Contemporary readers may find it hard to feel any pity at all for a character who in fact raped a high school girl and kept her as a virtual sex slave.

The fourth and final section is a kind of epilogue, a brief scene from the hopeless quest (and they know it's hopeless) of Lester and Ballard, who have been dispatched to New York by the three Eumenides— Gladys, Lois and Hazel—to seek Kyle, an Orestes who may feel no remorse at all. The funeral has passed, and they have hardly begun their door to door search. After the named streets of Manhattan there will be two-hundred-fifty numbered ones, and after Manhattan, there will be four other boroughs, the work of a lifetime, a hopeless quest for two xenophobic southerners. Ballard has begun to think of quitting, but Lester vows: "Son of a bitch if this goddamned town is going to make a monkey out of me" (328). But he has made a monkey out of himself. The Renshaws are indeed more throwbacks, at least to tribalism, than modern human beings.

William Humphrey told Ashby Crowder that *Proud Flesh* was a much better novel than its predecessors, and he obviously felt aggrieved at its failure: "It's a far better book, which is probably why it bombed. . ." (30). Reviews were scarce; only 24,000 copies were sold in the initial release in the United States, and it sold poorly in Britain. It has been discussed less than any other novel by Humphrey and critical opinion is not favorable. The *deus ex machina* of Greek archetypes seems not to have rescued the work, and no one has noticed the parallels. Humphrey had been impressed by the number of readers who had taken *Home from the Hill* as a kind of modern

Greek tragedy, but the parallels with Aeschylus and Sophocles went unnoticed in the new book.

In his *Oresteia* notebook, the novelist listed the elements that he thought gave a Greek atmosphere to the work. They included an obsession with burial rites, concern for dynastic continuity and racial purity, concern with hospitality, the defiance of authority, violence, and the use of choruses. To this the sympathetic reader could add the use of catalogues (especially of names) and the description of elaborate feasts. These are, however, southern concerns as well as Greek ones (even the choruses: the community has a choral function in other southern novels), and Humphrey was thought to be writing an exaggerated southern novel rather than something classical. It would have been useful if Humphrey had provided a quotation from one of the Greek tragedians as an epigraph for the book. He does refer to the three vengeful sisters as "Eumenides," but he also calls them the "weird sisters," after the witches in *Macbeth*, so the depth of the mythical allusion has been missed. Critics simply put the work in a southern Gothic category. Melvin Maddocks in *Time* said that the novel was southern in a formulaic way (94). In his 1992 pamphlet on Humphrey's work, Mark Royden Winchell says that in *Proud Flesh* "Humphrey combines the pseudo-Faulknerian melodrama of *Home from the Hill* with the structural chaos of *The*

Ordways" (22). However, Winchell does like the concluding scenes about the self-immolation of Amy, suggesting that "without seeming unduly derivative,
Humphrey achieves the blend of black humor and
grotesque spirituality that we associate with Flannery
O'Connor" (25). The most perceptive commentary on
the work is by John Grammer, who sees it as the most
powerful example of Humphrey's "rejection of the
aesthetic of memory: the spectacle of the mad
Renshaw family trying to preserve the corpse which
represents the old southern order could well serve as
a final word on the subject" (19).

The book certainly has flaws. The black characters are stereotypes and black-white relations are
stereotypical also. The white characters in the
Renshaw family are so numerous that not all of them
emerge as individuals. Among the sons, Russell is
distinguished only by his alcoholism, and Ballard is
simply truculent, but not as truculent as the impetu-
ous Lester. Amy's three sisters are all given distin-
guishing traits, like Hazel's stinginess, Lois's habit
of divorcing and remarrying the same man, and
Gladys's obesity. However, assigning a few character
traits to them does not make them memorable.

Humphrey kept advising himself not to overdo
the humor, but with Mrs. Shumlin's ruse to marry
Clifford (something out of a folktale, really), he in-
dulges, as Mark Royden Winchell says, in bad situa-

tion comedy. Clyde's obsession with his unruly penis is a character flaw presented as a comic trait. In the course of the novel he not only tries to cut it off, he asks the town pharmacist about the possibility of eating gunpowder for the saltpeter in it. Some problems of tone and proportion arise from the shift away from southern family epic to a kind of submerged mythical mode late in the novel. Humphrey thought of the novel as a short work for years, then under the influence of *The Oresteia* he decided that he had found his great theme—justice and revenge— and a powerful mythic way to convey it. But Humphrey was more at ease with destroying myths than with basing a plot on them. Although he considered the conclusion wild, he probably should have made it even wilder, breaking with realism more dramatically. Magic realism and other post-structuralist forms of fiction would exceed his wildness exponentially in the decade after his novel was published.

There is a jarring turn away from the comic adventures of Clyde and the grotesqueries of the mourners to the somber and rather mysterious cult of Amy, a section which introduces television and an elaborate satire on television into the relatively timeless world of the clan. Along with the shift in tone, there is a problem of proportion. Humphrey declared in one of his notebooks that each section would create its own laws, but he has ignored the law of proportion

by giving enormous weight to the last two sections,
Amy's self-immurement in Part 3, and the quest for
Kyle in Part 4. The section with Amy in the cellar is
dwarfed by the two parts that precede it, and the
manhunt in New York is very brief. He has no real
equivalent to the resolution of the conflict between
the archaic and civilized in Aeschylus: New York City
is not an Athens for his Eumenides and there is no
Athena to convene a court in New York competent to
adjudicate in this case. A novelist need not provide a
resolution, but when his model is Aeschylus it is surprising that Humphrey did not seek one here.
Humphrey's pessimism seems to have triumphed,
with Amy's inarticulate moans the only spiritual outlet, a futile catharsis for the hopeless. That kind of
judgment on our civilization implies that there is no
higher alternative to the proud flesh of the Renshaw
family, which means that justice is unavailable. The
book might have worked on some archetypal level if
it had managed to carry through with its Greek parallels in more detail. While it contains brilliant writing and strains toward an understanding of the
competing claims of kinship and society, ultimately
it fails to achieve a resolution. The puzzlement of his
readers is understandable, and his commentators
seem baffled as well. At the end of Part 3, the most
original part of the novel, the oracle moans in her
cell and falls silent, which is very different from the

conclusion of *The Oresteia*, in which even the Eumenides find their place in the order of the universe. Interesting as the novel is, the *deus ex machina* of Greek mythology has failed to rescue it.

7

Humphrey's "Intimations Ode":

Farther Off from Heaven

Proud Flesh was the first of Humphrey's books to sell poorly. Some of the reviews were good, but bad notices in *Time* and *The New York Times Book Review* were damaging. Lee Sullenger's favorable review in the *Library Journal* began by speaking of Humphrey as "a poor man's Faulkner" (1192) considerably worse than Frederick Hoffman's reference to Theron as a poor man's Ike McCaslin. Sullenger was a fellow-Texan, which must have added insult to the injury. The failure of *Proud Flesh* meant a financial crisis for the Humphreys and a crisis of confidence for William. When Ian Parsons heard just how serious their situation was, he immediately offered them an interest-free loan of $1000 in a letter dated 20 June 1973. He suggested that going back to teaching was probably not a good solution. Perhaps, he suggested, they could sell some of their antiques, and Bill could try short stories for ready money. Three days later, he had changed his mind about the teaching, proposing that it might be good to get out of the isolation of the house at High Meadow.

The failure of *Proud Flesh* must have left the author in a bitter mood. The October issue of *Esquire*, the magazine where he had most frequently published, was a special anniversary issue with fifty outstanding pieces which had appeared over the years. It did not include anything by William Humphrey, who subsequently wrote several angry letters to the editor, Harold Hayes. He had described Hayes to Fred and Andy Dupee as a pal a few years before. The focus for his anger was a well-known and rather amusing article by Nora Ephron called "A Few Words about My Breasts":

> If as Pascal said, the style is the man, then it is even more true that the writer is the man, and the man the writer. I should have thought you would have learned this in your experience as an editor. When have you

deeply offended a writer and remained friends with the man? I am flabbergasted at you saying, let's stay friends because the author-editor relationship is mostly horseshit anyhow. Not to me it isn't. If you can think, for instance, that Nora Ephron's article on the size of her tits is more worthy of inclusion in the issue of your magazine containing the fifty best things you've ever published than any of the six things I have sent you, then you're no friend of mine, nor are you the editor I thought you were. The meaning of my asking you to return the mss. of my novel is that you have seen the last of my writing and of me. We'll both survive this, I expect, but it saddens me—a poor reward for my [loyalty] to *Esquire* and for what I thought was *Esquire*'s loyalty to me. (13 October 1973)

Hayes wrote a conciliatory letter back, though he suggested that in this matter Humphrey was behaving more like an advertiser than a writer.

The financial crisis must have been eased somewhat the next year by a check from MGM. As part of the movie deal the author was entitled to a share of the eventual profits. Year after year Humphrey had been receiving rather enigmatic statements from

MGM but no money. Probably because of television sales he finally received a check for $21,488.00 for royalties from what the studio referred to as "Home from the Hills."

Humphrey did not return to academic life until 1976–77, when he became Elizabeth Drew Professor at Smith College, where his French translator, Jean Lambert, had long held an appointment. He and Dorothy had spent a long period in late 1975 and early 1976 in France, living first in an isolated village, Souvigny-en-Sologne, in the Loire, where Lambert had a house. In a letter to Fred and Andy Dupee, he suggests that "[b]eing what we are, rather reclusive types—we think we'll like it" (7 November 1975). But the isolation was too great, and they moved to Paris, where they were put up in the apartment of his recently deceased publisher, Gaston Gallimard. The French translation of *Proud Flesh* was published at this time and was well-received, which was consoling to an author who felt rejected by his American and British publics.

In 1977 he was offered a writer-in-residence job at North Texas State University, which he declined. A full-time writer's natural response to a career crisis is to write, though the crisis may weaken his writing by undermining his confidence. For whatever reason, Humphrey's next novel, referred to for some years as the Smoot novel, was the most profound kind of failure: a book which could not find a publisher.

For a while the Smoot novel was called "The Last Refuge," after Samuel Johnson's famous claim that "patriotism is the last refuge of a scoundrel." As that title implies, it is a political satire. The final title was "Horse Latitudes," referring to the legendary area in the Atlantic where Spanish ships were supposedly becalmed with cargos of horses, which would have to be thrown overboard. This legend of stagnation and waste is Humphrey's symbol of America during the Vietnam War period, especially the Nixon years. The book has two epigraphs, one from Richard III, "A horse, my kingdom for a horse!" and the other a phrase by Humphrey's friend, Theodore Weiss, "A book written with disgusto." Like an eighteenth-century satirist, Humphrey has chosen a persona through whom he can express some complicated feelings about America. Cecil Smoot is a Texas redneck with earthy opinions on politics and apocalyptic anxieties about nuclear annihilation. Fearing a breakdown of industrial civilization, he plans to organize a group of malcontents to buy up horses. He reads an article in *Newsweek* in which a Nobel Prize-winning physicist named Polykarp Kusch suggests that even the exhaustion of natural resources will not bring peace to the earth: without technology, men will still kill one another with bows and arrows. Smoot looks up the name "Polykarp" and discovers the Christian saint and martyr, who was put to death in 155 A.D., the oldest confirmed Christian martyr after St. Stephen, and the first to have his death officially commemorated with a feast day. What fascinates Smoot, and Humphrey as well, is Polykarp's habit of fleeing cities with his hands over his ears after detecting heresy in the local Christians. He would cry out, "Into what times, O Lord, hast Thou caused me to be born?" This makes a fine motto for a satirist.

Smoot's times, and Humphrey's by extension, are the Nixon years. The specific time is the summer of Nixon's resignation. The novel does contain some amusing satire on the Nixon administration, but it has so many problems of tone, plot, and plausibility that it really is unpublishable. The satire on Nixon dated rather quickly. Humphrey's longtime publishing house, Alfred A. Knopf, turned the book down in 1977. Humphrey had mentioned the book to Seymour Lawrence in a letter on Easter Sunday, 1975, saying that "after working all last year on a novel and accumulating nearly 300 pages of it, what I have got is a mess I myself don't know what to make of and which I may just walk away from." He submitted it to Lawrence, who had been trying to lure Humphrey to sign with him since 1966. Lawrence rather diplomatically turned it down, advising him in a letter (21 June 1979) to put it aside and work on his novel about the Cherokee Removal. Humphrey penciled a note on the

Smoot manuscript years later: "with the Cold War over we can now laugh at it." But the problem with the work is that it no longer seems very strong now that the events have passed: the topical interest has faded.

In the same period that he was struggling with "Horse Latitudes," Humphrey wrote one of his finest works, the memoir *Farther Off from Heaven*, a work as fluent as the novel was labored. It ranks high in comparison to other fine memoirs by novelists, like Wright Morris's *Will's Boy*, Tobias Wolff's *This Boy's Life*, and Wallace Stegner's *Wolf Willow*. It takes its place too among such specifically Texas memoirs as William Owens's *This Stubborn Soil*, A. C. Greene's *A Personal Country*, and Mary Karr's recent work, *The Liar's Club*. For a reader of Humphrey's early fiction, the book offers *deja vu* after *deja vu*. It tells us everything we need to know about Clarksville as a matrix for Humphrey's fiction. It also explains some of the traumas that influenced his work. The defining trauma in the book is the death of his father, but there are others: his mother's hand injury when she was three, something she brilliantly concealed; his birth injury, a deformed foot, concealed in all the family photographs; his torn knee cap; his sprained ankle; his near death by drowning. On the emotional plane, the growing crisis in his parents' marriage is a trauma almost on a level with his father's death. One task of the book is to reveal—often very gradually, but with foreshadowing—the way that the autobiographer was shaped by these experiences of pain and loss.

As usual, Humphrey had difficulty finding a title for the work. His early choices point to the formative nature of the early events: first he tried "Father of the Man," from Wordsworth's famous lines in the "Intimations of Immortality" ode, "The child is the father of the man." Indeed, his notebook on this work has that title. The subtitle was to be "a memoir," but that was crossed out in favor of "an evocation," which stresses both the subjective nature of the work and the desire to make the reader truly see (as Conrad famously put it) the events narrated. His alternative title was "Growing Pains," but his wife said this would suggest the sentimental novels of Booth Tarkington.

Musing in his notebook on the phrase, "father of the man," Humphrey realizes that not only is the child the father of the man—an interesting paradox—but the man is also the father of the child, as the individual writing about his life from the perspective of maturity inevitably alters his early experience in re-creating it. He rejects the possibility of writing entirely in the vocabulary of a child, a performance that would soon become tedious. He retains an awareness of his childhood ignorance, as in the passage about his father's attempts to explain the facts of life to an incredulous son. He also conceals from the reader certain things that he did not understand until later,

like the fate of the mysterious house in which he was
born, which apparently vanished from the earth. And
he withholds some events, like his "drowning" and
the details of the house fire, creating suspense.

His comments to Ashby Bland Crowder about
titles help explain his struggles to find the right one
for a book:

> Titles are devils of things to find. No author
> really likes to give a title to his book because
> any title he gives illuminates only one as-
> pect of the book, and he likes to think that
> his book has more than one aspect, so that
> any title is limiting unless it's something
> straight as *The Ordways*. (27)

The final title came when he discovered Thomas
Hood's poem, "I Remember," which nicely contrasts
the perceptions of childhood with adult awareness.
He liked using a line from the poem as a title because
his earlier alternatives had stressed the narrator's
life, while the book he envisioned would be as much
about his parents as about their child. He uses one
stanza from Hood as epigraph to the book, using capital letters for emphasis:

I REMEMBER, I REMEMBER
THE FIR TREES DARK AND HIGH;

I USED TO THINK THEIR SLENDER TOPS
WERE CLOSE AGAINST THE SKY:
IT WAS A CHILDISH IGNORANCE.
BUT NOW 'TIS LITTLE JOY
TO KNOW I'M FARTHER OFF FROM
HEAVEN
THAN WHEN I WAS A BOY.

The phrase, "I Remember," fits the memoir very well. Humphrey's memory of Clarksville, though fallible, is astonishing. I reviewed the memoir in 1978 in *Southwest Review*, and was surprised to receive a fan letter from the author, who was delighted that I had used his favorite saying from Henry James to describe his work. The letter (18 February 1978) says in part:

> I believe it is not *comme il faut* for a writer to thank a reviewer, but I have never done things *comme il faut* and it seems to me it would be unforgivable not to thank you for your review of *Farther Off from Heaven*. Believe me, it is not just for the high praise you give the book that I am thankful. No reviewer of any book of mine has ever seen more perceptively what I was trying to do and why I did it in the way I did.

> By coincidence you chose to say of me
> something which I have quoted to three gen-
> erations of students of creative writing:
> Henry James' "Strive to become a person on
> whom nothing is lost." To have it said that I
> am such a person is the highest compliment
> I could ever hope to be given.

Very little has been lost on Humphrey, though commitment to observation, natural in a writer who began as a realist, can be limiting.

There is certainly an element of the shaping
imagination in this memoir: the author is not merely
recording what he has seen. Much of the book recre-
ates events that happened before he was born, like
the childhood of his parents and the days and nights
of their courtship. He has praised a memoir by Sergei
Aksakov very highly in one of his interviews with
Ashby Bland Crowder. Aksakov is one of the great
Russian writers of the nineteenth century, the author of several classic memoirs. Humphrey says:

> If you are writing about childhood, well,
> it would be impossible for one to write a mem-
> oir of his childhood without the question of
> lost innocence, which is one of the things that
> happens in any childhood, southern or not.
> The story told may be an elegy to the lost

innocence, a lament for it, a depiction of a
world that once seemed perfect, only to turn
out to be something else. You're going to find
that in, I think, any childhood memoir; one
of my favorite ones of all time is called *A
Russian Gentleman*, by Aksakov, a writer of
the 1850s and 1860s, one of the truly su-
premely great autobiographies that I've read,
and one of the most penetrating insights into
childhood. And that of course is what it is;
it's a re-creation of a world that was to him
like an Eden, and it's all his joy, and all of his
life. (12)

In his introduction to the World's Classics edition of
A Russian Gentleman, Edward Crankshaw praises
the memoir for the skill with which Aksakov "moves
outside his own experience" (xii). The writer dealt with
matters that happened before his birth, reconstruct-
ing the world of his grandparents and parents through
hearsay, which is precisely what Humphrey does so
skillfully in *Farther Off from Heaven*. The reader can
easily forget that Humphrey was not present when
his father built his own primitive gun, or when his
parents went to dances in their courtship.

Humphrey's remembered heaven is defined in the
opening chapter: Clarksville itself, which he calls a
"Zion," a holy land which he remembers in exile. The

violent nature of his leaving it ensured that he would carry a map of it in his head for life. His refusal to attend his father's funeral scandalized the town, and left him with an open wound, an unresolved grief. He was left wondering, for example, why his father had suddenly started carrying a gun. Later in the book the narrator hears rumors that his father may have been carrying on a clandestine romance, so along with a sense of profound abandonment, there would be doubts about his father's morals.

The book begins *in medias res* with the awakening of young Humphrey by his mother at three in the morning after the Fourth of July, 1937, to tell him to get dressed because his father has been hurt. Each chapter of the book except for the second one, will open with a stage in the father's movement toward death. After creating some suspense by mentioning the gun that Clarence Humphrey had started to carry, the narrator takes us on a chilling ambulance ride with the mangled father to the nearest hospital, in Paris, thirty-five miles away. We can imagine the effect on the boy as his father kept calling out, "Turn out the lights" in the dark ambulance.

Humphrey carefully emphasizes the Fourth of July in the chapter. This was a special one for two reasons. First, it fell on a Sunday, which meant that the usual festive atmosphere of a Saturday market day in Clarksville was extended for two days. He evokes the atmosphere of the square (as he did in "Mouth of Brass"), the food, the bands, the speeches, one of them given by the young Lyndon Johnson. This holiday had a special intensity because people could sense that the Depression was coming to an end for the nation, and the Dust Bowl had given way to rain and a fine cotton harvest for Clarksville. We do learn later that the Fourth of July had been unlucky for Humphrey: on that day in 1933 he had sliced off his kneecap in an accident, one more of his childhood traumas. At the opening of the book, the emphasis is on the last joyous experiences in the city that the narrator would be leaving a few days later.

The second chapter is the only one which does not begin with a stage in the father's death and funeral: it is a kind of prose poem to Clarksville and its clock, Old Red, the center of the boy's universe. The clock seems to have received its mysterious name at its first striking, at 2:30, 27 May 1885. Though it was not colored red, Humphrey says that time always has a red coloration for him through the verbal association. Lives in Clarksville were regulated by that clock. The other strong sensory memory is the smell of cottonseed oil from the mill, a smell as pleasant as baking bread, though the product was not edible.

One of the high points of American autobiography, Wallace Stegner's *Wolf Willow*, offers interesting parallels with Humphrey's work. Stegner spent his childhood in Eastend, Saskatchewan, which he calls "Whitemud." He describes it as a good place in which to be a boy and a bad place to be an adult. Like Humphrey, he celebrates the town geography and evokes himself as "a sensuous little savage," which he says all boys are. For him, the town is linked forever to the scent of a local plant, "wolf willow." To describe the impact of Whitemud on his imagination, Stegner uses the analogy of a baby bird imprinting on its environment, suggesting that somewhere between the age of five and twelve a human being does the same. This is precisely Humphrey's situation. Humphrey and Stegner both came from families where the mothers saw academic achievement as an advancement for their sons. Both men had quarrelsome fathers, though Humphrey does not feel the hatred that Stegner expresses for his father. Ambivalence, but not hatred. Both writers returned to their home town after many years away and found that much had changed (a very common experience), and that some of the most intense memories had to be corrected. Humphrey's memoir has a focus that Stegner's, with its attempt to write the whole history of Western Canada, does not.

Humphrey defines himself in the second chapter as a rover. As the book progresses, we come to understand why. Shortly after his return visit, he wrote to Katherine Anne Porter, "my childhood had been pretty unhappy inside the house but very happy out on the streets" (14 July 1969). The first chapter described the town square. The second opens with a description of the courthouse and its clock, which served the child as the center of his little universe. Then he gives us a tour of the rest of town, using various routes that he took to school as a means of charting it all. He lived in various parts of town, so there were a number of routes to the school on the outskirts. The frightening route was through the "white trash" part of town, near the cemetery, and he recalls his mother's disgust with that area: Clarence Humphrey and Nell Varley started life as children of tenant farmers, the class most likely to be dismissed as white trash, a category at the bottom of the white social ladder. Humphrey's father escaped that fate by becoming a good mechanic. The parts of town that Humphrey never walked through were "Silk Stocking Street," the common term for the neighborhood of the well-to-do, and "Niggertown." As suggested before, *Home from the Hill* imaginatively transposes the Humphrey household to Silk Stocking Street: the tall landowner and hunter, Wade Hunnicutt, seems a fantasy version of Clarence Humphrey, who was a "sawed-off shotgun of a man" (11). The house he never saw but longed to know was the vanished house in which he was born: the reader quickly senses that the references to this house are the foreshadowing of a revelation.

After charting the routes to school, Humphrey talks about his school days, and the theme of social class is conspicuous: education is traditionally one route out of the working class, and a major theme of Texas memoirs. William Owens is a representative example: born in Pin Hook, Texas, not far from Clarksville, he makes education a major theme in his first memoir, *This Stubborn Soil*, and the central theme of its sequel, *A Season of Weathering*. John A. Lomax, the folk song collector, has a similar emphasis in his autobiography, *Adventures of a Ballad Hunter*. Lomax grew up in Bosque, Texas, about two hundred miles from Clarksville. Humphrey's own story, "Report Cards," comes to mind immediately in his account of his rivalry with Billy Barton. The Bartons, like the Spence family in the story, are a prominent family. Pathos arises when the author describes having to help his parents—who had only two years of schooling each—keep the books of the garage. And that family business, the subject of the conclusion of the chapter, is also linked with anxieties of social class. Boys love visiting garages, but Clarence Humphrey didn't want his son dropping by such a lower-class establishment. The son recounts how he became ambivalent about social status himself, not knowing whether to be proud or ashamed when he would see his father riding around town on the hood of a car with his ear to it in order to determine what was wrong with it, a detail readers of *Proud Flesh* will recall: Claude Renshaw is shot by an angry husband while doing exactly that.

One painful paradox of the memoir is the irony that Clarence escaped the brutal life of a sharecropper by becoming a mechanic and then died in a car accident. He began as a "shade tree mechanic," using farm tools to repair cars. "He could fix anything wrong with one of them long before he had the opportunity, except to test it, to drive one. When he began doing that, then along with the gift for repairing them came a zest for driving them as fast as they could go" (58).

The next chapter is a fine example of Humphrey's skill at construction: it begins with dawn in the Paris hospital, moves to memories of getting up early to hunt with his father, and then quite gracefully explains how hunting was his father's alternative to a brutally dull family life. Before he became a mechanic, Clarence Humphrey taught himself the woods, the wilderness of Sulphur Bottom, as a means of escaping oppressive farm life, and even tried making his own primitive rifle. He had begun teaching his woodlore to his son, and died one season before they were ready to go on the great trip together, hunting in Sulphur Bottom. The chapter is strongly reminiscent of *Home from the Hill*, down to the description of the development of a boy as a hunter rendered through the sizes of shotgun that he uses. Humphrey did not accompany his father in the pursuit of a murderer in Sulphur Bottom: he constructs the scene in his imagination, a scene similar to the one described in *Home from the Hill*, when Theron pursues Albert Halstead. In fact, Humphrey used a discarded passage from the novel as the basis of the episode, which, according to his *Farther Off from Heaven* notebook, he had from his father in only about twenty words. Edward Crankshaw's praise of Aksakov is relevant here: "It is impossible to tell where hearsay is supplemented by direct observation and where both are quickened by imagination" (xiii). Aksakov is revered for his ability to tell a story "without apparent artifice" but "with a simplicity which carries it to the highest peak of artistry" (xiii).

In one of his best scenes, Humphrey describes something he did witness: the killing of an alligator by his father and Wylie, the black assistant at the garage. It is a startling set piece, showing Humphrey's tremendous skill at describing physical action while exploring the larger theme of black-white relations in the South. The two men were both short, and when stripped to the waist seemed twins, with Wylie as the black carbon copy of Clarence. In his notebook, Humphrey suggested that his family's low social position would enable him to say things never said about race in the South before.

Wylie West: using him I can explore—through
his relationship with my father—something
never before said about southern life. The
reason I can is because nobody—nobody articulate—ever came from a class of southern
whites as close to the niggers as mine. The
incredible complication of it—like primitive
languages—the more primitive a language
the more complex it is.

The alligator scene is well-written, though perhaps
it is not as incredibly complicated as Humphrey would
have hoped. He does express the intense yet
unarticulated friendship of the two men, who are simultaneously risking their lives and having a fine
time doing it.

    The chapter is dominated by hunting, but it deals
with a number of other subjects. As an experienced
novelist, Humphrey is able to move with ease from
topic to topic, creating a seamless work. We learn
about Clarence's desolate home life, which is con-
trasted with the loving atmosphere created by his
Aunt Suzie, an affectionate and nurturing woman.
The boy runs off to Suzie's house whenever he can.
Running away, to Suzie or to the woods, becomes his
obsession until he is finally old enough to leave home
and stay away. We also learn about his father's schooling, about the butchering of hogs, about the intricacies

of making your own gun with minimal tools, about firearms in general, and about the hunting of quail and ducks. The chapter ends with a touching description of the boy's unspoken intimacy with his father.

The fourth chapter turns to the mother's side of the family, a subject introduced quite naturally by describing the arrival of her parents at the hospital. But it also introduces the father's violent side, a balance to the highly idealistic portrait of him in the previous section. Humphrey-as-child wants to tell them that he knows what they're thinking, that his father is not a reckless, violent man. But that makes him remember the summer in Arkansas when a drunk driver nearly killed father, mother, and child, and was then beaten unconscious by the angry Clarence. The chapter will end with a similar scene, known only by hearsay, the story of a fight over Nell at a dance, the incident that seems to have brought about the marriage. But the chapter is dominated by a portrait of the Varley grandparents. They are the prototypes for "The Hardys" and for parts of the portrait of Sam and Hester Ordway: the woman broods endlessly over her dead rival, Mr. Varley's first wife. The most interesting part of the portrait is the presentation of them as an exceedingly loving couple who manipulate their children: each appears to be selfless, constantly asking their offspring to do things for the other. In the long run, neither has to do anything, while appearing to be completely unselfish. Their children seem never to have caught on to the way that they are controlled: even after they have grown up, they continue to admire their parents' mutual love. In his interview with Jose Yglesias, Humphrey made an interesting comment on his book, which was dedicated to his mother:

> "My mother was very much hurt by that book," he says of his masterful *Farther Off from Heaven*, with the puzzlement authors feel when a truthful but loving portrait meets with disapproval. He can be gleeful when the reader "gets" the meanness subtly depicted in seemingly loving characters, as in the passages about his maternal grandparents in the same book. (64)

The grandfather was, like Mr. Hardy in the story, an Englishman. He left England as a boy after a dispute over his refusal to black his older brother's boots. This incident is used in *The Ordways*, and attributed to the first Ordway to come to America, Dismas.

The parents did not approve of Clarence Humphrey, whom they saw as a wild and disreputable young man. But they could refuse nothing to the pet of the family, the youngest child, and one who had been injured in an accident at the age of three, losing a finger in a game of riding the pulley in the barn. The injury was well concealed by Humphrey's mother, who would wear gloves or carry a handkerchief, so that her own husband didn't perceive the injury for five years, and her son was eight before he became aware of it. This incident introduces the theme of concealed injuries in the book, like Humphrey's own deformed foot, which was cured before he was old enough to remember it, and never mentioned to him. The gun carried by the father suggests another secret, though we never know what it is, because the son never learned. Families that keep secrets may be sick families: after a while we begin to sense the depth of the dysfunction in this one, for all the genuine love felt by the parents for each other, and the reciprocated love he felt for them.

Clarence and Nell did marry, and their son tells the story of their courtship well. They were fun-loving and hot-tempered, both being red-haired and therefore licensed by tradition to have tempers. Humphrey suggests that his father's willingness to fight over Nell in the early days was appealing to a woman of her background at this time and place, and he ends the chapter with a description of his father fighting at a dance and thereby sealing the relationship. This scene is balanced in Chapter 6 by a later one on the town square, after the marriage has gone sour. The wife simply ignores it: her cooling affection and the presence of her son make her embarrassed rather than passionate.

The fifth chapter deals with the mysteries of sex and death. It opens with the arrival of the paternal grandparents at the hospital. The boy has almost never seen both sets of grandparents together: after all, the Varleys feel superior to the Humphreys. He becomes aware that his father is likely to die, and that leads to a meditation on death, a memory of a boy who died by drowning, a fate which Humphrey teasingly suggests was his own. He describes visiting the dead boy's mother: the two of them weep together, but he is really weeping for himself, out of a new awareness of human loneliness and "unbridgeable isolation" (153). As the son waits for his father to die, he recalls his father's recent attempt to convey the facts about procreation. The memory is rather comic, as the boy could barely understand, but the discussion makes him realize in the hospital that the most appropriate person to share his grief, a brother or sister, will never be born.

The temporal period covered by the next chapter is three days at the Paris hospital, but now death has been admitted as a possibility, and the musings are dark ones, attributable to the adult Humphrey rather than to his younger self. He thinks about the decline in his parents' marriage, which coincides—though not in any easy causal way—with the Dust Bowl and the

Depression, situations which left the small businessman like Clarence Humphrey with thousands of dollars owed to him. In a painful scene, he despairingly
burns $10,000 worth of unpaid accounts. The gen-
eral social despair leads to the cult of the outlaw,
dealt with some years before in "The Ballad of Jesse
Neighbours." The growing tension in the marriage
increases the father's binges, and he begins to carry
a pistol. When a man makes drunken suggestions to
Nell one night on the town square, her husband beats
the man senseless, but this leads not to intensified
intimacy as it had in the country dance episode, but
to further estrangement: the presence of the child,
who witnesses the scene, makes all the difference.
For a moment there is hope when the family moves
to Mabry, and Nell, a resourceful country woman,
thrives, gardening and building a splendid chicken
house with her son's assistance. But the interlude is
brief. The landlord wants the house back, and the
family returns to town, where the father will die a
few weeks later.

The last chapter is a complex one: it covers the
father's death, and the funeral which young
Humphrey would not attend, while exploring the
past and taking the narrative ahead at last to the
author's visit in 1969. It seems crammed with incidents, and it clears up several mysteries. The end of
the previous chapter has emphasized the mother,

showing her spunk and skill. The final chapter seems
her chapter above all: we get to know her better than
before and she emerges as an admirable character.
We hear more about the fire that destroyed a house
in which they lived, and most of their memorabilia,
including the mysterious death certificate.
Humphrey deals with several of his physical traumas, which affect his mother deeply. There is the
disastrous fall on a stake that rips off his kneecap.
A surgeon sews it back on, and though the boy is
told he will never walk normally again, he recovers.
During his recuperation he becomes very close to
her, listening to Nell sing songs like "My Blue
Heaven," the celebration of cozy married love in
which "baby makes three." The grown-up Humphrey
knows that three also makes a crowd, that he took
some fun out of his parent's lives. He feels lucky to
have his mother, lucky to have the security of a family, unlike the outcasts in the country songs that she
sometimes sings in another mood, ballads of doom
and wretchedness. The reader understands that his
luck has changed radically with his father's accident.
During Humphrey's convalescence, he develops some
interest in reading, though his conversion to books
really comes later with the purchase of *Don Quixote*
in Dallas.

The memoirist presents himself as a rather accident-prone person, a tendency that shows up in

his later life, in incidents recounted in letters and
journals. Later in childhood he sprains his ankle, and
this time his mother collapses and tells the boy, who
has been bewildered by her apprehension, that he was
born crippled: hence the injury to that ankle devastates her. He learns the story of his mother's refusal
to accept what in their impoverished world would
seem to be fate: she sought out a doctor in Dallas who
could fit a brace, and by the time Humphrey was able
to remember anything, the foot was normal. Now he
understands why his foot never showed in early pictures, and it clear why his parents had difficulty pun-
ishing him. He also understands their reluctance to
have another child.

Immediately after the ankle episode, Humphrey
describes a catastrophic family dinner. The book is
filled with brilliant scenes, and this is one of the best.
The ritual of Sunday dinner is sacred, and all discord
should be hidden or suppressed in this unhappy family. But one Sunday Clarence comes home to dinner
very late, and drunk. After a row, he struggles with
his wife, who is dressed in her best clothes. Her pearl
necklace is broken and pearls—painted glass beads—
fly all around the room. After Clarence leaves, Nell
insists that the trembling boy eat his dinner. He takes
a bite of tomato soup, and finds that he has a pearl in
his mouth. Overcome, he runs from the house.

After the powerful emotion of this scene, the adult

writer is ready to tell us more about the fire and the drowning. He describes the fire obliquely, through the loss of a hobbyhorse, a magical one that seems to represent the lost joy of childhood. He recalls how one day his father saw an amazing sight in the country: an abandoned merry-go-round. At the boy's entreaty, the father removed one of the wooden horses and took it home. It was removed with hacksaw, painted and turned into something magnificent. Humphrey describes his father's decision that he should bring them all home and restore them for profit, but the magical event cannot be repeated: when he returns to the field, the merry-go-round has vanished. The unique horse, which becomes "almost a children's institution in Clarksville" vanishes in the fire.

It vanishes along with Humphrey's death certificate: he tells about his near-drowning at Crystal Lake, so near that the county coroner, an incompetent drunk who happened to be at the lake, filled out a death certificate from his pad. Humphrey as a child felt that the death certificate, kept as a souvenir, was proof of a charmed life. It was destroyed in the fire. By not dying in the blaze, he proved his charmed life again.

The only remaining mystery is the vanished house in which he was born, but the reader has to wait for that. There are pages that describe his unhappy feelings between his father's death and the funeral, his feeling of abandonment, his rejection of religion, his realization that he would become a new sort of person once he moved to Dallas with his mother. The funeral would be the funeral of his boyhood. It is a little hard to believe at this point that the thirteen-year-old boy takes stock of his past and predicts his future in the way that Humphrey describes: he shows himself predicting a personality change from openness to suspiciousness and skepticism. The reader is likely to sense hindsight here. At any rate, the religious confirmation scheduled for the following Sunday would not take place; Humphrey remained skeptical about Christianity. And he would seal off his happy childhood forever by leaving Clarksville.

But he did return eventually and the book ends with that return, though very briefly. He attributes this to "the salmon instinct," while alluding to Heraclitus, who said we can never ascend the same river twice. To his astonishment, his southern town has become western. Cotton has been dethroned, and cattle operations have replaced them, so that the Far West has replaced the Deep South, and the cotton lands have been reclaimed by grass. He visits the cemetery to pick out a grave for his eventual use. He sees two boys who offer to lead him to any grave he might want to see: "Looking at either of them was like looking at myself through the wrong end of the binoculars" (240). Remembering all the nickels he

was given as a child on the square, he gives them
each a half dollar, as if to compensate for inflation.
His guide, his favorite Varley uncle, says that it is
fitting for the grave to be so close to the house where
Humphrey was born. We have anticipated such a
moment: the house still exists, a mere hovel, and
the site is in the white trash part of town. The last
family secret has been revealed, one that emphasizes the terror of poverty and class humiliation. And
the involuntary distortions of memory emerge, too:
Old Red, it seems, never tolled "the four, eight, twelve
and sixteen chimes before the quarter, half, three-
quarters and the hour that I remembered." But the
sensation of red color that the clock always sum-
moned up in Humphrey is still with him, pervading
memories that we realize are sharp but, in the best
romantic fashion, half-perceived, half-created. We
have experienced Hum-phrey's own "Ode: Intimations of Immortality from Recollections of Early
Childhood." Like Wordsworth, he describes the "Delight and liberty" of childhood and also the way that
"Shades of the prison-house begin to close/Upon the
growing boy." But the last words of this powerful
memoir describe delight and liberty:

> The town had shrunk, fit closer, like old clothes
> long outgrown. So much smaller now than
> when measured by my ten-, eleven-, twelve-

year-old stride, and when, as Old Red told me then, I had all the time in the world. (241)

Although the book did win the 1977 Carr P. Collins Award from the Texas Institute of Letters, for the Best Non-Fiction Book by a Texan, sales were poor and the critics have given it very little attention. In an essay on Humphrey in *The Dictionary of Literary Biography*, James Ward Lee praises it highly and suggests that the portraits of Clarence and Nell Humphrey compare with parents portrayed in works of fiction by Virginia Woolf and James Agee:

> Writing with love and affection about one's parents—especially when one or both died early—is most difficult to do without bathing the whole work in a flood of sentimentality. It is so rarely done that after one has listed Virginia Woolf's *To the Lighthouse* and James Agee's *A Death in the Family* he is hard put to find many examples. To write such a book without benefit of the fictional distancing used by Woolf and Agee is doubly hard. But Humphrey has done it in *Farther Off from Heaven*. (152)

He also praises the style, calling it Humphrey's "best so far," noting its simplicity and the way that his "complex handling of time-shifts and shifts in mood is made to seem simple and unobtrusive" (152). In effect, Humphrey has learned La Rochefoucauld's maxim, "It is the height of art to conceal art."

The longest discussion about the memoir, by Mark Royden Winchell, deals with the work as a source for Humphrey's life, understandable when the reticence of the novelist about his biography is considered. It is a shame that the memoir has received so little attention: it is elegantly written and deeply felt—and it is the elegance that makes the depth of feeling real to the reader. Here is evidence that Ezra Pound was right when he spoke of style as the test of sincerity. Humphrey is less circumstantial in describing milieu than William Owens and more restrained in his picture of an unhappy family than Mary Karr, whose family must hold a record for dysfunction. Humphrey and Karr surely rank very high among the modern American autobiographers: for them, the local color is a way to universal human themes. Fortunately, the unhappiness of an interesting family can be the basis of a moving work of art. Clarence and Nell Humphrey were not Agamemnon and Clytemnestra, but their stories were worth telling. When Thomas Gray spoke in his *Elegy Written in a Country Churchyard* of "the short and simple annals of the poor," he spoke wrongly. Humphrey's family was poor, but their annals were neither short nor simple, and their son preserved their story until he could turn it into art.

8

Humphrey's Oedipus:

Hostages to Fortune

In 1976, Humphrey heard from Heywood Antone, who had been in grade school with him, in a class taught by Ida Mae McConnell Pinson. Antone had become an English professor at the University of Texas at El Paso, and then the director of the Texas Western Press. He wondered if his old schoolmate had anything he could publish in a deluxe edition by the press. Humphrey obliged with the text of a lecture he had given at Washington and Lee College during his 1963–64 appointment as a visiting professor, published in pamphlet form as *Ah Wilderness!* in 1977 and marked with a reading in El Paso in May, the same month that he was offered a post as writer-in-residence at North Texas State University, which he declined. The lecture is not a major contribution to the understanding of American literature. Mark Royden Winchell observes that "Humphrey says nothing that had not already been said better and more comprehensively by Leslie Fiedler in *Love and Death in the American Novel* or, for that matter, D. H. Lawrence in *Studies in Classic American Literature*" (*William Humphrey* 34). The work also shows the influence of Wright Morris's fine study, *The Territory Ahead*. Humphrey was a great admirer of Morris and late in 1957 sent him a special edition of Stendahl. Perhaps the most interesting comment in Humphrey's pamphlet comes at the beginning, when the author observes that there are few heroines in American literature. "We Americans seem, indeed, to have originated in *Moby-Dick* and *The Red Badge of Courage*" (7). Humphrey wonders where are our "Anna Karenina's" or "even our Lady Chatterley's?" He seems to forget Hester Prynne, but the comment is fair enough, and he himself has had trouble creating memorable female characters.

In November, 1977, the Humphreys went through the ordeal of Dorothy's major operation for intestinal cancer, with surgical complications afterward. As she was finally recovering, her husband had a massive infection of the jaw. Along with these health problems, they had to adjust to the poor sales of *Farther*

Off from Heaven.

For all its merits, *Farther Off from Heaven* failed
on both sides of the Atlantic. In a letter to Fred and
Andy Dupee (17 September 1977) Humphrey said
that he and Dorothy had returned from a holiday to
find that the book had been very favorably reviewed,
but the publisher seemed to have done nothing at all
to promote it. Only after Humphrey insisted did they
place ads, and only two of those. Humphrey soon saw
piles of remaindered copies of the book in New York,
and sales were so bad in England that Ian Parsons
took the unusual step of complaining in the press. In
a letter published in *The Bookseller* (7 January 1978)
entitled "Outstanding Merit," he noted that the British had neglected the first appearances of *The
Rubáiyát of Omar Khayyám*, *The Wind in the Wil-
lows*, Rupert Brooke's 1914 sonnets, and Mary Webb's
Precious Bane, and Humphrey's *Farther Off from
Heaven* had joined that honorable list:

> I'm prompted to ask this question because
> I'm equally at a loss to understand why the
> public of today will not, apparently, buy Wil-
> liam Humphrey's autobiography *Farther Off
> from Heaven*. This is a new book by a highly
> distinguished American author, with three
> novels and three non-fiction books to his
> credit, one of which—*The Spawning Run*—

sold like hot cakes here in 1970. But that book was a brief 10,000 word *jeu d'esprit*, compared with which *Farther Off from Heaven* is a masterpiece. By which I mean that it is a book in the same class as Scott Fitzgerald's *The Great Gatsby*, or William Faulkner's *The Bear* (two other classic American authors who had to wait a long time for any appreciable recognition here), or Hemingway's Parisian Reminiscences in *A Moveable Feast*. *Farther Off from Heaven* has affinities with all of them, in its humour, its vivid evocation of time and place, its compelling presentation of character, and above all the poignancy of the situation from which it springs, and which informs the book throughout. And yet it seems nobody wants to read it. I wish somebody would tell me why. (45)

Parsons told Humphrey that not even Hatchard's, the great London bookstore, could move the work in spite of giving it prominent display. At Christmas time, Peggy Ashcroft had chosen the book as her "Book of the Year" for the *Sunday Times*, but that did not help sales either.

The following year Humphrey would publish a delightful work—to be considered with his other sporting adventures—called *My Moby Dick*. Like its

famous predecessor, it has no female characters. He
made an important decision in 1981: he finally broke
with his long-time publisher, Knopf, and allied himself with the editor and publisher Seymour Lawrence,
who had been wanting him as an author since 1966.
In 1981–82, he held a one-year writer-in-residence
appointment at Princeton, which probably made it
easier to contemplate such a switch. Seymour
Lawrence would bring out *Hostages to Fortune*, *Open
Season*, *The Collected Stories*, and *No Resting Place*
as Delacorte/Seymour Lawrence books, and the most
recent title, *September Song*, as a Houghton Mifflin/
Seymour Lawrence book. Lawrence was experienced
at luring writers away from their publishers to com-
panies he worked with. He had separated Katherine
Anne Porter from Harcourt, Brace and World to Little,
Brown and Company, and later enticed her to change
to his own imprint. Lawrence inadvertently caused a
strain between Katherine Anne Porter and Humphrey
in 1970 when he included a note in her *Collected Essays* thanking a number of writers for helping as-
semble and proofread the book during one of Porter's
illnesses. Humphrey was on the list, and she was en-
raged with Lawrence and everyone he acknowledged.
But this did not end the friendship: Dorothy visited
Porter during one of her illnesses. She wrote her husband a very engrossing but undated letter about
Porter's southern grande dame ways, like her habit

of receiving visitors in her Christian Dior nightgown. When I asked Humphrey about the date of the visit, he replied that it was during "the second inauguration of Richard Milhous Nixon," a way of marking the date (6 January 1977) that makes it clear how Nixon's presidency weighed on his mind.

One noteworthy development at the start of the 1980s was the filming of the story, "The Last of the Caddoes," by the young film-maker, Ken Harrison. So far the twenty-nine-minute film has missed the notice of critics and bibliographers. Thanks to Harrison, Humphrey met the Texas writer William Owens, who taught at Columbia and lived along the Hudson at Nyack, and whose *This Stubborn Soil* Humphrey always admired. Owens knew Harrison, and served as an adviser on the film. He was able to suggest an Indian mound near Pin Hook for use as a location. The movie also had some shots of Clarksville and its courthouse. Humphrey's favorite uncle, Bernard Varley, who had been Vincente Minnelli's advisor on the location set of *Home from the Hill*, played the boy protagonist's grandfather. This is an interesting genetic twist, as the grandfather was actually based on William Humphrey's paternal grandfather. Humphrey was present during the shoot.

While serving as writer-in-residence at Princeton, William Humphrey formed a close friendship with the English poet Charles Tomlinson and his wife

Brenda, who both shared the Humphreys' love of Italy.
Tomlinson dedicated two poems to Humphrey. One,
first published in 1984 in *Notes from New York and
Other Poems* is called "Of the Winter Ball Game" and
seems to describe a football game at Princeton (*Collected Poems* 383). It is not one of Tomlinson's best—
American sports must have been obscure to him, but
he later wrote an elegant poem "for Bill and Dorothy,"
entitled "Hudson River School," collected in his 1989
volume, *Annunciations*. It evokes the Rip Van Winkle
spirit of the Catskills and the Hudson River Valley,
the idyllic atmosphere of an area beloved by painters
and still attuned to cycles like the migration of the
shad. The poem turns on a bit of folklore, that the
shad bushes in the area blossom just before the fish
arrive "to foison the river anew" (18).

The novelist made some use of the Princeton setting in his next novel, *Hostages to Fortune*, published
in 1984, a book marking an important transition in
his career. It is the first novel set somewhere other
than Texas, and no Texas character appears in it. Instead he uses the Hudson River area as his primary
setting, and the house of his protagonist, a novelist
named Ben Curtis, is modeled on his own house, with
its fine view and its collection of antiques. In this
novel, he gives up the folklore and history—the local
color—that mark so much of his work, but family tensions are still a major theme, although the family is

not a sprawling southern one like the Ordways and the Renshaws. It is hard to imagine a reader identifying Humphrey as the author of this novel in an anonymous test, unless the reader knew the fishing stories extremely well. The book is a psychological study, light on plot and heavy on complex motives, and the style is thoroughly analytical.

It was not finished quickly. Humphrey was a slow worker, and his very leisurely progress on *Hostages to Fortune* may have antagonized Lawrence, who would have preferred that Humphrey work on his historical novel about the Cherokee Removal, part of which Lawrence had seen. In the archive at the University of Texas, a letter (7 September 1983) has been preserved in which Toby Eady, Humphrey's English agent, wrote to Jackie Farber, an editor at Delacorte/Seymour Lawrence, complaining that Humphrey was being shamefully neglected. Eady noted that Lawrence knew that "Bill" was a slow writer. In letter written on 1 October 1987, Lawrence had to assure his anxious author that he was Humphrey's "publisher for life."

Hostages to Fortune is based on the experiences of two of Humphrey's oldest friends, Ted Thomas, who worked in advertising, and Andy Wanning, the Seventeenth Century scholar. Wanning's daughter had committed suicide in October, 1970, by leaping from a building. The notebook for *Hostages to Fortune* at the University of Texas (begun in 1977 and running to October 1982) contains letters from Ted discussing this terrible event. Later, Ted's own son committed suicide during his first term at Harvard. Humphrey's notebook, which charts the conception of the novel and reveals some of its sources, shows a writer struggling to re-invent his work and to survive emotionally in a time of deep discouragement.

After the novel appeared, Humphrey received letters from parents whose teenage children had committed suicide. Some of his replies survive in rough drafts, and in those, as well as in interviews, he points out that the book was not based on the suicide of a child of his own, as his correspondents assumed: he had no children, aside from a stepdaughter. But he consistently said that the central character, Ben Curtis, is himself. The novel uses Humphrey's own dark night of the soul, when he was struggling to finish *Proud Flesh*, to create the image of Ben Curtis (a novelist with a name as plain as "Bill Humphrey"), who falls into alcoholism and despair after his son's inexplicable death.

As he began his new work in 1977, he had also struggled for years with the Cecil Smoot novel and its multiple rejections, as well as the commercial failure of *Farther Off from Heaven*. It would have been bad taste if he had equated this experience with the suffering of a man whose child had committed suicide, but the equation was actually made by Ted Thomas himself, in a remarkably generous letter about the book. Humphrey was unsure whether he had the strength to continue his writing career. The "Sunday morning self-communion" quoted in the discussion of *Proud Flesh*, was despairing. There is a comparably bleak meditation in his *Hostages to Fortune* notebook, from 1977:

> I am fifty-two years old. I've written seven books. Each of them took a terrible toll of me. Now I'm thinking of trying to make something of one on which I worked—as always— like a slave and then was forced to abandon. A comic novel, yet—when I feel like being anything but funny. And, looking beyond that, a grim, even a grisly one. Back in 1958, when I was thirty-four years old, I projected two novels. And I wrote them both! I'm less resilient, less elastic now—and I've been battered, by reviewers, by life, now, as I hadn't been then. Can I do it? Have I the strength or the imagination? The will. No, I don't have. What do I do in order simply to stay alive. Not that I want to stay alive. But here I am.

In a draft of a letter to his admirer, Frederic Stout, cited in the introduction to this study, Humphrey had interesting things to say about *Hostages to Fortune*:

> Phew! that's just the response I wanted. My aim was merely to knock the reader's breath out of him and break his heart. I fashioned that book, paced it, as nearly as I could, so that it would be impossible for my ideal reader (and I write for that reader) to whip through it. I wanted it to be almost as hard for him to read as for me to write. And it was hard. For although both Tony Thayer and Ben Curtis are based on friends of mine, and although I have never had, much less lost through suicide a child, Ben Curtis is me. You are that ideal reader, and I am so grateful for you. And for your writing to tell me your response. I shall treasure it.

This novel had a title from the beginning, which perturbed an author who so often had found his titles only after a long struggle. For that very reason, he didn't trust it, and he contemplated others: "All Good Things," "The Savor of Salt," and a whole series of titles from Hamlet's "To Be or Not to Be" soliloquy. The best alternative was probably "The Savor of Salt," from the phrase by Jesus (Matthew 5:13) alluded to in the novel: "Ye are the salt of the earth: but if the salt have lost his savor, wherewith shall it be salted?"

Ben Curtis learns that life can lose its savor, and that his wife and friends, who are the "salt of the earth" to him, can also lose their appetite for life.

One comment in the notebook reveals the significance of the title for William Humphrey:

> Titles—if you can find one early on—give the book. *Hostages to Fortune* tells me that I am writing about a man reduced to nothingness—which is to say, to himself—the existential absurd & place myself in the Dostoyevskyan line. Whether I'm up to it is almost beside the point. But that does now seem to me my way out. To immerse myself in the destructive element and regard the immersion as the search for wisdom and if you sink—*c'est cè*. If there is any reason left for writing a novel it's as Lawrence said, the novel is the book of life. Life in Art—not art for itself. Surely in an age as desperate for guidance as ours that's the excuse for carrying on. Not that art is ever edification—but then I never meant to suggest that wisdom and edification had anything to do with each other. As I've said before, every novel sets out to solve the mystery of life,—and the bad ones succeed.

The passage echoes the celebrated moment in

Conrad's *Lord Jim* when Stein says that Jim's only hope after his disgrace is to take on a new task.

The title chosen has exactly the right emphasis. The source is Lord Bacon's essay "Of Marriage and the Single Life": "He that hath wife and children hath given hostages to fortune, for they are impediments to great enterprises, either of virtue or mischief." At first the title makes us think of the hostages themselves: Ben's son, Anthony, and wife, Cathy. His son dies literally, while Cathy dies as far as her marriage is concerned in a violent emotional reaction against love and intimacy as a result of her grief. But the focus of the novel is on Ben, who tries to understand their actions: we see the impact of the loss of his "hostages" on him. The third person limited narration is rigidly adhered to, making other people relatively insubstantial. This makes the narrative somewhat airless, but it is part of the effect. A parallel with Ben's case is his closest friend, Tony Thayer, whose daughter Christy had leaped to her death. Tony himself dies in an ice sailing accident which was not, in fact, an accident: no one has ever died in that sport before.

But initially the novel makes the reader think about the hostages to fortune, especially the brilliant son. The friend whose own son killed himself suggested in his letter about the book that it should have been promoted as a book on teenage suicide, and the letters Humphrey received from bereaved parents demonstrate that the book was immensely relevant to them. Between the pages of his notebook Humphrey tucked in an article from the 4 July 1977 issue of *Time* called "The Young Werthers," exploring teenage suicide. A notebook entry of 11 February 1977, shows how concerned Humphrey was with the subject:

> Dostoyevsky, in *Crime and Punishment*, went to one of the central problems of life, and one which his era had posed for it critically. The grand moral question: has one human being the right to decide that another shall die? An equally eternal question, has a human the right to take his own life? And one more to the point now than ever before in history— for suicide is the number one killer of today's young people. It is of course a reflection of the drying up in our time of meaningful reasons to go on living. That almost reasonless despair which grips us all.

But the very passage shows that just as his Russian predecessor could turn a crime story about a youth bludgeoning an old woman to death into a profound exploration of the soul, Humphrey is interested in more than a sociological problem. He is interested in the journalistic theme of the suicide of young people, but he also wants to probe "that almost reasonless despair which grips us all."

The narrative has a narrow focus which is new to Humphrey. The work is built around the protagonist making his first visit to his fishing club in a year. He is taking a risk doing this, because he has a potentially fatal allergy to the stings of bees, wasps, and hornets, and to the bites of deerflies. "Unlike other people, he did not absorb and shed the venom; in him it accumulated, and he had been stung so many times now he was full of it" (3). Humphrey debated having the novel begin with Ben's symbolic re-entry to life represented by buying a fishing license, or having it start with a moment in which he "anoints" himself with insect repellent. He settled on the almost magical anointing—protective, possibly healing. But the fishing license scene follows, and it is important. Ben Curtis's old fishing license had described him as "Age 48, Weight 205, Hair Black" (4). Now at age fifty he weighs 170 and his hair is white. The novel explains what has happened to him through a series of flashbacks. The flashbacks are natural enough, as Curtis has fallen into endless analyses of past events in an attempt to understand them. The first section, which occupies 180 pages of the 227-page total, tells the story of his day of fishing with two kinds of flashbacks incorporated: one set narrates the events of the afternoon and night before, from his arrival at the club till

breakfast; the other gives the complete story of his
son's death and the dissolution of his marriage—two
events that have filled him with venom—with other
events interpolated, like his wedding at the club and
the birth of the son. The flashbacks are handled with
subtlety and the reader is never lost in the labyrinth
of plot. In the second section, Curtis remembers his
own collapse, and in a final section we return to the
river, where he catches a fish, which in effect read-
mits him to the community of the living, at least as
the club represents it.

Humphrey's interest in codes and myths is apparent in the treatment of the club. Many of Curtis's
most important experiences, like his wedding and his
friendship with Tony and Pris Thayer, are associated
with it. By returning to the club, he is returning to
life, but he is acutely aware that the club is based on
a superficial notion of life. Its motto is "Thumbs Up,"
and the camaraderie of the members is a limited con-
viviality, not the full banquet of life. Members do not
bring their problems with them, and they do not discuss serious subjects.

> Should a dispute over politics, for example,
> erupt at the bar, the disputants were served
> one on the house, and as he set them down,
> Eddie pointed both thumbs up. It was a re-
> minder and something of a reprimand, and

it was all that was needed. Sometimes friend-
ships developed that extended beyond the
club, sometimes love affairs originated there,
but for the most part members knew, or cared
to know, little about one another except as
weekend fishing companions. Perhaps the
cheerful atmosphere of the place was owing
to the superficiality of their involvement with
each other. (7)

Humphrey was a passionate fisherman, and his files
are filled with letters from other anglers. This is a
world he knows very well, but he is clearly aware of
its limitations. This superficiality is exactly what
makes Curtis feel that he can risk a tentative return
to the larger world after his collapse: "Studiously
unnoticed, he felt like a ghost come back to the scene
of his former life" (7). The ghost theme is an important motif in the novel, as we shall see. A code can
have its value, but this sporting code omits large areas of human experience and Humphrey knows that,
though he is not concerned with destroying this particular myth because he has more important things
to deal with. Crucial to the character's mental sur-
vival will be his encounter with one club member, Ken
Howard, who ignores the code and insists on discussing Curtis's loss.

The book takes the form of a quest for knowl-

edge. Ben has devoted the time since his son's death
to trying to understand it. In his *Hostages to Fortune*
notebook, Humphrey says:

> I would make it something of a detective
> story—with a difference. A "detective story"
> in the way that *Oedipus Rex* is a detective
> story. The difference would be that it was a
> motive, not a criminal that my detective was
> in search of (this question haunts the minds
> of those who survive a suicide). (11 February
> 1977)

Oedipus seeks a murderer and finds it is himself. The crime is known but not the actor. In this
novel, the crime—self-murder—and the agent are
known, but not the motive. Oedipus questions others; Ben Curtis questions himself, and the flashbacks
show him doing it, as Humphrey indicates in his notebook: "Flashbacks would become the habit of mind of
my hero. He would dwell constantly on the boy—seeking clues to help explain what has happened—this
terrible [event], this mystery. Why? Why? This would
come to constitute his life." The mannerism used most
commonly in Curtis's quest for understanding is the
rhetorical question. Most pages have at least one such
question, and many have five or six, a device that
becomes wearisome. The narrator can find no con-

vincing clues to the self-murder; hence he keeps asking but finds no answers.

He inquires of Anthony's roommate and gets no clue. The same happens with Anthony's girlfriend. No one saw anything ominous in the boy's behavior. The wife, Catherine, has no part of this: our fashionable term "denial" fits her very well. She decides that it was a prank of some kind, assuming that the son had taken an overdose of sleeping pills. Curtis can't bring himself to tell her that Anthony hanged himself, a mode of suicide that leaves little chance for rescue.

He analyzes his son's character in great detail. The novelist prevents this inquiry from becoming too dry by using Anthony's interest in falconry as a way of explaining his obsessive, nature-loving temperament: animals were more important to him than people. The falconry episode is projected this way in the notebook:

> The hawk is the main clue to this boy. I will show that he was, as many boys are, a naturalist, with other concentrated interests before falconry. But in this one he finds himself. Then there is one hawk, his hawk. This is a hawk he captures, mans, breaks.
>
> It is when the father is recalling his boy and trying to understand him and account for his death that the story of the hawk is told.

Hawks have always been great symbols.

The long presentation of the hawk-taming (98–106) contains some of Humphrey's best writing. He had already devoted much of his time to sporting stories, and he knew how to make such complex processes clear. While the book seems heavily analytical, it contains rich passages about the physical world, especially the Hudson River Valley. The description of herring fishing is one of Humphrey's finest set-pieces, and he has an excellent account of ice-sailing. The hawk episode establishes that the boy is as independent and uncompromising as the falcon he trains, and it is here we see the symbolic value of the hawk. On leaving for Princeton, he has to release the hawk, a difficult act. He emerges in the episode as a rather narrow individual whose passions might make suicide possible, with the proper motive. Like the hawk, Humphrey tells us, the boy cannot endure failure. He is a perfectionist, tending to be proud and aloof. But his father can find no signs of failure in his life, so the mystery remains.

The notebook contains the passage from Valery's essay on Stendahl quoted in the introduction to this study. The quotation suggests that egotism may, in a convoluted process, lead to suicide. A horror of death and a craving to be Godlike increase the isolation of the individual, which may have helped Humphrey understand something of his character's motivation, but there is no suggestion in the notebook that the author of the novel has some secret insight into what "really happened." Anthony is a perfectionist and a loner, though he has in fact fallen in love by the time he kills himself. Valery says of the isolated, brilliant individual:

> In contact with, or at the memory of, other beings, they feel at times a particular distress, the sharp, abrupt sensation of which cuts into them and makes them shrink at once into an indefinable, intimate island. It is a reflex of inhumanity, of invincible antipathy, which may go as far as madness, as in the case of the emperor who wished that the whole human race had but one head that it might be severed at a single stroke. (117)

Or perhaps a desire to sever one's own head, another way of rejecting the whole human race. But a passage like this does not solve the mystery of the novel, a mystery which is closed to the novelist himself. What we get in the book is the quest of the father of the suicide to reconstruct the crime of self-murder, in a kind of Oedipus-drama in which he fears that he may, like his mythical model, find that he is responsible. As Humphrey puts it in his notebook: "My man's search would—despite him—prove him innocent. An innocence that he can never believe in or accept."

One book that Humphrey consulted during the writing of the novel was Leslie Farber's *Lying, Despair, Jealousy, Envy, Sex, Suicide, Drugs, and the Good Life*. Farber's essay, "Despair and the Life of Suicide," a sensitive treatment of the subject, would have been especially appealing to the novelist describing a quest for motives. Farber uses two images for the attempt to understand the suicide: the staircase and the trapdoor:

> Martin Buber once remarked: "The act of suicide—it is a trapdoor which suddenly springs open. What else can one say?" Well, one can say a great deal, to judge from psychiatric literature. But it is my impression that while to the man who kills himself the act of suicide may be a trapdoor suddenly sprung, to the analyst it seems rather to resemble a psychological staircase, leading step by logical step to an inescapable culmination. And although I don't wish to force the image, I must remark that whether this staircase goes down or up, it must always be traveled backwards. Confronted with the fact of suicide, the analyst must construct his explanation in reverse, laying motive upon

motive (hostility is favored here), and strategy upon strategy, until he reaches some final necessity. Having reached the end of his staircase, he may then retrace his steps forward, issuing those kitchen prescriptions for the heading-off of the act with which we are all familiar. (65)

Farber goes on to say that "this staircase, though a far more reassuring and manageable structure than the suicide's own trapdoor, exists principally in the analyst's head, not in the real world. On the other hand, the world is full of trapdoors. . . ." The staircase is comforting, as it explains and offers suggestions for prevention. But sometimes, he suggests, a linkage of causes is not an adequate description. The state of mind may not lead to the act; rather, the act may have a life of its own, a powerful fascination, something cherished and concealed, something with a demonic and seductive fascination over him. Anthony may be such a case. But his father must strive to construct the staircase, while drifting into a state of despair, moving toward his own trapdoor.

Farber also speaks of the more common variety of suicide, the individual who is in despair. Such a case is open to analytical understanding. Wounded by life, certain individuals retreat, isolate themselves from other human beings. Even before his son's death,

Curtis shows signs of becoming such a person: there is an estrangement from his wife that he does not understand, and his friendship with Tony and Pris Thayer has been undermined by their own despairing retreat from life after the suicide of their daughter. Farber says that the despairing person "slowly loses the power to be with other human beings. . . ." (69).

The protagonist learns of his son's death during his last trip with the Thayers on their yacht, the symbolically-named *Pandora*. In mythology, only hope is left when the blessings of the gods escape from the box. Curtis's own blessings escape when he learns of his son's death. It would seem that he has only despair left. The novel inquires into whether or not there is some hope at the bottom of the box. The ease with which he untangles himself from life after his son's death shows how weakly attached he was to it in his life as a writer. Humphrey had thought of making the character a professor, which would provide a "cast of characters," but a professor would not be able to break his ties with work and colleagues in the way that Curtis does. He also thought of using Ted Thomas's profession, advertising, but that too would make it difficult for the character to break all human ties. For similar reasons he chose to make Curtis an orphan. He rejects contact, then feels isolated, we are told, like the Oedipus of Sophocles's *Oedipus at*

Colonus. "No one liked to be reminded of the dark disasters of life" (119). He is so cut-off that when Thayer, his best friend, kills himself, the widow waits three months to tell him. The death of Thayer is presaged by a moment on the cruise when a drunken Tony Thayer almost kills them all. Humphrey emphasized this moment in a letter to Seymour Lawrence describing the novel: "I want Tony to have drunk himself into such a state that he ignores the chart, causing a collision that could have killed them all" (30 December 1982). Later Thayer will kill himself ice-sailing (this was a favorite sport of the primary model for the character, Andy Wanning), and Ben will come near death himself through a destructive addiction to alcohol.

Curtis's treatment of his wife after he learns of his son's death shows a deep alienation from her: he lets her finish her vacation, then tells her upon her return home. When she immediately locks herself in a bedroom for three days, he makes no attempt to talk to her. He is no more able to respond to her suffering than he could to the Thayers'. He turns to alcohol, disgusting her, and bringing on hallucinations of Anthony's presence in their lives as a mocking figure. The marriage breaks down; sexual life has ceased; she moves out.

He feels that in a way he has been cuckolded by his dead son. After all, this is a novel with undercur-

rents from the Oedipus story. The father and mother
have been estranged recently. Perhaps some Oedipal
conflict has been a factor. On one occasion when Curtis
imagines Anthony's ghost, it seems to rise with
Catherine and go with her to her room:

> He was seeing slightly double but this he
> saw clearly, and just as clearly he saw him-
> self and was appalled at the depravity of his
> mind. Yet why should he be? It was a mod-
> ern-day commonplace that sons lusted after
> their mothers and resented their fathers'
> possession of them, subconsciously wished to
> destroy their rivals, feared castration by them
> as punishment for their incestuous cravings
> and to prevent their consummating them.
> Another commonplace: afraid to destroy their
> fathers and tormented by guilt for their wish
> to do so, some destroyed themselves instead,
> perversely triumphing over their rivals from
> beyond the grave. "Long before you, many a
> man has lain with his mother in his dreams,"
> Jocasta tells her son and husband, Oedipus.
> "Who does not desire his father's death?" cries
> Ivan Karamazov. Once considered criminal
> psychopaths, both characters were now ac-
> cepted as spokespersons of normality. (160)

This speculation, too, fails to explain the unknowable motive.

The novelist was aware as he worked that Anthony had something in common with another of his characters, Theron Hunnicutt, who has a similar obsessive personality, with high demands and extreme idealism (Anthony was an environmentalist). The Oedipal triangle is certainly present in *Home from the Hill*: Hannah is entirely consumed by her love for her son, and the son eventually turns against the father when he realizes that his father has repeatedly betrayed his mother. Humphrey is particularly interested in the bizarre turns the "family romance" can take; but the unhappiness of the family does not seem a sufficient cause for Anthony's death.

Curtis's hallucinations are central to the novel. The book is haunted, especially by memories of Anthony, the dead son. Very early the novelist establishes the importance of certain images. When Curtis buys his fishing license at the store operated by the Kelly brothers, who are twins, they are shocked (and in a double image) to see how much he has changed in a year. They are "aghast," a word which we are told comes from the experience of seeing a ghost. The concluding paragraph of the passage is clearly foreshadowing but still a bit mysterious:

They could not know this, but the Kellys were

as much of a shock to him as he was to them.
There had been a time—the very time he was
here now to try to forget—when everybody
was twins to him, and, before that, a time
when he himself was. (6)

Later at the club, he feels estranged from himself
when he sees similar reactions of others to his
changed state: "He often caught such glimpses of
himself, as though he had stepped outside his body
and saw it with eyes other than his own" (19). And,
most ominously, when he catches a trout, he sees his
reflection in the water "blurred and indistinct at first,
sharpened as he neared it. It was as if a corpse,
drowned and bleached, was surfacing—his corpse"
(48).

Such passages establish a pattern of symbolism
that conveys what has happened to the character. The
symbols include double vision, twinship, mirror images, and the perception of himself as a ghost. There
are also allusions to *The Picture of Dorian Gray*, Os-
car Wilde's novel in which a character's twin is his
mysterious portrait. Humphrey is drawing on the
doppelgänger tradition in literature, as his notebook
makes clear. The *doppelgänger*, or double, has been a
major figure in German literature since Jean Paul's
novels of the eighteenth century, but it is also common in English literature (Dickens's *A Tale of Two*

Cities and Conrad's "The Secret Sharer"), and in American literature (in Poe's "William Wilson" as well as in works by Hawthorne and Melville). Dostoyevsky's *The Double* makes extraordinary use of it. The device of giving the protagonist a double is an excellent means for depicting a divided state of mind, and psychoanalytic studies of the *doppelgänger* theme have thrived since Otto Rank's classic study, *The Double*, a work tracing the figure in literature and anthropology. Conrad and Dostoyevsky are favorites of Humphrey's and he would have admired the skill with which they use the device to reveal the inner life. He does not indicate what he had been reading, but likely sources are Rank's study, with its anthropological chapter, and Ralph Tymms's pioneering work *Doubles in Literary Psychology*. Both of these works look closely at *The Picture of Dorian Gray*, a work that Humphrey alludes to frequently. In 1966 the novelist and critic (of Hardy), Albert Guerard, published an anthology, *Stories of the Double*, with a useful introduction and bibliographical footnotes.

Humphrey's notebook does not reveal what works he read for background on the theme, but it is clear that he did read some:

> The theme of the *doppelgänger* (an "Arch-romantic theme," according to Thomas Mann). A poltergeist in the house, which may

be that of Anthony, insidiously leading him
to death—showing him the way—or may be
his own double. Gothic—a house haunted by
your own self. What you will leave behind
when you are dead, urging you to hurry &
bring it to birth.

The split personality. Projection of the father into the son. Nothing supernatural
about it.

It is when we are all alone that we split in
two. A partner in life to share yourself is the
one thing to keep you whole.

In the *doppelgänger* literature and folklore is the double always malevolent toward
his host? (23 March 1977)

A passage likes this clarifies Curtis's breakdown experience after his wife leaves him. The *doppelgänger*
is almost always malevolent (Conrad's "The Secret
Sharer" is an exception). Curtis has perceived
Anthony's ghost even before Catherine's departure.
As Humphrey says in his notebook: "Haunted? Of
course. What family in which a son has committed
suicide does not live in a haunted house? Ghosts: it's
merely another name for memory." This is a very
Hardyesque view of ghosts. After a while the ghost
Curtis sees is himself. The reader is not asked to believe in the supernatural: mental disintegration and

drink are the explanation, as the notebook says: "Drink will have its share in this. When drunk one sees double. The brain is fuddled. One talks to oneself. And drink is a method of suicide."

The second part of the novel describes the breakdown. Alone in a house haunted by memories, Curtis becomes steadily more disoriented. He loses his glasses for the first time, leaving his vision distorted. When he finally peers into a mirror at close range, he feels like Dorian Gray looking at his portrait: the face returned is lifeless, its hair and beard tangled. Finally he has a vivid and threatening hallucination, but discovers that the figure which has come to fetch him to death is himself, not, as he had thought, his son. This is a turn comparable to the discovery made by Oedipus: that the murderer he seeks is Oedipus. Curtis begins as an Oedipus seeking his son's motive for the crime of self-murder; now he has learned that he himself has persistently been generating a motive for suicide.

He attempts death by an overdose but chooses to do so in the city, and he is discovered and resuscitated. The return to consciousness by stages begins with him in a state of apparent blindness: his eyelids are temporarily paralyzed. And when he does begin to see, one side-effect of the experience is a period when he sees everything double, so that he is surrounded in the hospital by people who appear to be twins dressed in white, an ironic echo of the ghost imagery, as these are savers-of-life, not malevolent ghosts.

The life has been saved, in the literal sense, but the question remaining is, what kind of life will the character live, after such losses? He has taken a first step, and one with some physical peril: he is allergic to bee stings, so the fishing trip offers physical perils as well as the emotional one of reviving old memories of happier times. Early in the planning of the novel Humphrey felt that an encounter with a sympathetic person would be useful:

> Chekhov's story "Grief" is the last word on a father losing his son and having no one to tell his sorrow to until finally he disburdens himself to his horse. I mustn't echo it. Yet I want to show my man close-up during the time he waits in Boston for his boy's body to be cremated. Some encounter with somebody. And on the road carrying the ashes to the burial ground.

But such an event would be too soon in the novel; grief has not yet had its full effect. The novelist found it more effective to use the burial scene in a grotesque way. Curtis has decided to bury his son's ashes on the grounds of his old prep school, and he does this without consulting the wife who has already left him. He recites the text that he believes his son would have wanted: Job's curse against life. (We should recall Humphrey's fondness for the darker parts of the Old Testament.) Although he has the permission of the headmaster to bury the ashes, he does it so stealthily that he is arrested as a suspicious character and forced to dig them up again, a touch of grotesque comedy in this dark novel.

The person he does meet in the novel is his fellow club member, Ken Howard, who clearly seeks him out to have lunch with him on the stream bank. At first Humphrey was unsure about the significance of this meeting, confiding to his notebook, "Either I am getting too little out of this episode or I am trying to get too much." Actually, he got exactly what he—or rather, his character—needed. Howard, unlike everyone else since Anthony's death, acknowledges the boy's existence. Anthony had a successful business tying flies, and Howard, who has caught a large trout with one of them, takes a drink from a flask and says, "To the memory of the fine boy who tied the fly that fooled the fish." Curtis's response is first to weep, then to say: "Thank you for that. Most people think they're doing you a favor not to mention him. It gets to seem as though you never had a son" (115).

Howard's insistence on raising the subject of the dead son arises from his own loss, his father's inexplicable death by suicide. Curtis has found someone else who has been haunted by such an act. If a son's suicide seems to deny the value of the gift of life, the suicide of a father seems to negate a son's existence. In both cases an ax has been taken to the root of life. But the conversation—a repudiation of the club's shallow motto, "Thumbs up," is cathartic for Curtis. He has found his true double: consider their similar names, Ben Curtis, Ken Howard. Both men have a deep experience of being told "thumbs down" by someone very close. Curtis has some chance of a modest affirmation of life.

The conclusion of Leslie Farber's essay, "Despair and the Life of Suicide" suggests that such affirmations are possible:

> But it is a redeeming paradox of the life of suicide that it does not always—and need not—make its exit from life via the trapdoor. The despairing man can return to life—alive. Many have done so, and some have left their accounts of that treacherous passage to remind us that salvation is never wholly out of reach, even in the farthest country of despair. (83)

In a restrained and paradoxical ending, Humphrey achieves a modest salvation. Curtis awakens from a

long nap—the Hudson is Rip Van Winkle country—
with such a start that he fears a bee has stung him.
He appreciates the irony of this: a man who wanted
to kill himself is now afraid of an insect bite. But that
fear shows some commitment to life. He has a new
conception of himself:

> An odd conception it was, and even odder was
> the fact that it should be not only not trou-
> bling but rather soothing. It struck him that
> his life was like a child contested in a divorce.
> Both his old contending selves had been
> judged unfit and the court had awarded cus-
> tody to a guardian with responsibility for the
> infant's welfare. He was now that guardian.
> Not even in the days when his hostile halves
> were warring had he felt more detached from
> himself, but now there was no sense of fric-
> tion, rather there was the sense that deci-
> sions were out of his hands. Things were as
> they were and what would be would be and
> the end would come when it came. He would
> just keep rolling along till the Judgment Day.
> (222)

He resumes fishing. The mayflies are active:
creatures that live for only a day, a rather natural
image for the evanescence of life. The fly fisherman

simulates this brief life with a lure that a trout may respond to. Curtis hooks a large trout and struggles successfully to land it. He thinks for a moment of releasing it, then, oddly enough, chooses life for himself in a way by killing it. By bringing back an impressive fish he will gain the approbation of the club, as much for their sake as his own. He has feared becoming a "sacred monster" like Oedipus:

> He changed his mind because into it had come thoughts of the moment on the clubhouse porch when everybody laid out his day's catch. If he appeared there with nothing they would all feel sorry for him, and God knew, people were tired of having to feel sorry for him. But if he brought in today's finest fish—and it was unlikely that anybody had caught a finer one than his—it would seem that he was proud of himself and pleased with his day. Nobody would envy him his luck. They would all be relieved. They would congratulate him and want to stand him a drink. At supper Eddie would serve the fish to some party with his compliments and from across the dining room they would gesture with thumbs up and he would respond in kind. Then it would seem to all that he had really rejoined the club. (227)

This is a measured conclusion. It takes the measure of the club and its code, for one thing. And the final "seemed" measures the limits of the final affirmation of life, the most that this Oedipus can attain.

Once the novel was in the hands of his publisher, it met with some resistance for the heavy use of poetry quotations. Along with flashbacks, Curtis has a habit of quoting poetry to himself, and the book is studded with allusions that range from single lines and phrases to entire stanzas from Hardy and Housman. His editor at Delacorte, Jackie Farber, was troubled by the abundance of them and made suggestions for cutting some of them. The most interesting exchanges were about Frost and Eliot. There is a quotation from Frost's "Two Tramps in Mudtime":

> But yield who will to their separation
> My object in living is to unite
> My avocation and my vocation
> As my two eyes make one in sight.

Humphrey responded to a proposal that he cut this quotation by echoing Melville's great review of Hawthorne: "No in thunder. The symbol of split vision is fundamental to the book." What appeared a casual quotation was in fact a *leitmotif*. Farber also questioned a passage quoting Eliot, concerned that the tone would be taken as patronizing. Humphrey replied with contempt for Eliot: "I don't mind in the least being patronizing to T. S. Eliot. He was much worse than that to his better, the above-mentioned Thomas Hardy."

Curtis's allusions help to establish him as a bookish character, and one drawn to poems that stick in the memory for their rhythm and rhyme as much as for their literary qualities. Along with grim commentaries by Hardy and Housman and Shakespeare, he recalls sentimental poems of loss like Thomas Hood's "Oft in the Stilly Night," and Charles Lamb's "Old Familiar Faces." He acquired the quoting habit from Tony Thayer, who suggested that they quote poems when duck-hunting, a pleasant diversion while sitting all day in a duck blind. The longest quotations are from Sir Walter Scott's "Hunting Song," which Tony Thayer liked to recite to wake up house guests, and William Cullen Bryant's schoolroom classic, "To a Waterfowl." After his losses, Curtis seems most fond of works of despair like Hardy's "I Look into My Glass," in which the speaker wishes that his heart had wasted away like his face. The allusion supports the *doppelgänger* motif effectively. Any well-read person would recognize many of the allusions immediately, and if curious could find nearly all of the other quotations in Granger's Poetry Index.

Some of Farber's other editorial queries have

bearings on the novel. She wondered why Curtis did not question whether or not his son had discussed suicide with Christy Thayer, the young woman who leaped to her death. Humphrey's reply addresses two matters:

> This goes to the same thing as, for example, your wanting some sort of final rupture scene between Ben & Cathy. Yes. You could follow out all these matters, but you'd have a different sort of novel from the one I aimed at. A lot longer, with a lot more loose ends tied up, more realistic—maybe even better—but not mine. Mine is about Ben Curtis. He couldn't possibly know whether his son & his goddaughter had ever discussed suicide.

Humphrey wanted a very narrow focus, something which gives the novel its purgatorial power, but also makes it harrowing to read. The lack of a confrontation scene between Catherine and Ben gives us a sense of his estrangement from human contact—he lets her drift away. But it also prevents us from learning what she has been thinking and feeling. In his *Hostages to Fortune* notebook, Humphrey worried about making Catherine a real enough character and about making the husband-wife relationship sufficiently dramatic. The sketchiness of Catherine is a

serious limitation of the novel. The lack of drama in
the marriage reveals a more important habit of mind
in Curtis than his abundant quotations from poetry.

The novel was not a success. It certainly lacked
the Texas exoticism of the previous books, and it is a
painful experience to read. Humphrey compared it in
his notebook to Hardy's *The Mayor of Casterbridge*
as a work which flows out of one event: the sale of
Henchard's wife in Hardy's book, the death of Anthony
in Humphrey's. Both books are relentlessly dark almost to the end, though Humphrey permits his hero
to find a limited peace denied to Henchard, who never
fully understands his fate. The novel was so sparsely
reviewed that his friend, Nick Lyons, sent letters to
at least sixteen reviewers and publications lamenting that it was being ignored, an act similar to Ian
Parsons's letter to *The Bookseller* about *Farther Off
from Heaven*.

The bleakness of the work, which even Hardy
might find excessive, must have contributed to its
paucity of notices. The unsigned one in the influential reviewing journal, *Kirkus Reviews*, was very accurate:

> Humphrey . . . doesn't allow Ben to probe
> deeply enough to shed much light on the trio
> of suicides here: there's a great deal of salt-
> in-wound repetition—and no real drama—

> along the way to Ben's emergence from his
> understandably acute depression. Yet the sin-
> cerity and restrained grace of Humphrey's
> mournful prose make this a gravely emphatic
> evocation of sheer misery: depressing, mono-
> tonic, but steady and authentic. (642)

Such comments would not make many people want
to read the book. And those who read it must surely
be irritated by the constant use of rhetorical questions.

An amusing mishap occurred in the preparation
of the dust jacket for Secker and Warburg's English
edition. The firm arranged for an American photographer to take a picture of a trout fishing fly of the
sort used in New York fishing lodges. After the dust
jacket was ready, Humphrey's editor discovered that
the fly was in fact a salmon fly, and worse, that it was
double-hooked, something illegal in the United States.
The editor, Barley Alison, claimed to have fainted
when he was told of the mistake by Humphrey's English agent, Toby Eady.

The work has received little attention. Mark
Royden Winchell is an exception. He has been hard
on Humphrey's earlier fiction, but his view of this
novel is quite different: "In *Hostages to Fortune* he
has finally earned his vision and found a voice dis-
tinctively his own" ("Beyond Regionalism" 292).

Winchell admires the narrow focus, through which he thinks Humphrey "achieves a unity and intensity that his other novels lack" ("Beyond Regionalism" 291). In his pamphlet on Humphrey, he suggests that the novel "is Humphrey's most accomplished book because it represents the first time in his fiction that he gains control of his materials without the semblance of manipulation" (*William Humphrey* 42). He does see some flaws: "Some readers may find the probing of Ben's psyche too discursive, and none is likely to find the character of his wife Cathy particularly memorable" (*William Humphrey* 41).

He also suggests that to some extent the influence of Hemingway has been substituted for that of Faulkner, though he finds the references unobtrusive (*William Humphrey* 42). In the great story, "Big Two-Hearted River," Hemingway's Nick Adams seeks solace from a profound trauma in fishing, but Hemingway was proud of writing a story about the war without mentioning the war, while Humphrey's protagonist can think of nothing but the insoluble riddle of his son's death. The styles of the two authors are hardly similar.

Humphrey strove to avoid writing the same sort of novel over and over. He moved from a southern tragedy in *Home from the Hill* to a picaresque narrative in *The Ordways* to a work with mythical underpinnings in *Proud Flesh*. In *Hostages to Fortune* he made his most radical departure yet, writing a psychological novel with no southern qualities at all. The change did not regain the readership he lost with *Proud Flesh*: it is too relentless in its probing of despair. Curtis suffers as much as Thomas Hardy's Henchard, without bringing it on himself. Unlike Henchard, he is not destroyed, but he comes very close, and the endless convalescence ("in recovery" is our trendy term) Curtis has in front of him is perhaps less cathartic than death itself would have been. *Hostages to Fortune* is a powerful book. It deserves readers, but it will never be popular.

9

This Sporting Life:

Open Season

In 1985, the year after *Hostages to Fortune*, Seymour Lawrence published *The Collected Stories of William Humphrey*. The volume reprinted *The Last Husband* and *A Time and a Place*, with two additional stories sandwiched between them. The two new stories are clearly placed before *A Time and a Place* to preserve that book's wholeness and impact, but they were written last. The collection received some respectful reviews, mostly in reviewing journals pitched at libraries. Janet Lundquist Black, writing in *The Wilson Library Bulletin*, described Humphrey as a "mythopoetic artist" and praised his imagery (71), and a notice in *The*

Virginia Quarterly Review said, acutely, that desperation was his "great theme," an observation that certainly fits many of the stories.

"Dolce Far' Niente" is a good and understated story. Humphrey has explained the genesis of the work in "Why Do I Write Fiction?" The story was based on comments made by an Italian neighbor about her life. Humphrey was interested in the fact that "a long life could be summed up in so few words" (187). In fact, it sums up two lives very briefly. The focus is the retirement dinner of Giorgio Donati, an immigrant carpenter who drifted into making coffins from scrap lumber. The dinner is an excellent focus for the story of Donati and his wife, Gina. They both remember the past, the frustrations of making a new life in America, the complications of the partial loss of one language and the acquisition of a new one as they raised a family and built a business. The farm sale in "The Hardys" served a similar purpose. Gina feels estranged from her language and her American-born children. Humphrey ends the story with his customary irony by telling us that in the boredom of retirement the coffin-maker has started making little boxes out of scrap lumber. The title, which means "It's sweet to be doing nothing," is clearly ironic: Giorgio will be working for the rest of his life, keeping his hands busy. The story shows Humphrey's ability to portray a social group very different from his usual Texas farmers and townsmen.

A more powerful story is "The Patience of a Saint." In this one the title itself turns out to be ironic. The setting is rural New York, along the Hudson River. There is a first person narrator, a rarity in Humphrey's work, but the focus of the story is on Ernest van Voorhees and his mother. Van Vorhees is not at all bright and works as a gardener and handyman to support the mother who lives with him in a trailer. He is, the narrator says, a "non-smoker, nondrinker, non-gambler, non-women chaser—a noneverything was Ernest van Voorhees: a model of the negative virtues" (184). He is admired and pitied for his devotion to his difficult mother. When they both come down with pneumonia he refuses medical treatment until it is too late to save the mother. Although the ground is frozen, he insists that she be buried immediately, an expensive request that everyone in the area admires as another example of his filial piety. But eventually the narrator learns from Ernest that he had in fact planned his mother's demise, risking death himself by refusing medical assistance for so long. The implication is that the immediate burial may be to be forestall an autopsy. Ernest resumes an activity that his senile mother had made impossible, bridge at the Grange Hall, and he even starts going to the bar.

The story appears to be a circumstantial sketch

of a local character, but it is carefully constructed with casual details that open up in the light of the ending: Ernest's skill at bridge, for example, implies that he is shrewder than his public reputation implies. The compassion of the cleaning woman, Giuseppina, who has expressed pity for Ernest early in the story, heightens the irony of the ending as she says—for the whole community—"He may not be quite all there, as they say, but he has feelings the same as anybody else and he's a brave soul to carry on as he does all alone in this terrible cruel world with nothing else to live for" (195). Humphrey has provided a means for a knowing exchange of ironic glances between narrator and reader. The narrator has no part in the plot, but his observations are essential. Humphrey makes ironic use of his interest in the Greek myths, patterns that he loves, in a passage stressing that the myths are pitched on a higher level than the banal story of Ernest and his mother.

I thought of Oedipus the King, of his horrendous self-punishment for his awful crimes, of Prince Orestes and the bloodthirsty Furies that pursued him. Or, rather, I tried to think of them but in their larger than life size, their exalted station, their superhuman suffering, those legendary figures eluded me. Unlike those of Oedipus, Ernest's bright blue eyes, still in their sockets, shone with the innocence of a child. Sister-sufferers though they were, I could not here in this tiny tin trailer with its color TV and its La-Z-Boy recliner, equate Clytemnestra and old lady van Voorhees. The high-flown word parricide that had entered so clamorously through the open door of my mind, finding itself woefully out of place, slunk quietly out the back. My brain spun, but not with horror and shock, but because it was all so down to earth. (194)

In the same year that *Collected Stories* appeared, Humphrey applied for a job at Louisiana State University, as head of the MFA program. He changed his mind, and his withdrawal from candidacy was regretfully acknowledged by Daniel Fogel in a letter dated 28 May 1985. He never returned to academic life.

In the following year, 1986, Seymour Lawrence brought out *Open Season: Sporting Adventures*. These pieces had appeared in periodicals ranging from *Sports Illustrated* and *True to Life* to *Town and Country*. "The Spawning Run" appeared in *Esquire* and "My Moby Dick" in *Sports Illustrated* before they came out as small books. The subtitle is useful: Humphrey writes excellent prose, and most of the narratives are too distinguished to be called "articles" or journalism, and the fashionable term, "creative non-fiction," is too ponderous. They are personal essays dealing with hunting or fishing, which makes them a little different from the nature writing so popular among essayists.

Critics have shown some uncertainty about these pieces. Mark Royden Winchell is one who seems to think them really important, seeing a "high degree of artistry" in them (*William Humphrey* 34). In his bibliography of Humphrey, Martin Kich concludes his brief introduction by saying, "I would particularly invite an examination of his fishing narratives that does not treat them as diversions from his novels, however interesting as diversions they might be found to be" (711). We don't generally think of fishing stories as enduring literature, but Humphrey admired the great exception, Isaak Walton, whose *The Compleat Angler* is the book most often reprinted in English, after the Bible and the Book of Common Prayer. Like Walton, he presents fishing stories that are more than sporting exploits or technical manuals. Both writers range freely in the manner of good familiar essayists, in the tradition of Montaigne pursuing all kinds of topics, alluding to history and poetry, and creating humor—sometimes self-deprecating humor. The humorous presentation of the persona is very important. Fishermen traditionally brag; as a Texan and a fisherman, Humphrey would be particularly sensitive on the subject of boasting. In an appreciative review, James Kilgo says:

> The actual literary genre of pieces like
> these has never found a satisfactory name.
> At least as old as William Elliott's *Carolina
> Sports by Land and Water* (1846), the form
> remains too reflective to be called anecdote,
> too given to narrative to be labeled personal
> essay. (Humphrey's subtitle shrewdly dodges
> the problem, calling his volume "sporting
> adventures.") Whatever their final classifi-
> cation, however, there can be no question that
> these are extremely well-crafted and engag-
> ing pieces of writing. (1051)

Whatever the genre—and the familiar essay is the
closest category—their merit is considerable.

His most amusing work is "The Salmon Run." In
a letter to Seymour Lawrence (20 June 1970) he said:

> Hope you saw my long essay on the sex
> life of salmon and salmon fishermen in the
> June *Esquire*. It's to be brought out as a book
> here and in England in the fall, and I'm get-
> ting inquiries about the film rights. Had more
> fun writing it than I ever had doing anything
> in my life. Hope it amuses you.

The work blends natural history about the life cycle of the salmon with an account of travel in pursuit of both trout and salmon in England and Wales. There is no easy term for the genre, but the method is that of a *New Yorker* article: the personal essay replete with information. We learn a great deal about salmon, but we also learn about persons and places, both of which are described with the skill of a novelist.

The work is cast as a diary, which enables Humphrey to use devices like suspense and foreshadowing, while keeping the illusion of verisimilitude: events seem to be just unfolding naturally. The device also works well to present a series of brief notations on British life, especially on the class system, which Humphrey describes through dialogue and character sketches, like his portrait of the surgeon, Mr. M., who takes the writer fishing one afternoon and relates the story of his life as a member of the professional classes who worked in Kenya. Early on, Humphrey describes a talk with fishermen in the public bar, The Pure Drop, in Dorset. He tells us by quoting a pamphlet on fishing that there are three kinds of fishing in Britain, and they correlate with class: game, sea, and coarse; "Read: upper, middle and lower." The men in the pub are coarse fishermen, and when he mentions trout, the reaction is quick: "Bill Turner, speaking for them all, says, 'Trout, is it? Ah, well, I wouldn't know, not being a toff meself'" (53).

Trout in Dorset are the reserve of those who can afford fishing rights, like the wealthy meat-pie king, Mr. "Porky" Mitchell, who sublets parts of his fishing stream to people like Mr. M. The identification of Mitchell with his pork pies gently suggests that he is an upstart plutocrat, not worthy of much respect.

The most amusing anecdote in the Dorset section of the work is the encounter with a parking lot attendant who had once been a driver for Mr. Hardy. Humphrey's love for Hardy immediately draws him into conversation, but it turns out that Mr. Hardy was Henry, the novelist's brother, not Thomas. The theme of the American innocent abroad is touched on very lightly in such passages. Humphrey presents himself as the bemused and amused observer who tries to learn the ways of the locals and manages to be witty about their snobberies and yet sympathetic.

The work moves to Wales via Ross-on-Wye, and at that first stop Humphrey occupies himself not with sketches of the people but with information about the salmon that he hopes to catch. His chief source is Professor Jones, author of *The Salmon* — the full name of the authority is John William Jones, appropriately a Welsh name. Humphrey's strategy is to introduce the complete life cycle of the salmon into his book, to inform the reader, but piecemeal, to avoid boring the reader. The author and his wife go to a posh hotel in Wales, which he calls The Redd, after the term for a

salmon's nest. There they park their Volkswagen between two Bentleys, which emphasizes that they are
not upper-class British. One of the peacocks that roam
the grounds pecks at himself in the bright hubcaps of
a Bentley, but scorns the little vehicle of the American tourists.

Those peacocks caused some anxiety at
Humphrey's English publisher, Chatto & Windus, a
bit of comedy worthy of inclusion in the book itself.
British laws of libel are much stricter than American
ones, and the editors worried that the peacocks would
identify the hotel and might lead to a lawsuit. So an
editor decided that the peacocks would have to be
replaced by another fowl, the guinea-hen, and made
inquiries about whether the substitute bird might
scream at night, as the book required. It does scream
nocturnally, and the substitution was made, but a
guinea-hen is not so amusing an image as a narcis-
sistic peacock.

The Humphreys enter a world of eccentrics and
fishing fanatics, like the old gentleman seen by Dorothy Humphrey in the act of banging a barometer on
the wall, who then complains that "They won't be biting tomorrow" (66). The narrator himself encounters
a woman in the garden who has a smoldering look,
but not for him. He then describes the nuptial flight
of mayflies, to increase the aura of sexuality. A little
later, accompanied by his wife, he takes his fishing

tackle and heads to a big pool to fish. However, the path is blocked by a startling sight: the smoldering woman and a man are copulating against the gate, standing up, fully-clothed, and in broad daylight. The *carpe diem* complexities are considerable: the fish will rise to snap at mayflies only as the brief mating ritual of the insects continues, but the way to the pool is barred by a couple engaged in a remarkably long ritual of their own. Finally, the lust for fishing overcomes Humphrey and he and his wife squeeze through the gate without disturbing the preoccupied man. In a brilliant touch, the woman opens her eyes just as the narrator comes close and simply smiles at him.

The male in this ritual is Holloway, known to the fishing set as "poor Holloway" because he has fished all over the British Isles and never caught a salmon, but as the cliché puts it, he has had other fish to fry. In an echo of Milton's "he for God only, she for God in him," Humphrey says "the salmon for the gentlemen, he for salmon widows" (71). At dinner the Americans meet the old man who was first seen banging the barometer: he is Admiral Blakey, who has been coming to The Redd for forty-two years. We learn that his wife responds to that claim with a smile that "looks forty-two years old" (73). The Admiral expresses pity for poor Holloway, who has fished the Usk, the Wye, and the Severn for twenty years with no success. Humphrey delights in giving the Admiral double-entendres: he says that Holloway "can't handle his rod," that he "never knows where his fly will light." But we know in a winking complicity with the narrator that Holloway handles his rod very well and that he casts his fly in many pools. Salmon, too, are cuckolded: a mature salmon male may have his chance for immortality stolen from him by an insolent young parr who darts in with his milt after the female sheds her 900 or so eggs into the water.

Dinner is salmon, through the generosity of Major Butler (this is a world of Admirals and Majors), who caught a twenty-seven pound cock salmon. But unfortunately the salmon is the victim of British cooking: poached in milk, it tastes like poached milk. After the diners retire, Humphrey breaks off a journal entry to say that he's heard the sound of a woman being murdered, a screaming repeated for much of the night. But the next morning no one mentions this sound, which the reader might associate with a human sex act. It turns out some pages later to be the scream of a peahen: sexuality yes, human no. Salmon are caught when they come upstream to spawn, peacocks mate loudly: sex seems everywhere, but on the human scene the enthusiasm is all for fishing, except for Holloway and the neglected wives of the fishermen.

A fishing story is incomplete without a story of a big fish; whether it is caught or not seems irrelevant.

Humphrey treats the reader to a long account of his struggle to land a big one, one that in fact gets away through a broken line. With that, he is ready to wrap up the account, giving readers a last glimpse of Holloway teaching a neglected young wife to fish, an activity that we are assured "was how Antony and Cleopatra also whiled away their leisure moments." We know from the narrative that some women return to the hotel even after their fishermen husbands have died, ostensibly for sentimental reasons but doubtlessly to see Holloway. Humphrey concludes with a droll passage that juxtaposes decrepit male salmon with their hardy widows, who can return to spawn repeatedly.

The other major piece in *Open Season* is "My Moby Dick," which first appeared as a small book in New York, published as a Nick Lyons Book by Doubleday in 1978. Lyons was Humphrey's student at Bard and a fellow fly-fishing devotee. He sometimes served as Humphrey's agent in placing sporting stories in magazines. The work was immediately reprinted in London by Chatto and Windus and issued in paperback the next year by Penguin. Ten years later, in an entry in one of his *September Song* diaries (21 July 1988), Humphrey recorded the sale of an excerpt to *Reader's Digest* with some puzzlement: "Counting the French version this is probably the eighth appearance of that little piece. It is not as good as *The Spawning Run*, and not as well liked by the public, yet it's been more popular. Odd!" The success of the piece is not odd at all: it is humorous, though not with the uproarious sexual comedy of the earlier work. It is a fishing story that those who do not fish can enjoy, for it takes readers into the obsessive world of the fly-fisherman without the snobbish in-group feeling of aficionado literature: Humphrey avoids the kind of condescending tone that mars Hemingway's book about bullfighting, *Death in the Afternoon*. It also ranges through classic American literature and makes an ecological point.

Humphrey uses a passage from Thoreau's *Walden* ("Time is but the stream I go a-fishing in") as the epigraph to *Open Season*. Like Thoreau, he manages to move rather far in space and time while situating his work beside a small stream, Shadow Brook, near Tanglewood, Massachusetts. Humphrey had been living in the area the winter before the narrative begins: he was teaching at Smith College and deepening his familiarity with American literature, he tells us. This particular brook, a branch of the Housatonic, is rich in associations, for it is a place where Hawthorne's family spent happy hours.

In the summer of 1850, the Hawthorne family met Herman Melville, who was brooding over *Moby-Dick*. The writing of the work was stimulated by the encounter with Hawthorne and his writing: one of the most famous reviews in American literature is "Hawthorne and His Mosses," written not long after they met. The review has the famous line, "No! in thunder," which Humphrey quoted to an editor who wanted to remove some allusions from *Hostages to Fortune*. The opening of *Moby-Dick* is more famous than the review, of course:

> Call me Ishmael. Some years ago—never mind how long precisely—having little or no money in my purse, and nothing particular to interest me on shore, I thought I would sail about a little and see the watery part of the world. It is a way I have of driving off the spleen, and regulating the circulation. Whenever I find myself growing grim about the mouth; whenever it is a damp, drizzly November in my soul; whenever I find myself involuntarily pausing before coffin warehouses, and bringing up the rear of every funeral I meet; and especially whenever my hypos get such an upper hand of me, that it requires a strong moral principle to prevent me from deliberately stepping into the street and methodically knocking people's hats off—then, I account it high time to get to sea as soon as I can.

My Moby Dick opens:

> Call me Bill. Some years ago—never mind
> how long precisely—I thought I would go fish-
> ing. It is a way I have of driving away the
> spleen, and after a winter spent in the Berk-
> shire Mountains of Massachusetts, I had a
> whale of a swollen spleen. Whenever this
> happens—whenever I find myself snarling at
> little children; whenever I stop being grate-
> ful that my bottle is half full and start grum-
> bling that it is half empty; whenever I get to
> thinking of committing myself to a mental
> institution like the handy one there in
> Stockbridge—then I account it high time to
> go fishing as soon as I can, as soon as the
> season opens, if it ever does. The poet who
> wrote, "If winter comes, can spring be far
> behind?" had never spent a winter waiting
> for spring to come to the Berkshires. (3)

The work is not a parody throughout, but the tone
has been set: playful, allusive, conscious of epic predecessors through the device of mock epic. Walton's
great *Compleat Angler* is a work filled with diverting
allusions to the classics and quotations from writers
like Donne and Wotton. Walton's book is often praised
as being quintessentially English. Humphrey's work

is quintessentially American in its setting, its ecological concerns, and its literary references to Melville, Hawthorne, and Whitman.

Along with *Moby-Dick*, he brings in one of Melville's most interesting tales for its ecological implications. In "The Tartarus of Maids" Melville presented a horrifying and surreal account of a paper mill and the pollution it caused by dumping effluent into "the Blood River," a river that Humphrey says was modeled on the Housatonic. The reason that the twentieth-century writer searches out a tributary of the Housatonic is that the main river has become "Shit Creek," a name given to it by a fisherman that he encounters. It has been poisoned by enterprises like the pulp mills at Dalton. Melville was familiar with Dalton: his trip to a paper mill there seems to have inspired "The Tartarus of Maids." Humphrey, like most sportsmen, is aware of the blight caused by pollution. In a letter to Fred and Andy Dupee (2 September 1975) he talks about the successful fight to keep a garbage dump from being built along his road in the Hudson Valley.

Fishing this stream, which has associations with literary giants like Melville and Hawthorne, Humphrey finds a fish of gargantuan proportions living in a pool under a bridge: "I got my binoculars from the car. What they showed me was a trout thirty feet long" (14). But this is mock epic, not the real thing:

the trout is big, but the eight power binoculars have magnified it. Still, at three to four feet long, it is a prodigy. Naturally, he conceives a passion to catch it, though unlike Captain Ahab he has not lost a leg to it. The fish is mutilated: it has only one eye. And the boys fishing under the bridge have been trying to catch it by using fish eyes as bait: the narrator sees bluegills lying on the ground with their eyes gouged out. The boys flee when the narrator approaches, but as the quest for the trout goes on day after day, one of them hovers around, as a kind of mocking commentator on the grownup's fishing strategies. In revulsion against the mutilation of the bluegills, Humphrey, who has been a worm fisherman—very low on the scale of sportsmen—decides that he will use artificial flies as bait.

We are taken through the mysteries of various techniques of fishing in the book: the worm and hook, the spinner, the dry-fly, the wet fly, the nymph. The dry-fly is most difficult to use and least likely to catch a fish, as trout feed on the surface of the water relatively seldom, taking perhaps ten percent of their food there. But that, the author tells us, is the appeal for the dry-fly aficionado: "His is the sport in its purest, most impractical, least material form" (18). Izaak Walton put it nicely in *The Compleat Angler*: "O Sir, doubt not that Angling is an Art; is it not an Art to deceive a Trout with an artificial Flie? a Trout! that is more sharp sighted than any Hawk you have nam'd, and more watchful and timorous than your high mettled Marlin is bold?" (37)

The world of dry-fly fishing is explored through a brief chapter summarizing the narrator's reading on the subject. He consults authors that he refers to as the Entomologist and the Efficiency Expert. The latter suggested that a stream should be approached with a microscope in order to determine what kind of insect larva are hatching at a given moment, so that the right kind of fly can be chosen for that very instant. Walton managed with the traditional twelve flies, one for each month of the year, but today a multitude of flies can be purchased. The proposal to analyze the insects of the stream collapses comically under its own weight, along with the suggestion that the elimination of drag in casting could increase the total fishing time by a week per season, in an unobtainably ideal world. The chapter draws to an end before the uninitiated can get bored. Indeed, the chapter ends with a little parody of Whitman's satire on pedantry, "When I had heard the learn'd astronomer." Whitman concludes his poem about an astronomy lecture:

> How soon unaccountable I became tired and
>   sick,
> Till rising and gliding out I wander'd off by

> myself,
> In the mystical moist night-air, and from time
>   to time,
> Look'd up in perfect silence at the stars.

Humphrey says:

> I, sitting, read the learned entomologist;
> Till rising and gliding out, I wandered off by
>   myself,
> In the mystical moist night air, and from time
>   to time,
> Swatted in perfect ignorance at the bugs. (56)

But the best way to fish, he decides, is to study the fish itself. With its one eye, it cannot detect him spying on it from its blind side. It becomes his supreme teacher, though he observes that he "remained ungrateful," for in his "increasing pride and vainglory" (43) he comes to believe that he can catch it.

Fishing stories end with the fish getting caught or getting away. The author observes that the bigger a fish is, the harder it is to catch: it must be a canny survivor. Furthermore, the fly has to be attached to a long and delicate leader, and a huge fish is likely to break it. And this happens, on the last day of the season, with the curious and jeering little boy watching. The writing is superb, both accurate and fanciful:

"More bird than fish he seemed as he hovered above the water, his spots and spangles patterned like plumage," the narrator says in good alliterative fashion, describing the leaping fish. "I half expected to see his sides unfold and spread in flight, as though, like the insects he fed upon, he had undergone metamorphosis and hatched." The fish breaks the leader with insolent ease, and the one spectator reacts with mockery: "'Dummy!' cried the boy on the bank. 'You had him and you let him get away.'"

William A. Owens thought the work was an allegory of the artist seeking his elusive masterpiece, as he told his fellow Texan in a letter (2 July 1980). The work is probably not so portentous: *Moby-Dick* is certainly about much more than whaling, but sometimes a fish story is about fishing. The epilogue suggests that the narrator's attitude has been changed forever by this particular fish. Walton's persona, the fisherman Piscator, consoles his friend the hunter, Venator, over the loss of a trout by saying, "Nay, the Trout is not lost, for pray take notice no man can lose what he never had." The conclusion of "My Moby Dick" is not so sophistical: the narrator says that he, not the fish, got away, for his attitude toward fishing has changed forever. "I have hooked and lost some big ones . . . but to each I have been able to say. 'Go your way. I have known your better, known him well, and there will never be his like again. You, however big you may be, are a mere minnow compared to my Moby Dick'" (48).

"The Spawning Run" and "My Moby Dick" are Humphrey's best fishing stories, but he has written others which have their own pleasures. A story first published in *Sports Illustrated*, "Bill Breaks His Duck," makes a natural supplement to "The Spawning Run." A reader of that work met Humphrey when he was writer in residence at Princeton in 1982 and invited him to go fishing on the Itchen in Hampshire, Izaak Walton's favorite river, where her husband and his brother-in-law owned the rights along a mile of the river. He also had an invitation to fish for trout on the Test, in the same region. He could hardly refuse. The resulting article is more for initiates than the longer works. But it manages to be an interesting exposition of countries and their distinctive codes as well as a description of fishing experiences. Naturally the tone is not satirical as in "The Spawning Run": a bread-and-butter note must be gracious, and the article is in part an expression of gratitude to generous hosts.

It is cast in the form of letters to friends back in the United States, and goes to some trouble to explore for their benefit the differences between American and British fishing practices. The differences clearly reflect deep differences in attitudes. The British consider wading into the river wrong, "presumably because it would make fishing easier," and it is unsporting to cast until a trout has actually been seen (177). Merely casting into the water over and over, the American practice, is "about like cruising in the dark for a streetwalker" (178). Wet-flies are too easy, and nymphs were not permitted until it became clear that they made fishing more difficult. The British way makes fishing an even more pure and impractical sport than American fly-fishing.

The essay provides some glimpses of the author's wife and gives a pleasant description of Winchester Cathedral, with its monument to Jane Austen and its stained glass windows in the Walton memorial chapel. But the focus is on fishing, and for once Humphrey, who talks about his "dismal record" as a fisherman in one of the letters, catches his fish. However, he thinks he is catching a fair-sized salmon, and only after a fine description of the whole process does he reveal that he has, in fact, caught a trout. So he can have it both ways: he can boast a little about his prowess, and still make mild fun of himself for mistaking the fish. The meaning of the title of the essay is revealed only then, when a new friend of his observes that "Bill has really broken his duck," a cricket phrase meaning that he has scored at last, because a "duck's egg" is a term for zero. He ends the work with a graceful tribute to his new English acquaintances. One of them, Graham Finlayson, became one of the Humphreys' most devoted correspondents.

The success of a fishing trip is never predictable. On behalf of *True* magazine Humphrey made a two-week trip to Ireland in 1972 to fish for salmon, and described it as a disaster; another salmon fishing trip to Scotland in 1977 also ended without success, unless we count an article called "Cast and Cast Again." The trip to Ireland ended, he told Katherine Anne Porter (16 June 1972), with only one salmon caught: a smoked one, courtesy of his hotel.

The trip for *True* to the Bahamas in 1971 had been more successful, resulting in a fine article, "The Rigors of Bonefishing." The bonefish is a peculiar fish, full of biological anomalies, which Humphrey describes very skillfully. It is hard to catch and not very good eating when it is. The real interest in the article is not in the description of the fishing—he has poor luck until the last day—but in the presentation of the setting and the excellent characterization of his guide, an elderly black man named Otto. Humphrey describes himself as a very unlucky fisherman and suggests that something dreadful always happens to him on a fishing trip. On his last day, the motor of the skiff dies and Humphrey finds out just how strong Otto is when it comes his turn to pole the boat. The two men finally take refuge on an island. The author has a plane to catch and fears that he will miss it and have to spend four more days bonefishing. His guide goes to find driftwood for a bonfire to signal searchers. But unfortunately he sets the whole island on fire and the pair has to take to the sea again for safety. And there they find bonefish, an abundance of them, driven from the coastal waters by the smoke and heat!

There is an interesting pair of fishing stories set in France. On 3 November 1975, Humphrey, who was staying in Paris, received a letter from Charles C. Ritz, who had been sent a copy of *The Spawning Run* by Nick Lyons, suggesting that they meet for a drink at his hotel, the celebrated Ritz. Charles of the Ritz, as he was usually known, was not only a famous hotelier who had known many famous writers, he was also a leading fly fisherman. Humphrey soon gave up trying to talk about literary figures with him after Ritz simply described Marcel Proust as a "flyswatter," that is to say, a man whose casting style is poor. The article growing out of the meeting with Ritz (who was in his eighties and died a few months later), "Cast and Cast Again," is much more a portrait of a man that Ritz introduced him to, Pierre Affre, who won the French national fly-casting championship at the age of twenty. This high-strung young perfectionist was someone Humphrey had in mind as a model for the character of Anthony in *Hostages to Fortune*. He rented three salmon boats in Scotland and invited Humphrey along. The American novelist had missed his chance to fish with Ritz, but he felt that this trip was a symbolic way of doing that. The fishing was poor, but the portrait of Affre captures his passion and his consummate skill.

The other article about fishing in France is in fact about fishing in Paris. It appeared in *Town and Country*, which is not a sporting magazine. The work deals with the eccentric and generally scorned men who angle for coarse fish in the Seine. They have long been figures of fun, and Humphrey does present the eccentricities of men like Pierrot le Plombier ("Pete the Plumber") and Paulo le Trépané, who suffered a head wound in the Algerian war. But he also respects them and the portraits have warmth. He particularly admires Albert Drashkovitch, a Yugoslavian who managed to discover a sport fish previously unknown in France, the sandre, or walleye pike, which had entered France via canals in the 1930s. Drashkovitch discovered that the fish were living at the bottom of the Seine and learned how to catch them.

The essay is leisurely and the tone is casual, sometimes dropping into the second person. It offers a tour of Paris as well as a look at some unusual fishermen. One route followed by Humphrey on his peregrinations was "the one taken by the young Hemingway en route from lunch at the Brasserie Lipp to the Closerie des Lilas, there to work on his fishing story, which is only incidentally about fishing, 'Big Two-Hearted River'" (223). In *Hostages to Fortune*, Humphrey wrote his own fishing story that is only

incidentally about fishing. In his article, the concluding section is devoted to Pierre Affre, with whom the
American often went fishing in Paris.

If there is anything a fisherman hates, it is the
destruction of the environment where he fishes. In
1970 Humphrey was asked to write an article about
soil conservation for *Life* and offered two thousand
dollars for it. His first reaction, recorded in a *Proud
Flesh* notebook (7 April 1970), was "Journalists are
nuts." But he did a fine job, going to Alabama with
the photographer Stan Wayman. He wrote Seymour
Lawrence (20 June 1970) that on the way back to New
York, he and Wayman stopped to see Katherine Anne
Porter in a Washington Hospital. It was a sunny day
but he wore a raincoat and smuggled in a bottle of
Virginia Gentleman bourbon. After the three of them
had almost finished it, Porter confided that she had
"a whole case more of the same medicine under her
bed."

The article, "Ditches Are Quicker," examines the
issue of "channelization," a practice promoted by
the Federal Soil Conservation Service to deepen and
regularize rivers to conserve soil and prevent flood-
ing. The article opens by mentioning the Faust story:
"By clearing a swamp in the service of humanity as
his last earthly deed, Goethe's Faust saves his soul
from the Devil to whom he had sold it," an "act of
public land reclamation" (233). The allusion is a good

one: the essayist wishes to challenge the assumption that draining swamps and turning back the sea are always benevolent acts. As a personal essayist, he is free to draw on his own experience as well as literary archetypes, and he draws as easily on the examples of his father and paternal grandfather as on Goethe. His grandfather was a sharecropper who struggled to make a living, an example which inclines the essayist toward the efforts of the Soil Conservation Agency on behalf of farmers. But his father, rebelling against the life of a sharecropper, hated cleared land and cities, preferring swamps, like the familiar Sulphur Bottom that figures so often in Humphrey's work. The efforts of the Agency destroyed the trees and the habitats for wildlife: the engineers see a stream as merely a conduit for water, not as part of the ecosystem. Humphrey's strategy in the essay is to challenge a familiar human ideal with nearly mythical status—the clearing of swamps—while first expressing sympathy with those who would approve, like his grandfather. But the case for preserving genuine rivers is strong: the river reduced to a mere ditch is "lifeless as one of the canals of Mars" (240).

He included a number of hunting stories in *Open Season*, placing them after the fishing pieces. All of them first appeared in *Sports Illustrated*. Two of them, centering on his father, found their way into the third section of *Farther Off from Heaven*: "Guardian

Dragon" (the account of the alligator hunt) and "The Guns of Boyhood." There is another essay based on memories of his father, "The Trick-Shot Artist," a fine variation of the traditional story of the modest local man who can surpass the expert in a shooting competition. It gives a good sketch of life in Clarksville during the Depression, when a trick-shot artist could pack in an audience at the fairground in order to demonstrate the merits of a company's firearms. Humphrey's laconic father outshoots the trick-shot artist, but he does not follow the man's advice to go on the road. Once again, Humphrey's father proves his tremendous skills as a hunter. His twelve-year-old son and a friend try to emulate his ability to hit a coin tossed in the air but eventually young Humphrey gets his thumbnail shot off with an air gun, an episode used in *Proud Flesh* when Lester shoots off Kyle's thumbnail. Humphrey's mother—as a reader of *Farther Off from Heaven* would expect, is dismayed, but the father is proud, assuring his son that he will grow another thumbnail.

> It was black for a long time afterward, a source of mutual embarrassment between my father and me. My new nail was just about fully grown in, only the tip of it still black, when, the following summer, my father died in the wreck of a speeding car.

In the more than forty years since then, I have grown many thumbnails, each of them with the identical dent where that pellet struck. I never rub it out but what it brings back to me these memories. (249)

"Birds of a Feather," an account of woodcock hunting, has some interesting autobiographical touches. The man who invites the author to hunt, Paul de Nemeseri-Kiss, or "Pauli," is someone he met casually at the intermission of *Don Carlo* at the Met. The poor boy from Texas had moved into a very different sphere: his letters contain a number of references to opera, something he and his wife saturated themselves in during their stays in London. Humphrey learns that woodcocks can be found in his area of New York, but he has never seen the elusive birds. Eventually a hunting trip is arranged.

Humphrey had little knowledge of woodcocks, so he had to read up on them, which makes a natural pretext for passing on what he learns to the reader. Most interesting is the set of parallels he draws between the bird and himself, following what he says is common belief that hunters "are attracted to a game species by a similarity of its disposition to their own." The passage is worth quoting in full for the insight it gives into this shy author:

Like the woodcock, I too am an odd bird; I
know I am, and I would change if I could,
because being odd is uncomfortable, but, no
more than the woodcock can, I can't, not any-
more—it's too late even to try. My brain, I
often think, must be upside down, so out of
step with the world am I. Like the woodcock,
I'm a loner. I don't sleep well of nights, either. It's true, I am bigger than my little mate,
but not by much. I don't migrate from south
to north annually, but I did it once, performed
my courtship rites, and settled in the nest.
The kind of terrain said to be favored by the
woodcock is terrain of a kind I favor, too. I
felt drawn to this queer little fellow creature
by everything I had read about him. Birds of
a feather.... For me, there was no contradic-
tion between that and my desire to kill some
of the *L'uomo è cacciatore*. (290–91)

True enough, Humphrey had settled into the isolation
of the Hudson Valley, a terrain where streams and woods
are nearby, threatened as they may be by developers
and pollution. And he had proven as elusive as a woodcock: Vicki Simons, editor of the *Hudson Independent*
told me in an e-note that "while we knew William
Humphrey lived in the area, every time we tried to do
something on him, he ducked us" (25 February 1997).

The essay suggests that its author thinks of himself as a poor shot: he spends a long while target-shooting for the hunt. He is not the hunter that his father was. However, he manages to bag five birds on the first day of hunting, while his experienced companion only gets one. An important element in the story is the forging of a friendship with Pauli: Humphrey worries a bit about that, because "you don't make a friend by badly outshooting a man over his dogs and on his grounds, and you don't inspire trust in your honesty or the uprightness of your character by doing it on what you claim is your first time." But Pauli proves magnanimous, if a bit suspicious. One reason the essay is so successful is that it has so many centers of interest: the social world of the Metropolitan Opera-goer, the bits of natural history, the self-portrait of the author, the descriptions of the wood, the clear description of the rather esoteric technique of wing-shooting, the look at male bonding and its complexities. A good personal essay in the tradition established by Michel de Montaigne—as opposed to mere sports-writing—it ranges freely, revealing the author as well as the subject. He has gone beyond the imitations of Faulknerian nature mysticism in an essay like this: the style does not seem derivative of the Mississippian at all. Nor is he uncomfortably close to Hemingway, whose style has the clarity and lucidity that we find in Humphrey, but seems more

mannered. Those who do not hunt will find the senti-
ments of Humphrey's conclusion a little foreign, but
he makes them understandable:

> By law wild game may not be sold. You
> must either get your own or else you must be
> given it. As a gift from a sportsman friend, it
> tastes good. But nothing else tastes as good
> as game you yourself have gotten. It savors
> of so much more than mere meat. It is food
> for the soul. In it are the sights, the sounds,
> and the smells of a landscape, the weather of
> a day, the companionship of a friend, your
> rapport with the dogs and theirs with each
> other, the moment when their ranging bells
> suddenly fall silent as they freeze on point,
> the memory of the rush of your blood as you
> walk in to make the flush and the heart-stop-
> ping instant when the bird bursts from cover
> and towers, the shot, the puff of feathers on
> the air, and, yes, that ineffable moment com-
> pounded in equal parts of self-satisfaction
> and self-reproach, when the dog brings it to
> you and you hold in your hand the creature
> you both love and love to kill. (301)

The final essay in *Open Season*, appropriately
enough, is a boar hunt. Humphrey's first novel, after

all, has a rather stylized boar hunt, one almost as formal as the hunt in Sir Gawain and the Green Knight. That hunt was imagined, not experienced, but in "Royal Game" he describes a real hunt in modern France, where they organize their hunts, using beaters and squads of hunters. This is not a Hunnicutt style of hunting. The essay incorporates some interesting background information, about the boar in literature and myth, and about the social and political history of the hunt (which was once the exclusive sport of royalty). The hunt itself is meticulously described, and there is much to tell, as it is organized on rather military lines. The author is unarmed—it is too complicated for foreigners to get permission to hunt in France—and he sees actual boars only when they have been killed somewhere out of his sight. But he gets to quote a poem by de Vigny containing a reference to "the hunter's adieu." This is a private reference, as Gallimard published *Home from the Hill* under the title, *L'adieu du chasseur*.

While Humphrey has no chance to perform like a Hunnicutt in the hunt, he does bring the essay to a fine conclusion. The Hunnicutts were royalty, in a southern way, in their tiny town. Humphrey and his wife are given a share of the meat by M. Hatte, the head of the hunt. As they talk with him, the house fills up with the strong scent of the boar. They are skeptical about eating it: the wife wants it thrown out. Its hide is so tough that "you could sole boots with it" (322). But after seven days of aging and two days of marination, they cook it for company and find "the best meat that any of us had tasted."

In a peculiar development, Humphrey's adopted area suddenly had an influx of wild boars in the spring of 1997. The animals apparently escaped from game farms, though whether or not they wandered in from "Loozyanner" is not known. They were sighted in three states, and on 13 May 1997, a boar was shot in the village of Rhinebeck not too far from the Humphrey home at High Meadow.

Most of the essays in the book appeared in sports magazines and other popular publications. The author never wrote down to these audiences, nor did he limit himself to mere descriptions of hunting and fishing. Like Walton before him, he provides information, literary references, and gentle humor (usually self-directed). When discussing his grim outlook with Ashby Crowder, Humphrey warned against "leaving out of consideration my essays on outdoor sports, which, when not comical, are a celebration of some of life's pleasures" (34). Certainly they establish that his vision of life includes more than unhappiness. *Open Season* is a work that should endure, as an achievement in the essay, not merely in sports journalism.

10

History of the Defeated:
No Resting Place

On 13 December 1986, a murder occurred which shocked Hudson, the town near the Humphrey's home at High Meadow. A seventeen-year-old named Wyley Gates notified the police that he had returned home that night and found the bodies of his father, his father's girlfriend, his brother, and his nephew, all shot to death. After an investigation, he was charged with the murders and eventually tried with his friend Damian Rossney. They were finally convicted, not of murder, but of conspiracy to murder Gates's father. In a foreshadowing of the O. J. Simpson case a decade later, they were later found responsible for all four murders in a civil trial brought by the mother of the girlfriend, Cheryl Brahm.

As a novelist Humphrey had dealt with murder and murder trials (admittedly, Sam Ordway is tried for the murder of someone who is not dead), but here was a genuine murder case in his own neighborhood. He kept two notebooks on the case, which was referred to in the papers both as "the Case of the Century" and "a small town murder case." The latter called one of his favorite novels to mind, as he records:

> I'm reminded of the opening words of that (fictional but not altogether so) small-town case of parricide, *The Brothers Karamazov*. Small town it was as regards the bungling of it by the local police. Keystone cops. Deplorable, but like so much that is socially deplorable, good material for fiction, or non-fiction.
>
> It would seem the Parable of the Talents for me to allow an event of such intensity to happen in my back yard and make no comment upon it. I'm told by all the critics that relations between parents and children, especially fathers and sons, is my theme.

Humphrey gathered materials, like the depositions of Wyley Gates, and examined police evidence. While he was an experienced hunter and a man who had written about acts of violence, he found that the police photographs of the crime scene sickened him. He made some experiments of his own with firearms to test theories about the crime. Like the press, he speculated that a game of Dungeons and Dragons might have been involved, but he also thought of the Greek myths about parricide. He became fascinated with the conflict between the concerns of the artist and the citizen. In his notebook he recorded his conversations on the moral position of the writer with his wife and with a defense expert:

> I said to Dorothy the other day. It's a paradoxical thing to be a writer. As a citizen you hope for the best. As a writer for the worst. The best makes life better, the worst is where your material is found. Social injustice, racial injustice are the very stuff of fiction, yet who, as citizen would not wish the alleviation of these ills? I said the same to Prof. Marchione. "If you succeed in proving this to be a case of psychopathology then I've lost a book. I'm interested in rational moral choice eventuating in mass murder. Yet at the same time I hope you prove your case. Let this boy be declared mad [and] save him from condemnation as a rational criminal and life long incarceration in some

place like Ithaca. He doesn't belong there."

Back on 11 March 1966, he had written to Katherine Anne Porter about Truman Capote's *In Cold
Blood*, a "non-fiction novel" about a celebrated murder case. He had not been impressed, feeling that the
characters failed to come alive and that "the fictional
devices were those of Wilkie Collins." Humphrey's
account of the Gates trial would probably not have
maintained the detached tone of Capote's work. Unfortunately, in spite of encouragement from Seymour
Lawrence, who felt that this was an American tragedy and that Humphrey's language would elevate it,
he was unable to finish the project. When I asked
him why in a letter, he simply mentioned his story,
"The Dead Languages," which deals with increasing
deafness, a problem that he himself suffered from.
Journalistic research would have required interviews
and careful attendance at the trial. A deaf man could
not have done it, Humphrey felt.

But there was another project that the novelist
had long been waiting to undertake. By December,
1982, he had been able to send four chapters of the
novel and a prospectus on a book about the Cherokee
Removals of 1838 to the Macmillan Company. He had
submitted some of the material years before to
Seymour Lawrence, who mentioned the Cherokee
novel when turning down "Horse Latitudes" in 1979.

An entry in his *Oresteia* notebook from the time of *Proud Flesh* (1965) states: "Certainly it's my last book based on my mother's family—and shouldn't I take leave of my place and my class with as big a book as I can make it? After this one—if I follow my present plan—I go to Oklahoma, and with the Indians, to my father's heritage." He had dealt with the Varleys through Sam and Hester Ordway. The similarity of the Renshaws to the same tenant farming relatives is a little obscure.

He had been fascinated with his father's Indian ancestry, something discussed in *Farther Off from Heaven,* and treated fictionally in "The Last of the Caddoes." Humphrey, like the boy in the story, had no knowledge of just what tribe his great-grandfather had belonged to. Unlike the boy, he did not choose to identify with the long-vanished Caddoes, but with the Cherokees, one of the five civilized tribes who were deported from the South to the Indian Territory, now known as Oklahoma, in 1838, with heavy loss of life through privation and disease. One route on the "Trail of Tears," the one followed by the Choctaw, ended not far from Clarksville. The Cherokee Removal would give him a chance to deal once again with his favorite theme of injustice, since the Cherokees were treated unjustly by the American government and by the Republic of Texas.

He gathered written materials. In 1978 he wrote

to Herman Gollob at Atheneum with a query about
Marion Starkey's excellent historical narrative of
1946, *The Cherokee Nation*, which had been published
by that company and which would be a major source
for *No Resting Place*. In his reply Gollob mentioned
not having heard of Mirabeau Lamar's crimes against
the Cherokee. Lamar was the second president of the
Republic of Texas, and he would provide a Texas connection for Humphrey's historical novel. There are
other novels on the Cherokee Removal, but Humphrey's is unique in its look at a neglected aspect of
the deportations.

Besides Starkey's book, Humphrey's archive at
the University of Texas mentions a number of other
background readings, ranging from books to brief
newspaper stories. Perhaps the most touching mark
of his research is the dried Cherokee rose that fell
out of a folder when it was opened. The rose had been
sent to Humphrey by one of his correspondents. The
Harry Ransom Center preserves everything: I showed
the flower to a curator, John Kirkpatrick, who took it
away to seal it in plastic and label it.

His sources included Grant Foreman's classic history, *Indian Removal*, with its superb maps. He also
used Jean Louis Berlandier's account of *The Indians
of Texas in 1830*. Berlandier, a French artist and natural historian, as much an ethnographer as a biolo-
gist, was just over twenty when he was hired by the

government of Mexico to lead a scientific expedition into the Texas territory. His account, published for the first time in 1969, offers a fine picture of the tribes living in Texas in 1830. The tribes in Texas included Cherokees who had fled there after a massacre of whites in Tennessee. They were led by their chief, Diwali (or Duwali), also known as "Chief Bowl" and "Colonel Bowles." The final section deals with Diwali's followers and the other tribes allied with them. Two books not mentioned in Humphrey's notes, but likely sources, are Mary Whatley Clarke's *Chief Bowles and the Texas Cherokees*, published in 1971, and Walter Prescott Webb's classic study *The Texas Rangers*, which appeared in 1935. Webb probably provided Humphrey with the historical incident on which the ending of the novel is based.

After writing a novel which scrupulously avoided all mention of Texas, and which had a protagonist from Kansas, Humphrey found himself dealing with Texas again, but not to celebrate it. The central section of the book moves from Georgia to the Indian Territory, now Oklahoma, but the framing story is set in Texas and the last episode of the novel takes place there, not far from the banks of the Red River and in the county named for it. The time is 1936, the centennial of Texas independence, an event to be marked in an unnamed town (which has to be Clarksville, the only sizable town in the county) by a pageant on San

Jacinto Day, April 21, reenacting the battle in which
President Santa Anna of Mexico was defeated, making the independence of Texas possible. The narrator,
a boy named Amos Smith IV, has been chosen to play
the improbably named Mirabeau Buonaparte Lamar,
a private who distinguished himself in the battle and
was made a colonel on the spot by the Texans' general, Sam Houston. Lamar rose quickly in the government of the Republic of Texas and became its
second president.

The pageant and the sketch of Texas history that
accompanies it give Humphrey a chance for his full-
est attack on the Texas myth. The pageant is part of
the indoctrination of students in the glories of their
history, which is a normal part of the education of
children in any society, but in Texas has been carried
rather far. In 1936 Texas erected an enormous obe-
lisk, the San Jacinto Monument, the largest poured
concrete structure yet created, and it was made a little
taller than the Washington Monument, showing the
Texas scale of values. As the narrator of *No Resting
Place* explains:

> It was during that centennial year of 1936
> that the chronic Texas patriotism turned
> acute and reached fever pitch. Indeed, one
> year was not time enough for it to run its
> course, be contained and subside. Both

> Dallas's Centennial Exposition and Fort
> Worth's rival Frontier Days were held over
> through 1937 by popular demand. I was
> taken with my class to both. We were re-
> minded that ours was the only one of the
> states that had been an independent coun-
> try all its own, and that before we were de-
> feated southerners we had been victorious
> Texans. (9)

For the Texas school child, "it was hard to believe that
Texas had begun in 1836; to us it seemed more as
though it had stopped then." Indeed, "in Sunday
school, there was a deliberate confounding of that
exodus led by Moses of Egypt with the one of Moses
Austin [founder of the Anglo-Texan colony] and of Sam
Houston at San Jacinto with Joshua at Jericho" (9).
These are the sorts of myths alluded to by T. R.
Fehrenbach in the introduction to his history of Texas.
Humphrey, the destroyer of myth, sought to demolish the shining history of the state and to reveal the
betrayal and ingratitude involved in its early years.
He lets the reader know in the opening that "the winds
of bombast, seldom still, blew over the land as incessantly as the dust storms." It is possible that the
severity of this critique owes something to his anger
over the Texas Sesquicentennial Conference discussed
in Chapter 1, although the novel had been conceived

long before the 1986 meeting.

The father of Humphrey's narrator is mysteriously immune to this "epidemic of patriotism," and the narrator calls him a throwback to the independent individuals who in fact created Texas, or rather, Anglo-Texas. The founders of the state were often troublesome individuals, "'G. T. T.,'—'Gone to Texas'—often just one step ahead of the law." In spite of his apparent indifference to the whole matter of patriotism, the father explodes when he discovers that his son is to play Lamar in the pageant and forbids it. The narrator is surprised to learn that his father knows who Lamar is, although the neighboring county is named for him. The novel will explain this puzzle, and give Humphrey a chance to attack the Texas myth, the story of valiant and noble individuals concerned with freedom. Amos Smith III tells his son a horrifying story of duplicity and ingratitude toward the Cherokees and their allies, one that he heard from his grandfather, the first Amos Smith, who has several other names in the novel. The first Smith was a participant in all the horrors of the forced relocation. The narrator's father astounds his son by singing "Amazing Grace," a song beloved by the Cherokee, in their language. He had long hesitated to hand down the tragic story to his son, but the mention of Mirabeau Lamar induces him to tell it. Only in the last section of the novel do we learn just why he hates the long-dead Lamar.

This device of a secret history handed down to a narrator is not uncommon in historical fiction. It gives an illusion of authenticity: the events are not merely narrated by an author; rather, they have been transmitted from a genuine witness, and the story is important enough to survive across the generations. The device creaks a little in this case, however. The elaborate reconstruction provided by Amos Smith IV stretches credibility, though we easily adapt to such conventions of story-telling, and it is clear that the narrator has elaborated the story through reading and through a trip in which he followed the Cherokee Trail. But it detracts from the immediacy of the story, especially when Humphrey occasionally interrupts the narrative to remind the reader of the frame story. Robert Morsberger's review in *Western American Literature* emphasizes this problem and unwittingly confirms how cumbersome the narrative is by confusing the names of the Smith characters (calling them Adam instead of Amos!) and getting the generations wrong: he adds an extra generation to the sequence of ancestors in his attempt to describe the framework. In his fine article, "Lament for the Vanishing," Larry R. Bowden speaks of the narrator as the son of Amos IV, and then on the following page quotes the conclusion of the novel, in which the narrator explicitly calls himself Amos IV (108–109).

Clearly Humphrey's apparatus is too complicated. John Clute in *The Times Literary Supplement* comments that one effect Humphrey aimed for is to show the impact of these distant events on someone close to us in time: the past has an enormous impact on him. Humphrey has made the first Amos Smith a boy of twelve at the opening of the novel, just one year younger than his great-great-grandson, who hears the tragic story and grieves over it. But Clute feels uneasy about this device, saying that "genocide should not be mooned over" (1338).

A mark of the contrivance required by the frame is the introduction of the Cherokee rose motif. The Cherokee rose is a species that began as a domesticated flower but can now be found growing wild in East Texas. The legend is that the roses were planted by Cherokees along the trail from Texas to the Indian Territory, the trail known in typical southern idiom as "the Cherokee Trace." The Cherokee rose has been the subject of a number of accounts, some of them quite romantic. One of Humphrey's sources for the Texas part of his narrative is Doyal T. Loyd's privately printed *A History of Upshur County, Texas*. Upshur is along the Cherokee Trace, and Loyd tells the story in some detail:

> The Cherokees selected one of their number who had an uncanny sense of direction.

He got on a horse and tied buffalo hides behind so that they dragged on the ground through the tall grass, then started out. He traveled in a generally straight direction with another group following blazing the trees and making the trail visible. Another group came along removing logs, underbrush and marking fords across the streams. A group of Indians followed him, blazing the trees to mark the trail.

At night they would camp together. Another group located springs and good camping places and marked them. After the road had been well established they planted Cherokee roses and honeysuckle which came from their homeland in the old states, so as to permanently mark the trace. (3)

This account must have energized Humphrey's imagination. He had a photocopy of it along with one of an article by Frank X. Tolbert, a professional Texan (founder of the Terlingua Chile Cook-Off) and newspaper columnist, an article based on an interview with Loyd. The novelist may well have been inspired further by an article in the *Gilmer Mirror*, 28 May 1970, by Sarah Greene, the editor of D. T. Loyd's history. In her very well-written piece, "Follow the Cherokee Trace: Roadmap for Trip in Time—Backwards,"

Greene discusses the roses, the Cherokees who were said to have planted them, and the role of Mirabeau Lamar in expelling the Cherokees from Texas.

In *No Resting Place*, the father, after pinning a rose in his son's buttonhole, begins to tell him the story of the two expulsions his grandfather experienced, first from the Cherokee lands in the southern United States, and then from the lands in the Republic of Texas. But the Cherokee Rose does not bloom at the time of the anniversary of San Jacinto, April 21. So Humphrey finds it necessary to have the roses bloom early. Ezra Pound claimed that "the natural object is always the best symbol," and the rose is a natural object, one found plentifully in the Red River Valley—but it must bloom unnaturally in order to provide the symbolism.

The narrator is thirteen years old in Part One, making him a year older than Humphrey was in 1936, and his father is remarkably like Clarence Humphrey. The narrator sets the revelation of the past in the Sulphur River Bottom, Clarence's favorite haunt. In a way, the novel is haunted again by William's father. It is a work of fiction, but Seymour Lawrence thought it should be labeled non-fiction, as a letter of his in Humphrey's archive makes clear (18 November 1987). His author wrote several letters in response. On 29 December 1982, he had sent Lawrence the opening of *No Resting Place* along with most of *Hostages to*

Fortune, and Lawrence had been much more interested in the Cherokee novel than in *Hostages*. At the
time, Humphrey had been unable to switch horses in
mid-stream, as he put it, and he continued with *Hostages to Fortune*, the work he was actively engaged
with. Now Lawrence decided that he did not like the
opening of the *No Resting Place*, a complete reversal
of his earlier view. Humphrey's first brief letter (18
October 1987) said: "I shall of course await your detailed criticisms of the book, but in the meantime I
can't help but be surprised at your suggestion that
the opening part be scrapped—it is so very different
from your original response." He enclosed a copy of
the original response, then wrote a longer, undated
letter:

> Thank you for your reading of *No Resting
> Place*, and for your offer to publish it should
> Delacorte refuse. However, I am dismayed at
> your suggestion that it be presented as non-
> fiction. The characters in it are caught up in
> a historical experience but they are not, nor
> are they based upon, actual people. It is not
> the story of my family, nor of anybody else's
> known to me. No real-life boy that I know of
> listened to the story of his people from his
> grandfather nor cast a magic spell upon a
> land-surveyor nor served as a doctor on the

Trail of Tears nor saw his father shot to death on Red River. No minister known to me lost his faith through that experience. These are fictional characters and events not drawn from recorded fact but imagined as being expressive of a historical happening. Indeed, as history the book is unreliable, for I have taken liberties with known facts and personages. A common experience that affects the lives of more persons than one is not thereby an impersonal experience. The right to an individual fate is the first right lost in genocide. It was this that I meant to convey. The novel can accommodate much variety. Mine may be a novel with a difference (I hope so) but it is still a novel. From this it will be seen that I would resist appending any subtitle to the book, no matter who should publish it.

The extension of the story into the present generation is a dramatization of Faulkner's dictum: The past is never dead—it isn't even past. I want my story to resonate beyond its local time and place and to affect people long afterwards. Were I to follow your suggestion and dispense with the opening section (the section which originally so stirred your imagination) that dimension would be lost. So would the rivalry between Houston and Lamar and the Bowl's part therein. So would an understanding of the end of the book.

To say that I am disappointed by your response is to say only a part of what I feel. I am bewildered, especially by your two antithetical responses to the opening section.

While Humphrey's justification is well-expressed, the need for it points to a problem in genre: he has written a book in which the novelistic elements seem subordinated to the history. Much of the work is a chronicle, based on actual events. It is a chronicle told in a complicated way, then: Amos Smith IV hears the story from his father, Amos III, who is repeating what he heard from his grandfather, Amos I. Amos IV relays it to us, elaborating the story with what he has apparently learned about Cherokee life and history in subsequent years. Once in a while as the story unfolds we are reminded of Amos III telling the story to his son in 1936 or even of Amos I confiding the story in his old age to Amos III. The principal male characters in the story of the removal are Amos I, who becomes Amos Smith only at the end, in bloody circumstances, but was born (in white nomenclature) as Amos Ferguson; his father, Abel Ferguson; Abel's father, Agiduda; and the Reverend Malcolm Mackenzie, a Scottish missionary who accompanies the Cherokees from Georgia to the Indian Territory. Mackenzie is said to have left an account of the Trail of Tears, published many years later as *The Missionary in Spite of Himself.* The mother and grandmother of Amos I are present in the book, as is the minister's wife, but they are shadowy characters. The frame may remind some readers of Alex Haley's book *Roots*, in which each generation confides the family's history— and the progenitor's name—to its successor.

The narration is often choppy and an image of a stylized bird is used to separate sections within chapters, increasing the episodic air of the text. What we read is a complex reconstruction of the story of Amos Ferguson and his family in the mind of his great grandson, who at one point even goes on a pilgrimage along the Trail of Tears, stopping at places like the Cherokee Trail Motor Lodge and Trading Post, and using maps handed down from his great-grandfather. An enormous amount of historical and ethnological information is transmitted by the descendent.

The opening of the reconstructed historical narrative, Part Two, is perhaps the best portion of the novel. The material is fresh: we learn a great deal about Cherokee culture. And we get a strong image of the way that the Cherokees are caught between two worlds. The section opens not with the original Amos but with a white man, the Reverend Mackenzie. The strategy is not unusual: we will learn about the

Cherokees through the experiences of a sympathetic outsider. The minister has come to Georgia in 1837 to convert the Indians, but he has failed to find any. His first convert is a young white boy, "sandy-haired, fair-skinned, freckled-faced and blue-eyed" (29) who presents himself for baptism. But when the boy strips himself he is covered with long scratches, the results of a Cherokee initiation rite that he has undergone not long before. The minister is baffled, and assumes that the boy is a white child taken captive and raised by Indians. But the boy explains that he is Jijalagiyai, one of "The Real People" (36).

One aim of the novel is to deconstruct ideas of race. Amos is racially mostly white, but culturally entirely Cherokee. For white America, one drop of non-white blood—this point is made several times—makes an individual a different race, and therefore inferior. The possession of all the strengths of white civilization means nothing: "Indian" equals "savage." The Cherokees had duplicated many features of white society: they had an alphabet (a superior one, at that), a constitution and government, a newspaper, all the trappings of civilization. When they were being pressured into leaving, they even sued in the United States Supreme Court and won. But Andrew Jackson, whose life had been saved by a Cherokee in the War of 1812, made his famous statement: "Chief Justice John Marshall has rendered his decision. Now let him enforce it."

But the Cherokees had retained much of their old culture. The boy seeking the white man's baptism had recently been initiated into the tribal wisdom by his grandfather, Agiduda, in ceremonies that included scratching his body. Amos Ferguson is known as Noquisi, or Bright Star, within his family. He has by custom a third name, known to no one else, not even his relatives, a name which he changes freely to mark occasions in his life. This fluidity of identity marks not only complexities of his culture, but also his membership in at least two worlds. The novel makes it clear that even among themselves the Cherokees of the early nineteenth century were a heterogenous people. Most of them did not speak English, yet some of their leaders hardly knew Cherokee. The process of acculturation into white concepts had gone far by the 1830s.

The description of the boy's initiation by his grandfather, which takes seven days, gives the novelist a chance to explain the customs of the Cherokee in a natural way, and Humphrey explains everything from mythology to bow-making through the vehicle of the grandfather's teachings. Noquisi has a white education but he still has a Cherokee imagination. He curses a land surveyor and assumes that the man will die. From time to time he believes that he can read the thoughts of other characters in the novel, a

power that the Cherokee believed they could exercise. Such an ability (or a belief by a character he has
it) is a narrative convenience for Humphrey, though
the reader is likely to feel too skeptical about it, which
makes it a stumbling block.

The interpolated passages about historical events
in the eight days of Noquisi's initiation seem arbi-
trarily added to the text. Humphrey goes into some
detail about the Battle of Horseshoe Bend in 1814, in
which Andrew Jackson was saved from defeat at the
hands of the Creeks, allies of the British, by
Junuluska, the Cherokee Chief. Present at the battle
was Sam Houston, who had lived among the Cherokees, a figure who becomes important in the last section of the novel without actually appearing. Two men
became national figures because of the victory at
Horseshoe Bend: Jackson, who became President of
the United States, and Houston, who became President of Texas. Jackson showed no gratitude toward
the Cherokees, but Houston remained sympathetic.
Near the end of the chapter Humphrey introduces
two flashbacks: one of the last assembly of the full
nation in Tennessee, the other of the meeting at New
Echota where the Removal Treaty was pushed
through by the U. S. authorities. The New Echota
meeting is introduced in a rather journalistic way:
"The time: late at night. The scene: the home of Elias
Boudinot, Ridge's nephew, in the former Cherokee

capital, New Echota" (64). At such moments the book reads more like a documentary than a novel.

While this section is readable and informative, the work is novelized history more than a novel based on history. An instructive contrast might be to consider a novel that Humphrey admired very much, Thomas Berger's deconstruction of the myth of the Old West, *Little Big Man*. Humphrey praised the book to Katherine Anne Porter and sent her a copy in December, 1965, and he corresponded with the author. Berger approaches the cowboy myth and the Indian Wars with bold invention, creating a frame story with a difference: his picaresque novel is narrated to a researcher by Jack Crabb, a man in a nursing home who claims to have participated in most of the great events of the Old West, including Custer's Last Stand. He also claims to be 111 years old. The book contains authentic ethnography and takes a strong pro-Native stance, but it avoids sentimentality, managing to be as irreverent about the Native Americans as about the whites. While no one would believe the adventures of Jack Crabb as any kind of truth, any more than we could accept the narratives of Jonathan Swift's Gulliver, Berger has told us something important about the gulf between the western hero in the popular imagination and the realities of life on the frontier, a subject that fascinates Humphrey.

Humphrey has not been so bold, and his book

suffers. The plight of the Cherokee is conveyed more powerfully in Starkey's *The Cherokee Nation*, a straight historical narrative. The characters in *No Resting Place* are excessively noble. Their station in life is meant to increase the pathos of their fall: Dr. Ferguson attended William and Mary College, and his house is full of books, like a reprint edition of *The Tatler*. The traditionalist grandfather, Agiduda, rather improbably reads to the family from *Robinson Crusoe* (a story of shipwreck) and *Paradise Lost* in the evenings. Part Three of the novel is devoted to the Ferguson home and the circumstances of their leaving it. Their land is taken by a white man, O. J. Blodgett, who builds a fence in order to dig a "gold mine." As the family is escorted away by the militia, they learn that Blodgett has actually dug up their family graveyard looking for gold jewelry. Blodgett has not understood that his neighbors were Cherokee until just before they are removed. He pays a racist compliment to Agiduda by saying, "Well, Chief, you sure fooled me. I took you to be a man like me" (124).

Part Three has some interpolated passages about Sam Houston's life among the Cherokees and a description of the Muscle Shoals Massacre of 1794, in which the Cherokee chief, Diwali was said to have killed thirteen whites. We are being prepared for the last section, in which Diwali, now living with a group of Cherokees in Texas, is the focus. Part Three ends with a description of life in what Humphrey anachronistically but accurately calls a concentration camp, a holding area where many of the deportees die of disease.

The narrative in Part Four becomes choppy, showing brief scenes along the Trail of Tears, a series of appalling episodes of suffering and persecution. Dr. Ferguson and his wife have gone ahead to the Indian Territory to find a place for Agiduda, his wife, and his grandson Amos to live. The three left behind set out, accompanied by Reverend Mackenzie and his wife. Mackenzie becomes very important. His faith and his charity are tested; his charity survives but his faith does not. He witnesses the death of his wife, among many others. When at the end of the section he attempts to say some pious words over the grave of Noquisi's grandfather, the boy interrupts him and says "You lie"—the only way to say "You are mistaken"—in Cherokee, and goes on to tell him that the god of the white man was not Agiduda's god, and that "Ours was taken from us and yours won't have us" (213).

This outburst deeply moves the minister, who years later writes in his story of the Removal: "Out of the mouths of babes," a statement that usually affirms faith. But Reverend Mackenzie loses his faith, not in God's existence, but in his goodness, which Humphrey suggests is a more desolate situation. He

lives out his life among the Cherokee, marrying a
Cherokee woman, and preaching consoling sermons
because it is what the people wish to hear. He is a
kind of Job who curses God and despairs. He had already noticed that those who had lost their faith were
the ones most sympathetic to him when his wife died.
Some still kept their faith, expressed in the favorite
hymn, "Amazing Grace":

> Most still affirmed in song that they were
> lost but now were found, were blind but now
> could see; but many showed in little acts of
> kindness and consideration their pity for him
> as the ill-rewarded servant of a thankless and
> hard-hearted master. He felt it was up to God,
> not him, to explain His ways, if he chose, to
> such unassailably primitive minds. (212)

"Primitive" in this passage is used ironically, of course.

The real protagonist of the march is Noquisi, who
gains more names along the way: Tad (for Tadpole),
Cap (for Captain), and, most important, Doc, because
he applies what he has learned about medicine from
his father after the official doctor dies. As in a disaster movie, we are provided with a group of characters
whose suffering we can sympathize with, and also as
in a disaster movie, many of them will perish. Noquisi
has to suffer through several losses. First, one of the

graves encountered on the Trail at a place called Beesville turns out to be his mother's. This discovery so devastates his grandmother that she despairs and dies. And finally his grandfather dies. Through all this suffering he ministers to the sick and even delivers a baby—it seems a cliché—whose mother dies in childbirth.

Humphrey's notebooks show that in writing the book he worried about making the boy too heroic. He was careful to make him a medic in the final battle in the novel rather than a participant. The character's tireless work for the sick is a kind of heroism in itself. William Butler Yeats notoriously excluded the World War I poets from his *Oxford Anthology of Modern Verse* on the grounds that their work presented passive suffering and therefore was not tragic. There is no scope for heroic action in the deportation: Humphrey would violate history if he changed the record of passive suffering to one of resistance. But the response to one's fellow victims need not be passive, and it would violate the dignity of the victims to assume that no one could act at all. Humphrey works to assert the individuality of his characters.

The novel also works to achieve some balance in the presentation of white characters. This is the sort of issue that arises quite naturally for the reader of such a polemical book. The Cherokees are treated very badly by the Georgia authorities, and much of the suffering on the Trail stems from corruption (bad food supplied by unscrupulous merchants) and incompetent planning of the Removal. But Humphrey does not present all white characters as evil. Mackenzie is clearly a good man, and some of the people who meet the victims on their march show compassion. The historical sources cite numerous examples of generosity and concern once the deportees left the areas where their lands were coveted, so Humphrey is not sentimentalizing. The commander of the Federal troops escorting Noquisi's party, Captain Donovan, is as humane as his peculiar assignment permits him to be. This reflects historical fact: the real abuse of the Cherokees was performed by state militiamen who started the evictions.

One issue he does not face with any balance: many of the most progressive Cherokees (from a white point of view) were slave-owners, and they often brought their slaves along on the relocation journey. The issue is raised only in passing. A brief reference is made to slaves ("captives of captives") in the middle of a paragraph describing some of the worst atrocities of the Relocation—a placement which minimizes the impact of the irony of captives who own slaves (133). Humphrey does mention briefly the contempt felt by the Cherokees for other Native Americans, something not learned from the whites, he admits: "In that the whites could have taken lessons from them" (96).

Just before the deaths of the grandparents, Humphrey provides a scene meant to arouse pathos, perhaps a little too palpably. To cheer up his wife, Agiduda describes their courtship at length, revealing an interesting custom. The old laws of Cherokee hospitality, frowned on by the missionaries, required a host to offer a male wayfarer remarkably full hospitality, including the chance to spend the night with any nubile daughter. The daughter might then choose the young man as a husband if by the next morning she found him suitable. The grandfather tells the story of his unusual courtship in a charming way. The grandmother's family was in fact 100% Scottish: they were Cherokees by choice, a decision made by many whites. Ironically, the five civilized tribes were the only Native Americans to imitate white civilization, and they were rejected by those they emulated.

The fifth and final section of the novel seems disproportionately short, as if the novelist were exhausted by the Trail of Tears himself and wanted to get through the novel quickly. It opens in a kind of flash-forward, with a short section anticipating Noquisi's flight with his father from Texas to the Indian Territory. We are told that the boy likes everything about Texas and that he felt like a Texan the moment he entered the new republic, when he was only about three years old. This prepares us for his deep disappointment with what happens to him there.

But then we move back in time to his reunion with his father, a potentially emotional moment which Humphrey slides over very quickly. Noquisi simply says, "You don't have to tell me about my mother. I found the grave" (219). This complete reticence of father and son, who have lost all their relatives, seems extremely implausible.

Once the pair hear about the assassination of pro-treaty leaders, they must flee the camp in the Indian Territory because Dr. Ferguson, unlike his traditionalist father, had reluctantly accepted the treaty, seeing no alternative. He realizes that he and his son may be murdered also. They find their way to the Texas Cherokees, led by Diwali. However, twice on the journey the reader has been told that the uprooted Indians can find "no resting place," and the Fergusons will prove this melancholy statement by what befalls them next. They arrive just as an order to leave Texas has been received in the Native encampment. Mirabeau Lamar, the new president and successor of Sam Houston, had promised to rid Texas of Indians if he won the election. Diwali has welcomed the new arrivals by saying "What's mine is yours," but unfortunately it will not be his for long.

The narrative moves quickly to a war council, a rather formal scene, in which the Cherokees and their allies vote first to fight, then to fight with Diwali, a man of eighty-three, as their leader. The narrator observes that Diwali would likely have been killed if he had refused the leadership, a point which the chief himself made in conversations with John Lacy, an Indian agent (Clarke 96). Young Noquisi, as an honored guest, is present when Diwali has his last meeting with the representative of President Lamar, General Thomas Jefferson Rusk. Humphrey takes advantage of the reputed Cherokee ability to read the thoughts of others to amplify Noquisi's understanding of the racial nuances of the meeting:

> Meanwhile Noquisi was doing what his Cherokee blood empowered him to do: thought-reading. Having entered the Chief's mind, he found him thinking that the hatred of somebody for you because of your difference from him was intensified by all the many inadmissible but undeniable resemblances that you bore to him. You, too, stood upright, had two eyes, were tailless, could utter speech, or some sort of sounds that to you passed for speech. That did not make you like him, but it made you too much like him.
>
> Inside the Commissioner's mind Noquisi found a refinement upon his distaste for the likes of himself. He was a mongrel, but just barely one. He might have concealed his Indian blood and passed for white; to be infe-

rior by choice was to be a creature beneath contempt. (231)

Somehow the chief's philosophical reflections seem anachronistic, while the prejudices of Rusk are timeless.

A moderate suspense is created by the absence of Grandgent, the courier sent to find Sam Houston on the assumption that he will intervene. He negotiated the treaty with the Indians permitting them to keep their lands in Texas after their helpful nonintervention at the time of San Jacinto. The suspense is not very effective because Humphrey has provided so much discussion of Houston in the novel that his failure to arrive is not surprising. This is not cowardice like Northumberland's failure to come to the aid of Hotspur and Worcester in *Henry IV*, Part 1. Houston is not temporizing: he has left on a trip to Tennessee. The cause of the Cherokees and their allies is hopeless. So much space has been devoted to Houston's personal history, including his sojourns among the Cherokees in the past, that Humphrey seems to have violated Chekov's famous dramatic law, which states that if a gun is on the wall at the start of a play it had better go off before the curtain falls. Houston is a gun which doesn't fire; he never even appears on the scene. The historical Houston returned to Texas and made "a savage speech" about the expulsion of the Indians, but it was too late (Clarke 117). As Auden says in "Spain," history can only say alas, not help or pardon.

The description of the preparation for battle and the battle itself are some of Humphrey's best writing. The battle known as the Battle of the Nueches, took place on 16 July 1839, near the present site of Tyler, Texas. Diwali prepares for action assuming that he will be defeated, but he is calm. His long reflections on the destiny of his people and his desire to be a Moses for them seem twentieth century, not nineteenth. In *Little Big Man* Thomas Berger attempted to use defamiliarization devices to convey the aboriginal thinking of his Cheyenne chief, Old Lodgeskins, and his character is more successful. Diwali's dignity in the novel has plenty of precedent in the sources: he seems to have been a remarkable man, and his demeanor on the battlefield won the admiration of witnesses on the other side. John Reagan, who later became a justice of the Texas Supreme Court and a U. S. Senator, spoke of him many years later as "a magnificent specimen of barbaric manhood" (29) and praised his character. Reagan accompanied the negotiators who dealt with Diwali and is the source of historical accounts of his death in battle. Parts of that battle are watched by Noquisi and his father, who have set up a field hospital. The novelist wanted to keep his young protagonist out of combat, saying in a notebook: "Might it not be better to keep the boy out of the battle? A medic. Having him engage in the conflict is, in the first place, unlikely, and to stain him with blood even in a just cause, is to stain him." The boy is a suffering witness, not a belligerent: he keeps a kind of innocence without ignorance.

Diwali's valor is hopeless—just before he is killed he is described as saying, as many Cherokees do in this novel: "This is a good day to die" (245). His body was mutilated, according to the sources, and Humphrey describes the desecration of the "magnificent specimen of barbaric manhood" by whites who could hardly be called civilized. His courage is meant to contrast with the imputed cowardice of Lamar, who was not in the state at the time of the battle. The anger of Amos Smith III toward the long-dead Mirabeau Lamar has been explained, and Humphrey has demonstrated the bloodshed and betrayal involved in the supposedly glorious history of his state. He alludes only briefly and dismissively to the Texans' belief that the Cherokees were inclined toward Mexico after Texas independence, though some historians would agree with the Texans. Once again he has sought to destroy a myth, and once again he has dealt with the theme of justice, or in this case, injustice.

But the novel has not yet been concluded. The ending is hasty and grows out of a minor historical incident, one reported in the press after the battle. It is cited by Walter Prescott Webb in his history of the Texas Rangers, describing the pursuit of the remnants of the Cherokees: "In August the papers reported that as the fugitives approached Red River they fell in with some hunters who gave them a farewell shot and killed four" (54). Humphrey has those four include Noquisi's father. The boy himself survives, caught by a hunter who assumes that he was an Indian captive, of whom there were so many in American history. The hunter decides to adopt him, and so he becomes Amos Smith, acquiring his last and least distinctive name. "We reach our resting places, we Americans, if we ever do, by roundabout routes and so, too, do some of us come by our lasting names" (248). Humphrey is stretching credibility here, having Noquisi accept an adoptive father who has killed his real one, though we are assured that this reflects an Indian custom and therefore seems fitting to Noquisi. It is dangerous to rely on the sudden introduction of an Indian custom as a kind of *deus ex machina* to settle the fugitive in Texas so that he can pass on his story. This ending is even more abrupt than the conclusion of *Home from the Hill*. Along with justice and the critique of myth, Humphrey was always interested in fathers and sons, but this novel leaves that complexity largely unexplored. We are left with a final glimpse of Cherokee roses in Red River County.

The special interest in this novel as a historical account lies in its linkage of the Cherokee Removal with the Cherokee War in Texas. There have been other novelizations of the Removal and several excellent non-fiction accounts of the War, but Humphrey is the first to provide a view of both, showing that Texas was hardly innocent of the sins committed in the United States. Indeed, the destruction of Indians, especially the Comanches, was remarkably thorough in Texas. But the question is, was a novel needed? While composing the work, Humphrey mused in a notebook on Aristotle's claim about poetry, a claim for literature in general, citing him in paraphrase: "Poetry is truer than history because history is only about what has been but poetry is about what might be." If the fictional account of events can reveal deeper truths than the literal one, then a historical novel may be the best way to deal with an event like the Cherokee Removal. Unfortunately, this novel is, as John Clute said in his review, "painful, decent, and slightly-fumble-footed" (1338), and in the words of Robert E. Morsberger, "instead of making it dramatic, he simply synopsizes much of the history" (392). His characters are idealized, even sentimentalized, and their thoughts often seem anachronistically modern. Mark Royden Winchell, who is always quick to belittle Humphrey, refers to Noquisi as "another literary half-breed whose adolescent identity crisis is exacerbated by racial schizophrenia" (44). Humphrey does not trivialize or exploit the historical events, as novelists portraying the Holocaust are often accused of doing, but his didactic take on them is overbearing. And he slides over the one relationship we would expect to receive full treatment in a novel by this writer: the relationship between Noquisi and his father. The final section is much foreshortened, giving an effect of haste, though the intention may have been to present a series of rapid actions in contrast with the drawn-out series of terrible events on the Trail of Tears. Humphrey has often been criticized for the endings of his novels: they are called melodramatic or contrived. This one seems hasty.

Humphrey's sympathies are decent, his research is thorough, and his efforts to understand something of the religious sensibilities of the Cherokee are laudable, but this novel does not improve on history. The best narrative of these events is still Marion Starkey's *The Cherokee Nation*.

11

Time's Laughingstocks:
September Song

William Humphrey's last book, *September Song*, has an autumnal atmosphere, as the title implies. In one of his notebooks from 1989, he speaks of his own "September Song" as a writer. He began working on the book at a time when *No Resting Place* had not succeeded very well in sales or reviews, and he and his wife were often ill and depressed. For a short time it appeared that the Cherokee novel would be a success, and Home Box Office flirted briefly with making a television movie of it, but nothing came of that. By the time Humphrey's publishers notified him that they would nominate the novel for the Pulitzer Prize, his reaction was simply,

"Hah!" *September Song* was published in 1992 by Houghton Mifflin, the latest publisher where Seymour Lawrence had moved his imprint.

Humphrey's misfortune in his old age had been advancing deafness, the complaint that made him give up the book on Wyley Gates. He says in a notebook entry from November, 1988:

> What it is to be totally deaf I don't know. It may be fatuous if not cruel of me, but I can imagine that there must a kind of resignation if not serenity to it compared to the maddening frustration of being able to hear people talking and being almost able, but unable, to understand what they are saying.

Despondency over his deafness led to a break with his old friend and fellow fisherman, Nick Lyons, who had published *My Moby Dick*. Lyons's wife held a show of her art and neither of the Humphreys felt up to going. Lyons was offended and wrote to say so.

One of the best stories in *September Song* deals with Humphrey's own experiences, modified slightly. The narrator of "The Dead Languages" is a reporter trying to cover a mass murder, something clearly based on the Wyley Gates case. He has been unable to distinguish the testimony, and he later learns from the doctor who examines him that the low hum of the electric typewriter may have been the cause. The story rather quickly drifts from the trial situation, giving up the pretense of being a work of fiction. The protagonist is clearly William Humphrey, a man who has traveled to Ireland and the Bahamas, and who reads Thomas Hardy. There is an interesting passage about *Jude the Obscure* (120–21): "He seized upon his new hearing aids as Jude the Obscure did upon the Greek and Latin grammars, expecting them to provide a key, a rule, a prescription which would enable him to change at will all words of the dead languages into his own. Jude was quickly disillusioned. 'He learnt that there was no law of transmutation'" (120–21). The hearing aids do not work well enough, and the central character becomes more and more disillusioned, not only with them, but with the possibilities of human contact. The deep alienation from others, even from his wife, is related very movingly, notwithstanding the grotesque touches offered by the misunderstandings that the hard of hearing suffer ("Go back off one noble size" turns out to mean "Gorbachev has won the Nobel Prize".) Even the sympathetic wife loses patience. The classical reference in the closing line carries on the allusions to "dead languages" and conveys just the right amount of pathos: "As for him, he would have dashed himself against the rocks happily to have heard the sirens sing" (125).

The tone of the collection is remarkably bleak.

There are three stories about suicide, and the miseries of the aged are a dominant theme. The book is Humphrey's equivalent of Thomas Hardy's anecdotal poems in collections like *Time's Laughingstocks* and *Satires of Circumstance*; as in *A Time and a Place*, the characters are often crushed by the conditions of their lives. The titles of the stories often emphasize the irony. He made sardonic use of literary allusions ("A Week in the Country"), or trite phrases ("A Labor of Love," "Mortal Enemies," "Be It Ever So Humble," and "Dead Weight") or references to the Bible ("An Eye for an Eye") or mythology ("The Apple of Discord").

But in the earlier book, the grinding circumstances were environmental. Human nature is generally the cause of suffering in *September Song*: flaws in characters or heartlessness in those around them. An exception is "A Tomb for the Living," a Dust Bowl story set in the Red River country. In the story, the narrator describes huddling in a storm cellar with his parents during a cyclone. The strain of listening to the wind and knowing what it is doing to the land is too much for the father. He makes a blasphemous reference to the Bible as the family sits in the dark: "Like Onan, I have spilled my seed upon the ground, and the Lord has smitten me" (162). After the storm is over, the wife and son discover that he has cut his throat with his pocketknife and died. This story would fit quite easily into *A Time and a Place*.

Suicide is the subject in a very short narrative, "Last Words," a note left behind by a woman who kills herself after reading the announcement of her ex-husband's marriage. It is also the theme of "Be It Ever So Humble," in which an elderly woman kills herself rather than go to a home for the elderly. These stories are so sketchy in characterization and so plot-driven that they lack all flavor, except for Humphrey's customary grimness. Another contrived and very brief story is a two page work, "Blood Ties," in which a man catches his wife in bed with his beloved brother and kills him:

> Joe was waiting for me in the yard. To support my testimony, he was still naked.
> I said, "Joe, I idolized you."
> I could barely see to shoot him for my tears. (182)

He spares his pregnant wife because he isn't sure if the child she carries is his or the brother's. Such stories are competent, but nothing more, as is "A Weekend in the Country," in which the narrator describes the fun he has pretending to be in the market for an expensive house so that he will be catered to by real estate men.

Another tale of ironic circumstance, "The Parish-

ioner," gives Humphrey a chance to indulge in his anti-
religious feelings. It is a very adroit tale of a smooth-
talking minister who seduces a parishioner whose
mother has died. He does it so skillfully that she
thinks of herself as the powerful seductress rather
than as the seduced. One text that the minister cites
to the woman when he comforts her about her mother
is from a rather unlikely source—unlikely for a Prot-
estant minister, that is, but not for William Humphrey: a passage of Ecclesiasticus, one alluded to in
Proud Flesh:

> In the first phase, Reverend Smith's text
> had been: "Let tears fall down over the dead.
> Weep bitterly and make great moan." Now
> from the same Biblical passage he drew this
> further bit: "Use lamentation, and that for a
> day or two, and then comfort thyself in thy
> heaviness. Thou shalt do the dead no good,
> but hurt thyself. When the dead is at rest, let
> remembrance rest." (131)

A much better story than any of these is the opening one, "Portrait of the Artist as an Old Man."
Humphrey always regarded inquiries about his life
and work as most people would regard an IRS audit.
In this story, a successful writer is interviewed in his
old age by a young woman. He rehearses the facts of

his early life with her—all of which, except for birth in "Sulphur Flats, Texas," are the facts of Humphrey's life. Then he realizes that she is in effect preparing his obituary, which is even less welcome than a tax audit. He begins to spoof her, claiming that his mother died in childbirth and that he was raised by a black mammy. He becomes quite creative, creating a fantasia on the Humphrey from *Open Season* essay, "The Trick Shot Artist." The old novelist recalls his career as a trick-shot performer with his father. Alas, he kills his father during a performance in Wichita Falls, Texas, and wanders for a while like Oedipus—a favorite myth of Humphrey's—until he decides that the only career open to him is as a writer. After the interviewer leaves, the novelist's wife reproaches him for his fabrications.

"But what are you going to say to people who know you when that yarn appears in print?"

"I won't be here." And he then explained to her what the reporter's assignment was. "In the trade they're called 'ghouls' or 'buzzards.' She was here to gather material for what they call an 'advance obituary.' Somebody's got to do it, but it is dirty work. What I didn't tell her was my last words."

"Oh, you've got them ready, have you?"

"Mmh."

"What are they?"

"They're the last words of a writer: 'In that case, I've got nothing more to say.'" (11)

A couple of stories are based rather closely on life, to the point of callousness. In "A Labor of Love," a man in retirement builds a house for his ungrateful and demanding sister, who is known to his wife as "The Praying Mantis." Humphrey mentions in a notebook that this story is his memorial to his late Aunt Bess, whose egotistical ways Humphrey despised. The story, "Vissi d'Arte," about a uxorious husband who auctions off his favorite fishing rods to pay for a kind of vanity art gallery show for his wife seems to be a story expressing a grudge over a quarrel with Nick Lyons. The title comes from an aria in Puccini's *Tosca*, in which the title character sings of her dedication to art and love. In a written response (1 May 1997), the author told me that he and Nick Lyons were no longer friends and commented, "Cf. Vissi d'Arte." However, the fishing rods episode is perhaps an unconscious echo of an occasion in 1955 when, according to Andy Dupee, William sold his hunting rifle to buy a camera for Dorothy.

The title work, "September Song," is also based on actual people. In a notebook he records the shocking break-up of the marriage of two old friends. The

wife, a grandmother and seventy-eight years old, decided to leave her husband of more than fifty years
for an old lover who reappeared after two decades.
The incongruity of this struck the writer:

> As a novelist, I'm supposed to know some-
> thing about people. I must be a bad novel-
> ist—people are continually surprising me.
> I thought the Wannings were both rather
> phlegmatic. I never could have imagined the
> latest scene I'm told. . . . Him preparing to
> leave the house to consult a lawyer about a
> divorce. Pat stopping him, a belt in her hand,
> saying, "Whip me."
> It's Russian! Beyond Chekhov.
> The Volga on the Hudson! A woman of
> seventy-eight! And of all women, Pat!

The story based on this episode is rather restrained,
a look into the woman's consciousness, stressing the
phlegmatism of the couple and ignoring the episode
with the belt. The story, which is a little too long and
circumstantial, ends on a Chekhovian note, with the
woman feeling pity for her husband and deciding not
to leave him.

Two of the stories on old age are particularly
moving and make use of his long experience as a
hunter. In the very brief story, "Mortal Enemies," an

elderly man who has shot "vermin" all his life finds that a woodchuck has been marauding in his vegetable garden. He asserts his continuing prowess as a hunter by shooting it. But after he hobbles over to it (he has a bad hip), he regrets having killed it: "He wanted everything to go on living. What they had in common had made peace between him and his old enemy" (111). The story does not state directly what they have in common: besides a love of vegetables, it must be mortality.

The other hunting story, "Buck Fever," momentarily summons up "My Moby Dick." The old hunter spots a magnificent old buck and decides to give himself one more season of hunting in order to try to kill it: he is hooked as surely as Humphrey is hooked by the big trout in the fishing narrative. He studies its ways with great care, just as Humphrey studied his Moby Dick. The title is an interesting play on words. The hunter has buck fever because he wants to hunt the buck, but idiomatically "buck fever" is the sort of nervousness felt by an inexperienced hunter.

What Humphrey's character feels is inexperience at dying: the reader will not fail to note the elegiac—but not mournful—overtones in the narrative. When the hunter at last encounters the buck, it is being attacked by a pack of wild dogs, two of which he shoots. The truism in "Birds of a Feather," that the hunter loves the thing he kills, gets a new twist here: the hunter defends the thing he loves. And he dies in a snowstorm shortly afterwards, slipping away like Rip Van Winkle, whose famous sleep took place in the Hudson Valley woods that Humphrey knew so well. This denouement is not horrifying: the hunter has made a good death. The story is one of Humphrey's best, achieving pathos without sentimentality.

Another touching treatment of old age comes in the concluding story, "A Heart in Hiding," in which a widower can find no expression of his grief until he comes across a trivial object in a drugstore, a bamboo backscratcher. It reminds him of the many times his wife had scratched his back, and suddenly he can cry. This is the kind of tiny domestic detail that his master, Hardy, used so tellingly in poems about grief.

Not all of the stories are about old age. "The Farmer's Daughter" is a tale of young love gone wrong in Texas. A young man working his way through school has a serious fall from a power pole which he is repairing. He is taken in by a kindly farmer and his daughter. The daughter and the young man both know French and conduct a bit of courtship in it, but nothing comes of their mutual infatuation: he is too poor to offer her marriage, and they never quite come to talk of love. The ending of the story is a tear-jerker: he climbs on a train and we are told in a line worthy of country music, "No sound was so sad and lonesome as the whistle of a departing train to one left behind" (24).

The great failure in the book is "An Eye for an Eye." The story was described by one reviewer as a rewriting of *Ethan Frome,* and that seems very just. It is an *Ethan Frome* with a touch of horror movie contrivance about it, and perhaps an allusion to Chaucer's "The Merchant's Tale," in which an old man regains his sight long enough to spot his wife and a lover naked in a pear tree. Humphrey's story has three narrators—James, his wife, and Ursula—fitting for a story about a love triangle. At one point in the story, the blind wife regains her sight long enough to realize that James has been carrying on an affair with Ursula, her hired companion. She finds her way to Ursula's room in the dark and pours sulfuric acid on her face. After her release from the hospital, Ursula has nowhere to go but back to the house of misfortune, so James, like Ethan Frome—but under far worse circumstances—has to care for them both.

Another very short story, "Virgin and Child," is based on an incident from Dorothy Humphrey's youth. A young girl is babysitting for an aunt and her husband. The man returns, having pretended to be ill, and makes a pass at his niece. She defends herself by holding up the baby, which shames him and brings him to his senses. This lean story is told with a classic understatement, making it better than most of the longer ones. Another story of family conflict is "Auntie," in which a woman who has been honest all her life is corrupted by her love for a worthless and criminal nephew, who needs an alibi. This one is more predictable than "Virgin and Child."

There is one story which returns to the baroque extravagance of *Proud Flesh* and *The Ordways*. "Dead Weight" is another parody of the *As I Lay Dying* theme of the transportation of the dead. This time Humphrey's protagonist is not a wounded Civil War veteran, but an antique dealer from upstate New York who travels in a camper. His friend Kelly, a diabetic with one leg, relies on the narrator to take him back to the northeastern United States from Dallas. But Kelly dies on the toilet of the camper, giving Humphrey the chance to indulge in some bathroom humor. The narrator finds that Kelly has made a will leaving him all his property and that he deliberately stopped taking his insulin. The will was meant to compensate the narrator for his efforts in taking Kelly's body back home. But the narrator decides that the authorities will likely suspect foul play—the intimidation and murder of a helpless diabetic—so he burns the will.

Still, he feels a duty to take Kelly back to the northeast, and begins a cross-country journey as wild as that of the Bundrens in *As I Lay Dying*. He even stops off in one town to take part in a centennial celebration baseball game. Humphrey has dealt with similar situations before. At least the Renshaws packed their mother's body in ice, but this antique dealer simply leaves the body in the toilet of the camper. Humphrey's story is rather grisly, but exuberant nevertheless, oddly reminiscent of Kerouac's *On the Road*. And the protagonist becomes a kind of local hero when he is finally caught back home in New York. Fortunately, there is not enough evidence for murder charges. Humphrey seems to have wanted to pay a last tribute to the southern grotesque—and he picked a northerner as his speaker, as if to say he had become something of a Yankee writer at last.

The most ambitious story in the book, one which Humphrey took enormous pains with, is "Apple of Discord." He originally called it "Comfort Me with Apples," a line out of *The Song of Solomon*. It is not one of his best stories, over-weighted as it is with symbolism from *King Lear* and the Bible. The third person limited narration shows us the struggle of Seth Bennett, a Hudson River Valley apple farmer, to pass down his splendid orchards to his own seed. "Seed" is a revealing term: he thinks of his family as apples, and fears that his breed will die out. He has three daughters, but they refuse to take over the farm. The eldest daughter has married a preacher, the second an undertaker. Most of the action centers on Bennett's attempt to persuade his third daughter, Janet, to marry Pete, the son of a neighbor, Tom Jeffers, who shot himself in the heart after being wiped out by hail.

The story keeps us in some suspense about an injury to Bennett's right hand. Much of the action is given in flashbacks as he shaves on Janet's wedding day, showing how he must struggle to shave with an electric razor because of the injury. One point of the story is that he has been unable to find a right-hand man: Pete has failed to win Janet, and she is about to wed the very real estate man who sold the farm to developers on behalf of the despondent Seth Bennett. The farm, known as Garden of Eden Orchards, has been desecrated by the developers: Humphrey had a particular dislike for the defacement of the Hudson Valley, and he had an apple orchard of his own, so the description of the destruction of the trees is very powerful. Bennett finally realizes that his neighbors perceive of him as the spoiler of the American Dream.

The Eden symbolism in the story is quite clear. "Seth" is the name of Adam's third son, and "Bennett" is a plain enough name to represent the human race. The daughters have gone to Vassar College, thanks to their father's work, but the knowledge they gain there does not induce them to live in the Garden. As Bennett muses on his daughters' marriages, he thinks of them as stepdaughters of Eve. The marriage of the eldest to a preacher—a profession that Humphrey clearly does not respect—leads Bennett to some reflections on God's dislike for farmers, especially apple farmers, whose attempts to earn their bread by the sweat of their brows is complicated by such acts of God as hail and diseases like mold and blight. In fact, Humphrey describes the tribulations of farmers in such relentless detail that he could easily be talking about the afflictions of Texas dirt farmers.

In one of his late notebooks (November 1998) Humphrey discusses the Eden symbolism:

> In my original notebook on this material I find something which I should keep foremost in mind although it is a thing I should allow to speak for itself.
>
> Eve and the apple. He—my man—becomes in his effort to entice, inveigh his daughter into the marriage of his wish the serpent tempting her with an apple. He is her father, God was Eve's. It was not God who tempted Eve with the apple—it was Satan, the Serpent, and the serpent knows his doing so would bring about her expulsion from the orchard. But I like my switch on it: Her father tempting her with the apples (millions of them) that will keep her in the orchard. And this Eve refuses the bait. And refuses to tempt her Adam with it. She is not Eve, she [is] a daughter of Eve, profiting by the mistake of her ancestress. The daughter is outraged when he tries to pressure her into

marrying Pete by offering her the entire farm, which would disinherit her sisters.

The King Lear symbolism is also clear: three sisters, a kingdom, a petulant old man threatening disinheritance. In his notes for the story Humphrey observes that Bennett is a king of sorts. Like Cordelia, the youngest daughter is quite affectionate—until she is estranged by her father's bullying and his insistence on bloodlines: "You're no father, you're . . . you're a breeder. A stock-breeder" (59). The accusation shocks him but he can see the truth in it. Ironically, this Cordelia's betrothed is the despised real estate man, Rodney Jones, whose commission for selling the farm enables him to seek a wife. Bennett ruefully thinks that he has introduced the serpent into the garden, though he himself is the serpent.

Lear had his storm; Seth Bennett has his motorcycle accident, which injures his hand. He is weakened but not reformed by this misfortune. One valedictory note for the author: we get several looks at a family cemetery in the course of the story. Bennett has already had a stone put in place for himself and his wife, both of whom are still living. This is not as eccentric as the stone and empty grave that Hannah Hunnicutt prepares for herself in the Clarksville cemetery, nor are there any eccentric Bennetts described in the manner of the cemetery section of *The Ordways*.

Bennett visits the family cemetery just before the
wedding, when he tries to get the crews demolishing
the farm to reduce their noise level so that the wedding can take place in the house again. He has wrecked
his own paradise. He will visit the cemetery again at
the end of the story.

In Shakespeare's *King Lear*, the tendency is to
characterize people through animal imagery. For
Bennett, the dominant metaphor is the apple. Just
before the wedding he has these reflections about the
ancestors buried in the family cemetery:

> He had not bred true to type, and his fail-
> ure made him feel beholden to these, his and
> his daughters' ancestors. He did not regret
> having had daughters but he could not help
> regretting having had the daughters he had.
> He blamed each for the dereliction of all,
> particularly Janet, the one given the oppor-
> tunity to redeem the others and make her-
> self—as she had been until then—the apple
> of his eye. A sense not of the impermanence
> of life but of his long lineage, of his deep-delv-
> ing roots in this consecrated earth, was what
> he had always felt when straying among
> these graves. Now he would come here no
> more until he came forever. (71)

He does not wish, like Lear, that his disobedient daughters had never been born, but he is extremely patriarchal, even when he might appear progressive. The daughters are educated because education is impractical: a male heir would have simply been taught the apple-growing business. His repeated patriarchal mistake with Janet is to assume that he understands how she thinks better than she does herself.

He spoils the wedding and estranges the family by making it into melodrama, reading his will and forcing his daughters publicly to accept the checks for their share of the sale of the farm. Unlike Lear, he does divide the spoiled kingdom equally, but by stressing this he insults them: he insists that they look at the checks to verify that they are equal. The scene is surely meant to recall Lear's histrionic division of the kingdom in Shakespeare's play, and it goes awry for him as it did for the British king. Janet tears her check to pieces, and when she leaves, she gives him a cold kiss on the cheek. Cordelia, who loved her father deeply, offended him by saying he would get only his due from her; Janet is quite literally giving her father only his due and he feels it deeply.

The only recourse for this pathetic Lear is death. He was sure that he would visit the family cemetery only once more, and we learn what this means when he leans against his tombstone at the end of story

and attempts to shoot himself. "That right hand of
his was good for nothing." The purpose of this ending
is obvious enough: he has botched everything, but the
ending seems too bathetic. And the story as a whole
suffers from predictability: between the garden of
Eden and the Lear parallels, too much is foreseen by
the reader. The classical parallel invoked by the title
is not carried very far. There are indeed three daughters, but no Paris to judge a beauty contest. The story
is overlong, and that, combined with its predictability, keeps it from being one of Humphrey's best efforts, in spite of his ambitions in writing it. Jane
Smiley's magnificent retelling of the Lear story in *A
Thousand Acres* perhaps makes any story suffer by
comparison, at least for our time. What lingers in the
mind are the elegiac description of the orchard and
the appalling destruction wrought by the developers.
In this story, Humphrey has proven his citizenship
in upstate New York, by long tenure and by allegiance
to its threatened beauties.

The tone of the entire book often goes beyond even
Humphrey's usual grimness. Sympathy is never missing from his beloved Thomas Hardy, no matter how
grim the material. Elizabeth Tebeaux saw compassion in Humphrey's earlier stories, but no one is likely
to see that quality in *September Song*. The failed suicide attempt of Bennett in "The Apple of Discord" is
pathetic rather than pitiable; the portrait of the

painter and her husband in "Vissi d'Arte" is spiteful, and "An Eye for an Eye" has the cynicism of an Ambrose Bierce, not the rueful irony of a Hardy. Only in "Virgin and Child," based on his wife's experience, and in his portraits of aging hunters (likely self-portraits), does he seem to show much sympathy.

He concluded the book of stories on 18 November 1991, according to a journal. At the same time he made an intriguing entry. He was changing address books and noticed that many people in the old book had died or ceased to be friends. A dedicated writer can make a book out of anything, and it occurred to him to write a novel using the format of a man going through his address book and counting losses: "What more beautiful arrangement than the alphabet? The dead. The defectors. Some who he cannot place. Nothing wrong with getting a touch of glamour in it." One of his late notebooks contains a sad meditation on the transience of friendship, a sketch entitled "Damon and Pythias."

He also described his desire to take up the writing of poetry in his old age, something for which there is a fine precedent in Thomas Hardy. Humphrey recorded this exchange with an old friend:

> This to Ted Weiss—I'm thinking of taking a home-study course in writing verse. Not with you. You're too modern for me. I want to

rhyme.

He: who wouldn't like to? Why doesn't anyone? The rhymes are all used up.

The rhymes are all used up!

But William Humphrey did not create a new career for himself as a poet.

12

The Highest Sort of Courage

In 1996 William Humphrey received a lifetime achievement award from the Texas Institute of Letters, an appropriate prize for a writer nearing the end of his career. The $1500 prize was named for his old benefactor, Lon Tinkle, which made it even more appropriate. By 1997, Dorothy Humphrey was seriously ill, and her husband was dying of cancer, which may explain why this thoroughly private man cooperated with this study, feeling perhaps that it was time for retrospectives, though his direct responses to queries were very brief. One heartening development for him in recent years was the reprinting of *Home from the Hill* in 1996 and *The Ordways* in 1997, in a series that includes such southern writers as Allen Tate, Robert Penn Warren, Elizabeth Spencer, and Peter Taylor.

Humphrey, as we have seen, regarded the purpose of his work as a destruction of myths. One myth that he himself seemed to embody in his early career was the myth of the young writer who comes from the backwoods (or a small town) to the metropolis, seeks out a mentor (as Hemingway and Faulkner sought out Sherwood Anderson), writes a book which is accepted by a great publishing house, makes the best-seller lists and is carried by the book clubs, sells his book to Hollywood, then goes off to Europe like F. Scott Fitzgerald to meet the rich and famous.

In a jubilant letter to Katherine Anne Porter on 28 February 1958, giving her the news that his first novel was a best-seller and had been sold to Hollywood, Humphrey copied out a passage from Balzac's *Cousin Bette* (205–206) that summed up his commitment to writing. Humphrey omitted a few sentences pertaining to the plot of the novel, and his version is quoted here:

> This quality that above all deserves this greatest glory in art is courage, courage of a kind of which common men have no conception. To plan, dream and imagine fine works

is a pleasant occupation to be sure. It is like
smoking magic cigars, like leading the life of
a whore who pleases only herself. The work
is then envisaged in all the grace of infancy
in the wild delight of its conception, in fra-
grant, flowerlike beauty, with the ripe juices
of the fruit savoured in anticipation. The man
who can explain his design in words passes
for an extraordinary man. All artists and
writers possess this faculty. But to produce,
to bring to birth, to bring up the infant work
with labor, to take it up again every morning
with inexhaustible maternal love, to lick it
clean, to dress it a hundred times in lovely
garments that it tears up again and again;
never to be discouraged by the convulsions
of this mad life, and to make of it a living
masterpiece that speaks to all eyes in sculp-
ture, or to all minds in literature, to all memories in painting, to all hearts in music—that
is the task of execution. The hand must be
ready at every instant to obey the mind. And
the creative moments of the mind do not come
to order. These, like the moments of love, are
discontinuous.

Humphrey sent this to Porter with the suggestion that she had the courage, the maternal love for

her work, and the patience (which he defined as "the highest sort of courage") to persevere at a time when she was struggling with her novel, *Ship of Fools*, which was for thirty years the most famous unfinished work in American literature. Humphrey would also need patience as he struggled with *The Ordways* and *Proud Flesh*. He often experienced the truth of Balzac's statement, "the creative moments of the mind do not come to order." He quoted Hoffmansthal's claim that the writer is "one for whom writing is harder than it is for other people" to Alfred A. Knopf, in 1961, and cited it again in his interview with Jose Yglesias in 1989 (64). The effort was heroic, but the rewards of fame diminished.

The enduring books are likely to be *Home from the Hill*, *The Ordways*, *A Time and a Place*, and *Farther Off from Heaven*. The first novel is derivative and overwritten, but it does recreate a unique social world—East Texas before the sweeping changes of desegregation—with power and gusto. The second novel makes the southern aspects of Texas clear in an entertaining way, and it leaps brilliantly from southern tragedy to western comedy. In *A Time and a Place*, Humphrey creates a relentless and sardonic portrait of the 1930s Dust Bowl world. All three of these works show him in his role as a destroyer of myths. In *Farther Off from Heaven,* he wrote one of the finest American memoirs, a shamefully underestimated book. The sporting adventures in *Open Season* are excellent works. Their genre, not the writer's style, makes them minor.

The other works are honorable failures, though future critics may make more of *Proud Flesh* once its mythic understructure is known. It is certainly his greatest failure in the Faulknerian sense: a work whose ambitions outrun mortal achievement. Faulkner failed at a higher level in *The Sound and the Fury*, the work he called his "most splendid failure." The background that Humphrey shares with the Mississippian (and some echoes of style) make the work seem derivative, for all of Humphrey's desire to avoid echoes. In *Hostages to Fortune* he turned to an introspective novel with no traces of the southern ambiance. It is not a novel that many would want to read twice, so tortured is its theme, but it is still worth reading. In *No Resting Place,* his good intentions could not redeem a historical tale that slights the novel in favor of history and hurries to an unsatisfying conclusion. The Texas frame gives Humphrey a last shot at the Texas myth, but it also seems to complicate the novel unnecessarily. The stories in *September Song* are a little weary of humanity: Job's patience has worn too thin; the sneering mask of Ecclesiastes/ Ecclesiasticus is not very appealing.

He could not continue to mine his past indefinitely. A. C. Greene's observation in *The Fifty Best*

Books on Texas is a good one: "Humphrey spent most of his writing life abroad or on the Eastern seaboard. . . . I wish he could have spared Texas a few years of residence somewhere in there. His commentary (fictional) on our much changed society could have been priceless" (65). But he did not witness the changes in Texas, its move toward the urban, and he quite honorably decided to avoid repeating himself.

In spite of the late stories and *Hostages to Fortune*, William Humphrey remained a Texas writer in his most important work, as his lifetime achievement award attests. Perhaps one reason that the best work succeeds is that he never had a limiting desire to be a regional writer, a minor writer, a parochial writer, though the work fulfills his inscription of *Home from the Hill* to Katherine Anne Porter: "the place and the life and the speech to which he was born is his place and his subject and his speech."

Works Cited

PRIMARY SOURCES
(chronologically arranged)

BOOKS AND ARTICLES

The Last Husband, and Other Stories. New York: Morrow, 1953; London: Chatto & Windus, 1953; Books for Libraries P, 1970.

Home from the Hill. New York: Knopf, 1958; Baton Rouge: Louisiana State UP, 1996.

The Ordways. New York: Knopf, 1965; Baton Rouge: Louisiana State UP, 1997.

A Time and a Place. New York: Knopf, 1968; London: Chatto & Windus, 1969.

Proud Flesh. New York: Knopf, 1969; London: Chatto & Windus, 1973.

The Spawning Run: A Fable. New York: Knopf, 1970; London: Chatto & Windus, 1970.

Farther Off from Heaven. New York, Knopf, 1977; London: Chatto & Windus, 1977.

Ah, Wilderness! El Paso: Texas Western P, 1977.

My Moby Dick. Garden City: Doubleday, 1978; London: Chatto & Windus, 1979.

Hostages to Fortune. New York: Delacorte/Seymour Lawrence, 1984; London: Secker & Warburg, 1985.

The Collected Stories of William Humphrey. New York: Delacorte/Seymour Lawrence, 1985.

Open Season: Sporting Adventures. New York: Delacorte/Seymour Lawrence, 1986.

No Resting Place. New York: Delacorte/Seymour Lawrence, 1989.

"Why Do I Write Fiction?" In Ashby Bland Crowder, *Writing in the Southern Tradition: Interviews with Five Contemporary Authors*. Amsterdam, Atlanta: Rodopi, 1990. 183–89.

September Song. Boston: Houghton Mifflin/Seymour Lawrence, 1992.

ARCHIVES

The Harry Ransom Humanities Research Center at the University of Texas has William Humphrey's personal archives: nineteen boxes of documents. The letters exchanged between Humphrey and Katherine Anne Porter are held in the McKeldin Library, University of Maryland. Columbia University has the files of Humphrey's agent, Annie Laurie Williams, and many of his letters to F. W. and Barbara ("Andy") Dupee. Barbara Dupee has other letters in her possession and generously made copies available for this study. The University of Mississippi holds the letters of Humphrey to Seymour Lawrence in The Mississippi Collection.

SECONDARY SOURCES

BIBLIOGRAPHY

Kich, Martin. *Western American Novelists*. Vol. 1. New York and London: Garland, 1995. Annotated. 707–802.

BOOKS AND ARTICLES

Aksakov, Sergei. *A Russian Gentleman*. New York: Oxford UP, 1982.

Almon, Bert. "William Humphrey's Blue Heaven." *Southwest Review* 63 (Winter 1978): 84–86.

_____. "William Humphrey's 'Broken-Backed Novel': Parody in *The Ordways*." *The Southern Quarterly* 32.4 (Summer 1994): 107–16.

Arrowsmith, William, Introduction to *Orestes. Euripides IV*. Chicago and London: U of Chicago P, 1958. 1–31.

Bayley, John. *An Essay on Thomas Hardy*. Cambridge: Cambridge UP, 1978.

Berger, Thomas. *Little Big Man*. New York: The Dial Press, 1964.

Black, Janet Lundquist. Rev. of *The Collected Stories of William Humphrey. Wilson Library Bulletin* (November 1985): 71.

Bleikasten, André. *Faulkner's As I Lay Dying*. Bloomington: Indiana UP, 1975.

Bowden, Larry R. "A Lament for the Vanishing." *Cross Currents* 41.1 (Spring 1991): 107–15.

Bowen, Elizabeth. "Texas Beyond the Oil Wells." *The Tatler* 227 (12 March 1958): 506.

Bowers, Eugene, and Evelyn Oppenheimer. *Red River Dust: True Tales of an American Yesterday.* Waco: Word Books, 1968.

Busby, Mark. *Larry McMurtry and the West: An Ambivalent Relationship.* Denton, Texas: U of North Texas P, 1995.

_____. "Rewriting History." *Texas Books in Review* 16.3/4 (Fall/Winter 1996): 11.

Cervantes, Miguel de. *Don Quixote of the Mancha.* Ed. Charles W. Eliot. The Harvard Classics ("Dr. Eliot's Five–Foot Shelf of Books"). New York: P. F. Collier & Son, 1909.

Chaney, L. Dwight. "William Humphrey, Regionalist: Southern or Southwestern?" *Journal of the American Studies Association of Texas* 19 (1988): 91–98.

Clifford, Craig Edward. *In the Deep Heart's Core: Reflections on Life, Letters, and Texas.* College Station: Texas A & M UP, 1985.

Clute, John. Rev. of *No Resting Place. The Times Literary Supplement.* 1 Dec. 1989: 1338.

Rev. of *Collected Stories. Virginia Quarterly Review* 62.1 (Winter 1986): 91.

"Cornua Longa, Ars Brevis." *Time* November 14, 1955: 114, 116.

Cooper, Stephen. "William Humphrey." *Contemporary Fiction Writers of the South: A Bio-Bibliographical Sourcebook.* Ed. Joseph M. Flora and Robert Bain. Westport, CT: Greenwood P, 1993. 234–43.

Davenport, Gary. "The Desertion of William Humphrey's Circus Animals." *Southern Review* 23 (1987): 494–503.

Dickey, James. "Notes on the Decline of Outrage." *South: Modern Southern Literature in Its Cultural Setting*. Ed. Louis D. Rubin, Jr., and Robert Jacobs. Westport, CT: Greenwood P, 1961. 76–94.

Eliot, T. S. *The Letters of T. S. Eliot 1898–1922*. Ed. Valerie Eliot. London: Faber, 1988.

Ephron, Nora. "A Few Words about My Breasts." *Esquire* October 1973: 278–80+.

Farber, Leslie. *Lying, Despair, Jealousy, Envy, Sex, Suicide, Drugs, and the Good Life*. New York: Basic Books, 1976.

Faulkner, William. *Absalom, Absalom!* 1936. New York: Random House, 1964.

_____. *As I Lay Dying*. 1930. New York: Vintage, 1987.

_____. *Go Down, Moses*. 1942. New York: Vintage, 1964.

_____. *The Hamlet*. 1931. New York: Vintage, 1964.

Fehrenbach, T. R. *Lone Star: A History of Texas and the Texans*. New York: 1968.

Frantz, Joe B., and Julian Ernest Choate, Jr. *The American Cowboy: The Myth & the Reality*. Norman: U of Oklahoma P, 1955.

Freud, Sigmund. "Contributions to the Psychology of Love: On the Most Prevalent Form of Degradation in Erotic Life." *Collected Papers*. Vol. 4. Ed. Ernest Jones. New York: Basic Books, 1959. 203–16.

_____. "Dostoyevsky and Parricide." *Collected Papers*. Vol. 5. Ed. James Strachey. New York: Basic Books, 1959. 223–42.

Givner, Joan, ed. *Katherine Anne Porter: Conversations*. Jackson and London: UP of Mississippi, 1987.

_____. *Katherine Anne Porter: A Life*. New York: Simon and Schuster, 1982.

_____. "Katherine Anne Porter: The Old Order and the New." *The Texas Literary Tradition: Fiction, Folklore, History*. Ed. Don Graham, et al. Austin: U of Texas, 1983. 58–68.

Goyen, William. *Selected Letters from a Writer's Life*. Ed. Robert Phillips. Austin: U of Texas P, 1995.

Grammer, John M. "Where the South Draws Up to a Stop: The Fiction of William Humphrey." *Mississippi Quarterly* 44 (Winter 1990–91): 5–21.

Greene, A. C. *The Fifty Best Books on Texas*. Dallas: Pressworks, 1982.

Greene, Sarah. "Roadmap for Trip in Time—Backwards." *Gilmer Mirror* 28 May 1970: 1+.

_____ "Sideglances in the Mirror." *Gilmer Mirror* 21 May 1997: A4.

Grider, Sylvia, and Elizabeth Tebeaux. "Blessings into Curses: Sardonic Humor and Irony in 'A Job of the Plains.'" *Studies in Short Fiction* 23.3 (Summer 1986): 297–306.

Guerard, Albert, ed. *Stories of the Double*. Philadelphia: Lippincott, 1967.

Gussow, Mel. "William Humphrey, 73, Writer of Novels about Rural Texas." *New York Times* 21 Aug. 1997, natl. ed.: A17.

Havighurst, Walter. Rev. of *Home from the Hill*. *Saturday Review* 11 (January 1958): 15.

Hiers, John T. "The Graveyard Epiphany in Modern Southern Fiction: Transcendence of Selfhood." *Southern Humanities Review* 9.4 (1975): 389–403.

Hoffman, Frederick J. *The Art of Southern Fiction*. Carbondale and Edwardsville: Southern Illinois UP, 1967.

Rev. of *Hostages to Fortune*. *Kirkus Reviews* 15 July 1984: 641–42.

Hudziak, Craig. "William Humphrey." *Contemporary Novelists*. Fourth Edition. Ed. D. L. Kirkpatrick. New York: St. Martin's P, 1986. 447–49.

Janeway, Elizabeth. "Journey through Time." *The New York Times Book Review* 31 January 1965: 1+.

Jeane, D. Gregory. "Cemeteries." *Encyclopedia of Southern Culture*. Ed. Charles Reagan Wilson and William Ferris. Chapel Hill and London: The U of North Carolina P, 1989. 463–65.

Kappler, Frank. "Texas with Another Accent." *Life* 5 February 1965: 17.

Karr, Mary. *The Liar's Club*. New York: Viking, 1995.

Kilgo, James P. Rev. of *Open Season*. *Georgia Review* 40 (Winter 1976): 1051–2.

Lattimore, Richmond. "Introduction to The Oresteia." *Aeschylus I: Oresteia*. Chicago: U of Chicago P, 1953. 1–31.

Lee, James Ward. *Classics of Texas Fiction*. Dallas: E-Heart P, 1987.

_____. *William Humphrey*. Austin: Steck-Vaughn, 1967.

_____. "William Humphrey." *Dictionary of Literary Biography*, Volume 6: *American Novelists since World War II*, Second Series. 148–53.

Lomax, John A. *Adventures of a Ballad Hunter*. New York: Macmillan, 1947.

Loyd, Doyal T. *A History of Upshur County, Texas*. Ed. Sarah Greene. Gilmer, TX: Privately Printed, 1966.

Luce, Clothilde. "Texas, Paris." *Texas Monthly* 24 (February 1996): 98–101.

Maddocks, Melvin. "Ten-Gallon Gothic." *Time* 30 April 1973: 94.

McMurtry, Larry. "Southwestern Literature?" *In a Narrow Grave*. Austin: Encino P, 1968. 31–54.

_____, and Diana Ossana. *Pretty Boy Floyd*. New York: Simon & Schuster, 1994.

_____, and Diana Ossana. *Zeke and Ned*. New York: Simon & Schuster, 1997.

Morsberger, Robert. E. Rev. of *No Resting Place*. *Western American Literature* 24/4 (Winter 1990): 391–92.

Mullen, Patrick B. "Myth and Folklore in The Ordways." *Hunters and Healers: Folklore Types and Topics*. Publications of the Texas Folklore Society, Vol 35. Ed. Wilson M. Hudson. Austin: Encino P, 1971. 133–45.

Owens, William A. *A Season of Weathering*. New York: Scribner's, 1973.

_____. *This Stubborn Soil*. New York: Scribner's, 1966.

Parsons, Ian. "Outstanding Merit." *The Bookseller* 7 January 1978: 45.

Pyron, Darden Asbury. "Gone with the Wind." *Encyclopedia of Southern Culture*. Ed. Charles Reagan Wilson and William Ferris. Chapel Hill and London: The U of North Carolina P, 1989. 958–59.

Rank, Otto. *The Double: A Psychoanalytic Study*. Chapel Hill: U of North Carolina P, 1971.

Reagan, John H. "The Expulsion of the Cherokees from East Texas." *Quarterly of the Texas State Historical Association* I (1897): 38–46.

Rubin, Louis D. *The Curious Death of the Novel: Essays in American Literature*. Baton Rouge: Louisiana State UP, 1967.

Starkey, Marion L. *The Cherokee Nation*. New York: Alfred A. Knopf, 1946.

Steckmesser, Kent Ladd. *The Western Hero in History and Legend*. Norman: U of Oklahoma P, 1965.

Stegner, Wallace. *Wolf Willow*. New York: Viking, 1962.

Stevenson, David L. "Ceremony of Prose." *Nation* 22 February 1958: 172–74.

Sullenger, Lee. Rev. of Proud Flesh. *Library Journal* 98.7 (1 Apr. 1973): 1192.

Sullivan, Walter. "The Continuing Renascence: Southern Fiction in the Fifties." *South: Modern Southern Literature in Its Cultural Setting*. 376–91. Ed. Louis D. Rubin, Jr., and Robert Jacobs. Westport, CT: Greenwood P, 1961. 376–91.

Tebeaux, Elizabeth. "Irony as Art: The Short Fiction of William Humphrey." *Studies in Short Fiction* 26.3 (Summer 1989): 323–34.

Tolbert, Frank X. "Following Trail of Roses Planted by 1821 Cherokees." *The Dallas Morning News* 8 June 1969: 31A.

Tomlinson, Charles. *Annunciations*. Oxford: Oxford UP, 1989.

_____. *Collected Poems*. Oxford: Oxford UP, 1987.

Tymms, Ralph. *Doubles in Literary Psychology*. Cambridge: Bowes & Bowes, 1949.

Valery, Paul. "Stendahl." *Variety: Second Series*. Trans. William Aspenwall Bradley. New York: Harcourt, Brace, 1938. 101–54.

Van Ghent, Dorothy. *The English Novel: Form and Function*. New York: Holt Rinehart and Winston, 1953.

Vellacott, Philip. "Introduction" to *Aeschylus, The Oresteian Trilogy*. Harmondsworth, England: Penguin Books, 1956, 1959. 9–37.

Walton, Izaak. *The Compleat Angler, or The Contemplative Man's Recreation*. London: Oxford, 1967.

Warren, Robert Penn. "Katherine Anne Porter: Irony with a Center." *Selected Essays*. New York: Random House, 1958. 136–55.

Webb, Walter Prescott. *The Texas Rangers: A Century of Frontier Defense*. Boston & New York: Houghton Mifflin, 1935.

Weiss, Theodore. *The Last Day and the First*. New York: Macmillan, 1968.

Welty, Eudora. *The Eye of the Story: Selected Essays and Reviews*. New York: Vintage, 1979.

Winchell, Mark Royden. "Beyond Regionalism: The Growth of William Humphrey." *Sewanee Review* 96(1988): 287–92.

_____. *William Humphrey*. Boise, Idaho: Western Writers Series, 1992.

FILM TREATMENTS

Home from the Hill. Vincente Minnelli, Director. MGM, 1958.
The Last of the Caddoes. Ken Harrison, Director. Phoenix Films, 1981.

INTERVIEWS

Crowder, Ashby Bland. *Writing in the Southern Tradition: Interviews with Five Contemporary Authors*. Amsterdam, Atlanta, GA: Rodopi, 1990.
Dupee, Barbara. Telephone interview with Bert Almon. 12 May 1997.
Harrison, Ken. Telephone interview with Bert Almon. 14 May 1997.
Ligon, Betty. "Novelist Finds Time Does Not Heal Wounds." *The El Paso Herald-Post* 6 May 1977: 3.
Yglesias, Jose. "William Humphrey." *Publishers Weekly*. 235.22 (June 1989): 64–65.

Index

450